Pathways to Multilingualism

BILINGUAL EDUCATION AND BILINGUALISM
Series Editors: Professor Colin Baker, *University of Wales, Bangor, Wales, Great Britain*
and Professor Nancy H. Hornberger, *University of Pennsylvania, Philadelphia, USA*

Recent Books in the Series
Bilingualism and Language Pedagogy
Janina Brutt-Griffler and Manka Varghese (eds)
Language Learning and Teacher Education: A Sociocultural Approach
Margaret R. Hawkins (ed.)
The English Vernacular Divide: Postcolonial Language Politics and Practice
Vaidehi Ramanathan
Bilingual Education in South America
Anne-Marie de Mejía (ed.)
Teacher Collaboration and Talk in Multilingual Classrooms
Angela Creese
Words and Worlds: World Languages Review
F. Martí, P. Ortega, I. Idiazabal, A. Barreña, P. Juaristi, C. Junyent, B. Uranga and E. Amorrortu
Language and Aging in Multilingual Contexts
Kees de Bot and Sinfree Makoni
Foundations of Bilingual Education and Bilingualism (4th edn)
Colin Baker
Bilingual Minds: Emotional Experience, Expression and Representation
Aneta Pavlenko (ed.)
Raising Bilingual-Biliterate Children in Monolingual Cultures
Stephen J. Caldas
Language, Space and Power: A Critical Look at Bilingual Education
Samina Hadi-Tabassum
Developing Minority Language Resources
Guadalupe Valdés, Joshua A. Fishman, Rebecca Chávez and William Pérez
Language Loyalty, Language Planning and Language Revitalization: Recent Writings
and Reflections from Joshua A. Fishman
Nancy H. Hornberger and Martin Pütz (eds)
Language Loyalty, Continuity and Change: Joshua A. Fishman's Contributions to
International Sociolinguistics
Ofelia Garcia, Rakhmiel Peltz and Harold Schiffman
Bilingual Education: An Introductory Reader
Ofelia García and Colin Baker (eds)
Disinventing and Reconstituting Languages
Sinfree Makoni and Alastair Pennycook (eds)
Language and Identity in a Dual Immersion School
Kim Potowski
Bilingual Education in China: Practices, Policies and Concepts
Anwei Feng (ed.)
English Learners Left Behind: Standardized Testing as Language Policy
Kate Menken
Biliteracy and Globalization: English Language Education in India
Viniti Vaish

For more details of these or any other of our publications, please contact:
Multilingual Matters, Frankfurt Lodge, Clevedon Hall,
Victoria Road, Clevedon, BS21 7HH, England
http://www.multilingual-matters.com

BILINGUAL EDUCATION AND BILINGUALISM 66
Series Editors: Colin Baker and Nancy H. Hornberger

Pathways to Multilingualism
Evolving Perspectives on Immersion Education

Edited by
Tara Williams Fortune and Diane J. Tedick

MULTILINGUAL MATTERS LTD
Clevedon • Buffalo • Toronto

Library of Congress Cataloging in Publication Data
Pathways to Multilingualism: Evolving Perspectives on Immersion Education
Edited by Tara Williams Fortune and Diane J. Tedick.
Bilingual Education and Bilingualism: 66.
Includes bibliographical references and index.
1. Immersion education (Language teaching). I. Fortune, Tara Williams.
II. Tedick, Diane J.
P53.44.P38 2008
418.0071–dc22   2007029774

British Library Cataloguing in Publication Data
A catalogue entry for this book is available from the British Library.

ISBN-13: 978-1-84769-036-4 (hbk)
ISBN-13: 978-1-84769-035-7 (pbk)

Multilingual Matters Ltd
UK: Frankfurt Lodge, Clevedon Hall, Victoria Road, Clevedon BS21 7HH.
USA: UTP, 2250 Military Road, Tonawanda, NY 14150, USA.
Canada: UTP, 5201 Dufferin Street, North York, Ontario M3H 5T8, Canada.

The policy of Multilingual Matters/Channel View Publications is to use papers that
are natural, renewable and recyclable products, made from wood grown in
sustainable forests. In the manufacturing process of our books, and to further support
our policy, preference is given to printers that have FSC and PEFC Chain of Custody
certification. The FSC and/or PEFC logos will appear on those books where full
certification has been granted to the printer concerned.

Typeset by Wordworks Ltd.
Printed and bound in Great Britain by The Cromwell Press Ltd.

Dedicated to those talented educators who enter immersion classrooms, programs and schools day in and day out, breathing new language life into future multilingual citizens of the world.

Contents

Part 2: Evolving Perspectives on Language Development in Immersion Classrooms

Part 3: Evolving Perspectives on Social Context and its Impact on Immersion Programs

Synthesis for the Volume

The Contributors

Barbara Burnaby (PhD, University of Toronto) has taught English as a foreign language in Japan, and English as a second language to adult immigrants in Toronto. She first joined the faculty in the Department of Adult Education at the Ontario Institute for Studies in Education (OISE) at the University of Toronto and later moved to the Modern Language Centre at OISE. She served as Dean of the Faculty of Education at Memorial University of Newfoundland (2000–2002), and is currently an Honorary Research Professor, working with Marguerite MacKenzie on a grant on language development among the Innu in Labrador.

Donna Christian is president of the Center for Applied Linguistics in Washington, DC (www.cal.org). Her work focuses on the role of language in education, with special interests in second language learning, dialect diversity and policy. She has published extensively on those topics, including co-authored or co-edited publications such as *Educating English Language Learners: A Synthesis of Research Evidence* (Cambridge University Press), *Bilingual Education* (TESOL), *Dialects, Schools, and Communities* (Lawrence Erlbaum), and *Profiles in Two-Way Immersion Education* (CAL/ Delta Systems).

Diane Dagenais is Associate Professor in the Faculty of Education at Simon Fraser University. She teaches courses in French and in English in the area of second language education. Her teaching load is distributed in the graduate, undergraduate, in-service and pre-service teacher education programs. She is coordinator of the French graduate cohorts in curriculum studies. She has received funding from several sources to support her research and has published on learning and teaching a second language, bilingual and minority education including French immersion and Francophone programs, multilingualism, multiliterate practices of children from immigrant families, language diversity and language awareness development.

Deborah Dubiner (MS in TESOL, University of Southern California) is a doctoral student in Second Language Acquisition at Carnegie Mellon University. Her research interests include trilingualism and third language acquisition, second language reading and second language fluency. Her dissertation focuses on the impact of incipient trilinguality on the linguistic and affective development of elementary school children in Israel. It examines an innovative program that teaches Jewish children Arabic as a third language, in addition to Hebrew and English. Currently ESL instructor at the Kinneret College in Israel, she has taught ESL for over 20 years, and Hebrew and Portuguese also.

Tara Williams Fortune, Immersion Projects Coordinator for CARLA, one of several Language Resource Centers in the US, is engaged in the preparation and continuing education of language immersion professionals through CARLA and as a member of the graduate faculty in Second Languages and Cultures Education at the University of Minnesota. Tara lectures and consults on immersion education throughout the US and abroad. She is founding editor of The ACIE (American Council of Immersion Education) Newsletter. Recent projects target struggling immersion learners and oral proficiency assessment. Her own research examines the dynamics of language use and peer interaction in immersion classrooms.

Fred Genesee is Professor in the Psychology Department at McGill University in Montreal. He has carried out extensive research on alternative approaches to bilingual education, including second/foreign language immersion for language majority students and alternative forms of bilingual education for language minority students. His current work focuses on simultaneous acquisition of two languages during early infancy and childhood, language development in international adoptees, and the language and literacy development of children at-risk for reading and language impairment in immersion programs.

Philip Hoare is an Associate Professor in the Department of English in the Hong Kong Institute of Education. He has studied in the universities of Leeds, London, Edinburgh and Hong Kong. He worked in a number of countries including Tuvalu, Mongolia and Bahrain before coming to Hong Kong, where he has worked with English immersion teachers for many years. With Stella Kong, he is currently advising and researching content-based English teaching projects in Mainland China.

Liz Howard is an assistant professor of bilingual education in the Neag School of Education at the University of Connecticut. Formerly, she was a senior research associate with the Center for Applied Linguistics, where she directed a number of studies related to two-way immersion education and biliteracy development. She has authored several publications on two-way immersion, including the recent book *Realizing the Vision of Two-Way*

Immersion: Fostering Effective Programs and Classrooms, which she co-authored with Julie Sugarman. She has worked as a bilingual elementary school teacher in California and as an adult literacy/ESL instructor as a Peace Corps Volunteer in Costa Rica.

Stella Kong is an associate professor in the Department of English in the Hong Kong Institute of Education, where she has been working as a teacher educator for 15 years. She specialises in immersion teacher education. Her teaching and research interests are in immersion education pedagogies, content–language relationships and writing-to-learn across the curriculum. She has extensive experience working with English immersion teachers in Hong Kong.

Sharon Lapkin is Professor Emerita in the Modern Language Centre and Second Language Education program of the Ontario Institute for Studies in Education at the University of Toronto. Her research focuses on French as a second language (FSL) education in all its forms and ranges from large-scale program evaluation to micro-analysis of second language learning in progress. For nearly ten years, she co-edited the *Canadian Modern Language Review*, and is currently Past President of the Canadian Association of Applied Linguistics. She was recently awarded the Prix Robert Roy in recognition of her contributions to FSL by the Canadian Association of Second Language Teachers.

Kathryn Lindholm-Leary is Professor of Child and Adolescent Development at San Jose State University, where she has taught for 19 years. At San Jose State, Kathryn received a Teacher-Scholar award, was a finalist for the President's Scholar award, and was a San Jose State nominee for the prestigious Wang Family Excellence award. She has worked with more than 50 two-way and developmental bilingual programs over the past 22 years and has written books and journal articles, and given presentations to researchers, educators and parents on the topics of two-way immersion education and child bilingualism.

Roy Lyster is Professor of Second Language Education in the Department of Integrated Studies Education at McGill University in Montreal. His research focuses primarily on immersion and content-based classrooms, including both observational and experimental studies of teacher-student interaction, form-focused instruction and corrective feedback. An executive member of the Canadian Association of Applied Linguistics (President 2006–2008, Co-President 2004–2006), he is author of *Learning and Teaching Languages Through Content: A Counterbalanced Approach*, published by John Benjamins in 2007.

Myriam Met is a senior research associate at the National Foreign Language Center, University of Maryland, where her work focuses primarily on K–12 (kindergarten to grade 12) foreign language policy. Her previous positions include supervisor of foreign language programs K–12, English for Speakers of Other Languages, and bilingual education for major urban and suburban school districts. She has served as President of the National Association of District Supervisors of Foreign Languages and the National Network for Early Language Learning. She was a co-chair of the New Visions in Foreign Language Education and has served on the Executive Council of the American Council on the Teaching of Foreign Languages.

Hirohide Mori is Associate Professor in the College of Economics at Nihon University. He has conducted research widely on the effects of input, interaction and feedback on second language acquisition, especially in Japanese immersion public elementary schools. He has also published articles on language transfer, language universals, and teachers' beliefs about language teaching. His current research interests include the role of individual differences in child second language acquisition.

Deborah Palmer is an Assistant Professor in Bilingual/Bicultural Education in the Department of Curriculum and Instruction at the University of Texas at Austin. Her research is qualitative in nature, and her interests include bilingual education policy and politics in the United States, dual immersion enrichment education, teacher preparation for diverse and multilingual classrooms and ethnography and discourse analysis.

Merle Richards is a professor of education at Brock University, Ontario, Canada. Her interests in language and cross-cultural education have led to research in Heritage Language teaching, Aboriginal language revitalization, and bilingual education programs. For two decades, she has been deeply involved in Aboriginal teacher education and language development, working mainly with Hotinohsonni (Iroquois) and Anishnaabek (Ojibwa) educators in Ontario.

Margareta Södergård is Senior Lecturer in the Department of Early Childhood Education at Åbo Akademi University in Finland. Before joining Åbo Akademi, she was engaged in research on Swedish immersion in the Department of Scandinavian Languages at the University of Vaasa, where she also served as Professor of Swedish Immersion Education. Her current research involves a longitudinal study of Swedish immersion in which she is following the same immersion pupils from kindergarten to grade 9.

Merrill Swain is Professor Emerita in the Second Language Education Program at the Ontario Institute for Studies in Education at the University of Toronto, where she has taught and conducted research for 36 years. Her present research focuses on the role of collaborative dialogue and 'languaging' in second language learning within a sociocultural framework. She was President of the American Association of Applied Linguistics (AAAL) in 1998–99, and a Vice President of the International Association of Applied Linguistics from 1999–2005. She is recipient of the 2003 Canadian Robert Roy Award and AAAL's 2004 Distinguished Scholarship and Service Award. She has authored books and many book chapters, as well as over 150 refereed articles.

Diane J. Tedick is Associate Professor in the Second Languages and Cultures Education program in the College of Education and Human Development at the University of Minnesota. She is a teacher educator for second language contexts including immersion and bilingual education, foreign language education, and English as a Second Language. She serves as a consultant and conducts program evaluations in immersion and language programs around the US and internationally. Her research focuses on the pedagogy required for balancing language and content in instruction. Recent publications include an edited volume entitled *Second Language Teacher Education: International Perspectives* (2005, Lawrence Erlbaum).

G. Richard Tucker is Paul Mellon University Professor of Applied Linguistics at Carnegie Mellon University. Before joining Carnegie Mellon, he was President of the Center for Applied Linguistics in Washington, DC (1978–1991), and Professor of Psychology and Linguistics at McGill University (1969–1978). He has published more than 200 books, articles or reviews concerning diverse aspects of second language learning and teaching. In addition to his work in North America, he spent five years living and working as a Language Education advisor for the Ford Foundation in Southeast Asia and in the Middle East and North Africa.

Constance L. Walker (PhD, University of Illinois, Urbana-Champaign) is a faculty member in Second Languages and Cultures Education, College of Education and Human Development at the University of Minnesota, where she is involved in the preparation of teachers for second language contexts. Her research interests lie in the experiences of teachers who work with culturally and linguistically diverse populations, and issues of school policy and practice related to second language learners. She is currently directing the TEAM UP Project, a Title III teacher development project that focuses on collaborative processes for serving students learning English as a second language.

Foreword

DONNA CHRISTIAN

Themes of globalization and diversity permeate current discussions in commerce, diplomacy, security, individual advancement and many other domains. In our global society, individuals and groups from diverse backgrounds come into contact much more regularly than in the past. Whether they seek to collaborate or to compete, they need to understand one another. Although English is widely used as a common language internationally, there is a growing demand for products and services adapted to local languages and cultures around the world. New technologies provide broad and instantaneous access to ideas, information, and interaction for individuals who have the needed language skills. And, to serve our common welfare, communication in diverse languages is essential for sensitive discussions on critical world issues such as the environment, health and terrorism. Now more than ever, communication across languages and cultures is vital to success in today's world for nations, societies and individuals. This fact underscores the importance of competence in languages on a wide scale.

Demand and supply are not well matched, however, in many areas. In the United States, for example, the lack of language resources has become painfully apparent in recent years. Of the relatively small number of individuals in the United States who learn languages other than English, an even smaller number achieve a high level of proficiency in the language(s) they study. Developing a cadre of professionals with high levels of proficiency in both English and another language is essential for meeting the challenges of today's world. In other nations, individual multilingualism may be more common, but additional language skills could be beneficial, particularly in expanding opportunities to interact with the world outside their local communities.

Schools can and should play a major role in meeting the need for language skills by offering learners the opportunity to acquire them via 'pathways' through the system that lead to multilingualism. Paths that foster growth in multiple languages would include the following basic elements, among others:

- early language learning opportunities for young learners so that they develop an appreciation for languages and have a foundation for getting to higher levels of proficiency in a second language and for adding more languages;
- sustained and intensive language development, from pre-school to elementary to secondary to university and beyond;
- integration of language and content instruction and use of other effective pedagogical strategies that cultivate high levels of proficiency in meaningful contexts;
- support for native languages, so that additional languages do not adversely affect their maintenance and development.

All of these elements can be found in immersion programs. Language immersion education is a powerful ingredient in an overall plan to promote the development of multilingualism in our schools. It fosters additive bilingualism, which, as Fred Genesee points out in his contribution to this volume, has beneficial social psychological, psycholinguistic and educational effects for students. While the approach may still be widely considered 'innovative,' it has claimed its place in educational programming as an effective way to give students a high quality education *and* the opportunity to become proficient in more than one language.

The value of language immersion programs has been recognized in growing numbers of communities in Canada, the United States and around the world since the St Lambert experiment began over 40 years ago. The Center for Applied Linguistics, in databases maintained on its website (www.cal.org), documents nearly 600 schools in the United States with immersion programs (one-way and two-way), representing well over 100,000 students. While these totals represent a small percentage of the larger US student population, the numbers are significant nonetheless and growing.

As immersion programs have spread, they have also evolved to suit different communities. One-way (foreign language) immersion programs have been joined by 'two-way' immersion programs where students from two different language backgrounds learn together through both languages, so that each group has an immersion experience in the other's language. This development is significant in part because it provides a positive response to two important challenges facing many societies: the need for increased language resources and the need to educate learners from minority language backgrounds well. While there are important differences between immersion programs in different contexts, many pedagogical and programmatic strategies can work well in both. It is a credit to this volume that various strands of immersion education are brought together so that experience and research can be shared. It is also extremely helpful that the editors have identified the core features of immersion programs and clarified terminology for these and related (or similar-sounding) educational approaches. As is often the case, dispersion of the model has led to variability in labeling, which makes it difficult to accumulate knowledge about it.

The diversity of student populations and unclear terminology are just some of the many challenges faced by immersion educators. As our under-standing of immersion education in different contexts has deepened, so has our appreciation of the questions that have yet to be fully resolved, including a number of instructional and programmatic concerns:

- What are the effects of implementation differences (decisions on how program languages are allocated – for example by time, by teacher, by content area)?
- What is the impact of sociocultural context on immersion programs?
- How can language learning opportunities in the classroom be opti-mized?
- How can immersion instruction better support high levels of academic achievement?
- What pedagogical strategies are most effective for promoting second language learning in immersion classrooms?
- What design characteristics work best to create long sequences of language learning (preK–16) that include immersion?

Many of these issues are addressed in the contributions to this collection.

In today's and tomorrow's world, well-marked pathways to multi-lingualism are more important than ever. Language immersion programs play a central role in achieving the goal of multilingualism through schooling. Thus, the time is right for a volume such as this one, which takes stock of what we've learned about how to do immersion education, contributes fresh insights from well-established immersion settings, and introduces us to its practice in new and varied contexts. Tara Fortune and Diane Tedick have assembled reports of research and practice that deal with immersion education both broadly and deeply. From studies of Spanish immersion in the United States, to English immersion in Hong Kong, to aboriginal language immersion in Canada, the chapters offer research-based discussions that can inform practice. They remind us to pay attention to diversity in the immersion classroom, to plan carefully for language development, to integrate content and language instruction in meaningful ways, and to honor the goals of the local community for the program – and they give us insight into ways of doing this. The volume makes an important contribution to the field of immersion education, as a type of bilingual education, by integrating research and practice and moving us forward in both domains. It will be a significant reference work for educators and researchers alike for years to come.

The editors and authors are to be congratulated for preparing a set of articles grounded in research that can help us see what can be done to make immersion an effective path to multilingualism and to academic success. We should act now to apply their findings and to extend them through further research.

Acknowledgements

It has been said that the journey of a thousand miles begins with a single step. And such is the case with this book. When we first stepped into the field of immersion education we found ourselves surrounded by generous and knowledgeable scholars who welcomed us and have offered mentoring guideposts along the way. We would like to especially recognize Merrill Swain who has served as CARLA's Immersion Projects External Advisor for many years. Her professional insights, field expertise and authentic communication style have greatly influenced the CARLA Immersion Projects and this publication from the outset.

Donna Christian and Fred Genesee are among the very few scholars that bring a deep understanding of and commitment to the various branches of immersion education addressed in this volume. We turned to them to situate this volume within the broader field of dual language education. We so appreciate that Donna accepted our invitation to write the foreword. In addition to contributing an introductory chapter, Fred led us to two Canadian scholars who were able to offer a chapter representing the indigenous immersion perspective, and for that connection we are grateful. Dick Tucker and Deborah Dubiner graciously agreed to write the synthesis chapter, which involved a very short turn-around time after digesting the entire manuscript. It is an honor to have one of the researchers from the French immersion pilot program in St Lambert, Quebec, weighing in with historical perspective. We'd also like to thank our colleagues, Siv Björklund, Michele de Courcy and Ann Snow for reading and reviewing the final manuscript for the publishers.

A number of individuals impacted the organization and shaping of the volume. We are grateful to Merrill Swain, Kathy Lindholm-Leary and Mimi Met for providing thoughtful feedback on the book prospectus. The series editors, Colin Baker and Nancy Hornberger, offered exceptional guidance and vision. We benefited tremendously from their wisdom and the questions they challenged us to consider after reading the first draft. The book is much stronger as a result of their time, attentiveness and scholarship.

We are also deeply indebted to each of our contributing authors, who carefully responded to feedback and suggestions on earlier drafts of their chapters. We genuinely appreciated contributors' patience and prompt replies throughout the editing process. Most importantly, we gratefully acknowledge their willingness to support the vision that grounds this edited volume, that is, the importance of bringing together research carried out in various immersion settings so that the field as a whole might benefit from a shared knowledge base while remaining mindful of the need for certain context-specific adaptations.

It has been such a pleasure to work with the staff at Multilingual Matters. From our initial interaction with Michael Grover to ongoing support from Tommi Grover, to our work with the editorial staff including Marjukka Grover, Ken Hall, Anne Gray and others, our experience has been so very positive and productive.

Finally, we are grateful for the enduring support and encouragement from those family members and friends who are nearest and dearest to us, Alissa, Brendan, Ryan and Connor Fortune, Bill Pilicer and Mike Lind. Thanks for your patience with those late nights, a less-than-fabulous meal program, and for supporting those much-needed chunks of time away that allowed us to devote the focused energy required to bring this volume to completion.

Tara Williams Fortune and Diane J. Tedick

Introduction to the Volume

Chapter 1

One-Way, Two-Way and Indigenous Immersion: A Call for Cross-Fertilization

TARA WILLIAMS FORTUNE and DIANE J. TEDICK

> *If names are not correct,*
> *language will not be in accordance with the truth of things.*
> Kung Fu-tzu Confucius (551–479 BC),
> Chinese Ethical Teacher – Founder of Confucianism

Foreign language immersion. Two-way immersion. Indigenous immersion. Early double immersion. Early total immersion. Structured English immersion. One-way partial immersion. Dual language immersion. What do these names actually mean?

Coming to terms with terminology can be difficult. When discussing schooling experiences in language and culture education on a global scale, the naming task becomes even more daunting. Public schools as dynamic social institutions are inherently messy places. They and the language immersion programs that exist within them welcome all students and families and develop in response to local needs and sociocultural contexts. Because of these pre-conditions, educational programs, in particular those that teach two or more languages through content, do not lend themselves well to simple categorization or labeling. However, given researcher interest in disseminating program-specific findings and educator interest in replicating successful models, labeling programs accurately and ensuring that program design and implementation cohere with the elected program's key characteristics become critical.

The challenge of assigning names to program models that exists for many bilingual and immersion educators and researchers is hardly surprising. Consider, for example, the following complexities:

- global exportation and proliferation of the Canadian French immersion program model and other forms of bilingual education, and the need for context-specific adaptation;
- use of public monies for school-based maintenance of minority

languages and cultures,[1] and the impact of local and national legislation and political agendas;

- vernacular use of the term 'immersion' to describe a teaching and learning methodology as opposed to an educational program model with distinct characteristics, and the confusion that naturally arises from such doublespeak; and
- negative connotations that evolve over time with labels such as 'bilingual' and 'English immersion' education in the US, and the misinformation that results.

To facilitate a clear use of terminology in this edited volume, we begin this introduction by briefly offering a literature-based, research-friendly description of 'immersion education.' We aim to ground this description in what immersion researchers have reported in earlier investigations and to explicitly identify defining core characteristics as well as acceptable programmatic variations. Such practices support accurate use of program labels and this, in turn, upholds the integrity of research findings published under the name of immersion education or as we suggest, its 'research-friendliness.' Within this section, we also present background information on the three types of immersion programs discussed within this volume: one-way foreign language immersion, two-way immersion and indigenous immersion. As volume editors, our characterization of immersion education delimits use of the term to programs that adhere to specific goals as well as well-defined program design and implementation features, which we identify. We then go on to articulate our rationale for bringing these various strands of immersion education together in one research-focused volume. Finally, we preview the contents and organization of individual chapters by section.

Immersion Education: A Literature-Based, Research-Friendly Description

The programs discussed in this volume were modeled after and inspired by one of two grassroots language education efforts, both of which emerged on North American soil in the 1960s: St-Lambert, Quebec's French immersion program in Canada (Peritz, 2006) and Miami-Dade County, Florida's Spanish/English bilingual program in the US (Ovando, 2003).

Canadian French immersion education

Canada's foreign language immersion program model originated during conversations among a small group of disgruntled English-speaking parents. Concerned about the growing importance of French/

English bilingualism in their community and motivated by a desire to bridge the cultural divide between Canadian Anglophones and Francophones (Lambert, 1995), they determined to create a more effective way to develop their English-speaking children's bilingualism and biliteracy. Engaging the expertise of a few local academics, this visionary parent group designed an elementary 'language bath' program alternative to the traditional 'Core' French program, lobbied hard and after two years launched the French immersion program with 26 English-speaking kindergarteners at Margaret Pendlebury Elementary School. The words 'language immersion' were adopted in October 1963 because the words 'language bath' did not seem sufficiently sophisticated for schooling (Peritz, 2006).

The first French early total immersion classrooms in Canada offered all subject matter instruction in students' second language (L2), French (Lambert & Tucker, 1972). Content instruction in French only continued through grade 3, and French was the language of initial literacy as well. Beginning in grade 3 or 4, programs introduced some subject matter instruction in English, gradually increasing the time allotted to English to 50% by grades 5–6. At the time, one of the key criteria identified as essential to this program's success was the language background of incoming students. All students entered the program with limited to no proficiency in the immersion language (IL) (Lambert, 1984). Researchers pointed out that this design feature facilitated teachers' ability to make appropriate modifications to their IL use and instructional practices for increased comprehensibility among learners.

Having a linguistically homogeneous student group also meant that all students were moving together *in one direction* towards proficiency in French. In this volume use of the descriptors 'one-way' and 'two-way' references the linguistic background of the target student audience.[2] 'One-way' foreign language immersion programs, modeled after Canadian French immersion programs, serve a majority language group in the process of acquiring the same second language (e.g. Japanese immersion in the US or English immersion in Hong Kong).

Miami-Dade County's two-way bilingual program

While Canadians experimented with French immersion education for English-speaking children, to the south of Canada Cuban parents exiled from their home country and living in Florida worked together to establish the first two-way bilingual education program at Coral Way Elementary School in Miami-Dade County. Believing that their situation was only temporary, these parents were interested in maintaining schooling support for their children's native Spanish as they acquired the new language, English (Ovando, 2003). The model they adopted with the support of Coral Way school officials brought together English-speaking Spanish learners and Spanish-speaking English learners in one classroom. The instructional day was divided between the two languages and subject matter was taught in both languages with the goal of developing bilingual, biliterate and bicultural children. The success of this program model spurred the development of similar programs in Florida and elsewhere in the US.

Thus, in contrast to one-way immersion programs, two-way programs serve a linguistically heterogeneous group. In these programs students speak one of the two languages of instruction and are in the process of acquiring the other as their 'partner' (Lindholm-Leary and Howard, Chapter 9 this volume) language. Thus, two-way students are moving in two distinct directions, towards the native language of their linguistically-different peers.

National and international growth

Since the birth of these two forms of bilingual education in Canada and the US, both program models have spread within their countries and around the world. Canadian Parents for French (CPF, 2006) reports a total of 300,628 French immersion students as of 2004–2005, with immersion students in every Canadian province except for Nunavut, where no programs are offered. Immersion programs have also been implemented with Canadian Aboriginal languages such as Mohawk (see Richards and Burnaby, Chapter 11 this volume). In addition to in-country expansion, a 2003 CPF report details exportation of the Canadian immersion program internationally to countries such as the United States (1972, Spanish immersion in Culver City, California; 1974, French immersion in Montgomery County, Maryland), Finland (1987, Swedish immersion in Vaasa, Finland), Germany (1996, English immersion in Kiel, Germany), Spain (1983, Catalan immersion in Catalonia, Spain), and elsewhere. In most of these countries, as in Canada, the languages being acquired in immersion programs are few. However, in the US one-way immersion programs exist in 18 different languages including the more commonly taught (e.g. Spanish, French and German), the less commonly taught (e.g. Arabic, Mandarin and Russian) and indigenous languages (e.g. Diné, Ojibwe and Yup'ik). Lenker and Rhodes (2007) report awareness of 310 one-way foreign language programs spread across 33 states and 83 school districts.

Compared with the one-way immersion model, growth of the two-way bilingual program model has been relatively recent and as a public school program is still largely limited to the US context (for a more in-depth discussion of similar bilingual models around the world, see Baker, 2001). In the mid- to late-1980s, US interest in the two-way immersion model grew as a result of factors such as increased attention on research-supported educational models for minority language and majority language students and the availability of federal and state funding (Christian, 1994). During the 1990s the number of two-way immersion programs swelled from 41 in 1990 to 284 in the year 2000 (CAL, 2006). Today the Center for Applied Linguistics' two-way immersion directory reports some 338 programs in 29 states across the US, including the District of Columbia. While Spanish/English programs are by far the most common, there are also eight other languages partnering with English such as Cantonese, Mandarin, Korean, Navajo, Japanese and French.

As decades have passed both one-way foreign language immersion and two-way bilingual immersion models have adapted themselves to better meet the needs of the local school and community contexts they intend to serve. For a discussion of programmatic variations in one-way foreign language immersion, see Chapter 2 by Genesee in this volume, and to read more about two-way immersion program variants, see Lindholm-Leary and Howard's Chapter 9.

Immersion education: A category within dual language education

The dramatic increase in two-way bilingual program numbers during the 1990s was accompanied by a similar increase in program labels. For example, some researchers referred to 'two-way bilingual immersion' or simply 'two-way immersion"; others used identifiers such as 'dual language' or 'dual language immersion.' As anti-bilingual education legislation gained momentum and was adopted by a few states, e.g. California (Proposition 227, in 1998), Arizona (Proposition 203, in 2000) and Massachusetts (2002), the tendency to more systematically replace the term 'bilingual' with less-politically-charged labels such as 'immersion' or 'dual language' grew stronger.

Today, the term 'dual language education' is increasingly used by US and Canadian educators and researchers as a categorical term to differentiate a subgroup of bilingual and immersion programs whose goals, fundamental principles and basic design and implementation features are largely similar. Among the first to name program models that merit the dual language education descriptor, Cloud *et al.* (2000) include the following three: one-way foreign language immersion, two-way immersion, and developmental or maintenance bilingual. Writing from an international perspective, Swain and Johnson (1997) and Baker (2001) identify these programs as falling in the bilingual education category. Baker (2001: 194) does, however, group these same models together and refer to them as 'strong forms of education for bilingualism and biliteracy.'

According to Cloud *et al.* (2000), dual language programs support 'enriched education' by adhering to the principle of additive bilingualism and providing content-based instruction through the medium of a second language (L2) for a minimum of 50% of the instructional day preK–5/6 (from prekindergarten to grades 5/6), while offering sufficient schooling support for the continued development of students' first language (L1). Within this book the descriptor 'dual language education' is used in this manner (e.g. see Chapter 2 by Genesee and Chapter 9 by Lindholm-Leary & Howard).

Departing slightly from Cloud *et al.*'s identification of dual language education models, we argue for the inclusion of indigenous immersion as a fourth stand-alone branch within dual language education. Indigenous immersion programs are dedicated to cultural and linguistic revitalization for Native or Aboriginal groups around the world. Their design and implementation practices meet and in some cases exceed the critical criteria for dual language education outlined above (e.g. preK–12 Hawaiian in the US and preK–12 Maori immersion in New Zealand). In other cases, however, programs struggle to adhere to the defining features outlined below. See, for example, some program models described by Richards and Burnaby in Chapter 11 of this volume. As culture and language revitalization programs intended for entire Native communities, indigenous immersion targets a broader learner spectrum beginning perhaps with preschoolers, or elementary age students and, in certain communities, with adults. Because of the unique needs of these diverse audiences and the profound challenges confronting these programs, some indigenous immersion efforts employ the term 'immersion' to describe culture- and language-driven programs that may at times incorporate more traditional, grammar-based language teaching. This contrasts with the academic content-driven, less analytical immersion model referenced elsewhere in this publication.

Currently immersion programs serving Native students in the US are designated as one-way foreign language or two-way immersion programs depending on the make up of their student population. Linguistically similar to the one-way immersion student audience, one-way indigenous program audiences primarily comprise majority language speakers. However, unlike most one-way foreign language immersion programs, indigenous immersion places significant emphasis on developing student understanding of cultural practices and perspectives for a particular Native group and may withhold the introduction of English until the upper elementary grades or later (Wilson & Kamanā, 2001). Furthermore, in some indigenous immersion programs, English is only taught as a subject and is not used to teach other academic subjects. The same holds true in two-way indigenous immersion settings. Thus, given the expansion and importance of indigenous immersion programs as a means of revitalizing Native language and cultures around the world, we believe these programs merit inclusion under the dual language umbrella. Moreover, given the unique challenges they face and the myriad ways those challenges are addressed in program design and implementation, we believe they belong in a category of their own.

It is important to keep in mind that the more recent meaning assigned to the term 'dual language education' and used by contributors to this publication is not simply another name for a two-way immersion program, as has been the case in many parts of the US. Nor is this term limited to programs that include minority language students, as some have suggested (see for example, Freeman *et al.*, 2005). Two of the four dual language branches, foreign language and indigenous immersion, primarily serve majority language students and a third branch, two-way immersion, seeks to attract English-speaking students for half of its student population.

To promote consistent use of terminology, ensure greater dual language education program integrity and avoid some of the earlier pitfalls that rapid spread and too few program implementation parameters created for researching bilingual education in the US, Canadian and US second language educators and researchers today are working together to reach greater consensus on definitive dual language program characteristics and standards.[3] A few recent publications and resources contribute positively towards this important goal (CARLA's Immersion Projects, 2006; Genesee, 1999; Howard *et al.*, 2005).

We are in full support of these collaborative efforts among dual language educators and researchers. However, because contributors to this volume present research carried out predominantly in one of the three language immersion contexts described above, either one-way, two-way or indigenous, we return our focus to clearly defining this form of dual language education at this time.

What language immersion education is

Building on earlier immersion program characterizations (e.g. Christian, 1996; Lindholm, 1990; Lindholm-Leary, 2001; Swain & Johnson, 1997; Swain & Lapkin, 2005), we confine use of 'immersion' to those educational programs committed to the following practices:

- instructional use of the immersion language (IL) to teach subject matter for at least 50% of the preschool or elementary day (typically up to grade 5 or 6); if continued at the middle/secondary level a minimum of two year-long content courses is customary, and during that time all instruction occurs in the IL;

- promotion of additive bi- or multilingualism and bi- or multilingual literacy with sustained and enriched instruction through at least two languages;
- employment of teachers who are fully proficient in the language(s) they use for instruction;
- reliance on support for the majority language in the community at large for majority language speakers and home language support for the minority language for minority language speakers;
- clear separation of teacher use of one language versus another for sustained periods of time.

Immersion programs are choice-based educational alternatives offered within a larger public school system. Program success and long-term viability is measured primarily by immersion students' academic achievement relative to non-immersion peers as measured by standardized tests administered in the country's majority language (Genesee *et al.*, 2004).[4] Other distinguishing features of well-implemented immersion programs have to do with curricular and instructional elements. For example,

- curriculum is content-driven and language-attentive;
- language, culture and content are integrated;
- classroom tasks are designed to challenge students both cognitively and linguistically;
- instructional strategies reflect linguistically and developmentally-appropriate scaffolding and elicit frequent use of the immersion language;
- classroom interactional dynamics encourage peer–peer communication;
- cooperative learning techniques seek to build more equitable and socially respectful student relationships.

The end goals of an immersion education include academic achievement, bi- or multilingualism, literacy in at least two languages, and enhanced levels of intercultural sensitivity. Within these parameters, program purpose and student population vary. This volume brings together three main branches:

(1) foreign language or 'one-way' immersion intended for speakers of the majority language;

(2) bilingual or 'two-way' immersion for speakers of a minority language and the majority language;
(3) indigenous immersion or 'Aboriginal' immersion for Native Peoples.

One-way foreign language programs primarily aim to create highly proficient IL speakers who better understand and appreciate cultural diversity in their community. Two-way immersion programs also hold these goals. Additionally, they offer language minority children a research-supported path to higher levels of academic language and literacy development in English. Indigenous immersion education seeks to renew a sense of ethnic identity and empowerment through revitalization of endangered and formerly oppressed Native languages and cultures. All three of these immersion branches develop language proficiency in more than one language while positively supporting academic achievement over time.

What language immersion education is *not*

Immersion, the process of completely surrounding oneself with something in an effort to quickly bring about a powerful personal transformation, has long been seen as a highly effective approach to acquiring new identities and competencies. If your goal is to become a musician, immerse yourself in the world of sound and music-making; if you want to become a swimmer, immerse yourself in a pool of water and swim with swimmers; and if you want to become proficient in another language and culture, immerse yourself in a place where you will encounter that language and culture as much as possible and surround yourself with native speakers and culturally authentic experiences. It seems the term 'immersion' for many individuals is synonymous with getting farther towards one's goal faster – arguably a good thing. Small wonder that people have opted to teach and learn through immersion experiences for millennia.

Clearly, many people make use of the word 'immersion' as described above. Even those in the field of language education can and have overextended its use resulting in the need for immersion and bilingual researchers to provide in-depth explanations about appropriate and inappropriate use (see for example, Cohen & Swain, 1976; Hernandez-Chavez, 1984; Lambert, 1984; Mora *et al.*, 2001; Wink, 1991). As an example, some use the 'immersion' label to describe any language program that teaches the language by using the language all or most of the time, a practice that typically necessitates the teacher's adoption of a number of immersion strategies and techniques. Program use of such immersion methodologies, while necessary, is not sufficient. Others, such as US educators implementing 'English immersion,' use the term even though the end goal of the program is schooling in and language and literacy support for one language, the majority language. Exclusive use of an L2 to teach subject matter and develop literacy for minority language children is also insufficient.

Witnessing the misappropriation of the term 'immersion' during the early 1980s, Wallace Lambert (1984), one of two academics consulted for the French immersion pilot program in Canada, published a chapter widely disseminated in the US to clearly articulate the intended meaning of 'immersion.' Coining the terms 'additive bilingualism' to describe language immersion education for majority language children and 'subtractive bilingualism' to describe many bilingual education programs for minority language children, he clarified:

> Immersion programs were not designed or meant for ethnolinguistic groups in North America that have some language other than English as the main language used in the home. To place such children in an initially all-English instructional program would be to misapply the immersion process in a harmful, subtractive way. Their personal identities, their early conceptual development, their chances of competing or succeeding in schools or in occupations, and their interest in trying to succeed would all be hampered by an immersion-in-English program. (Lambert, 1984: 26)

Lambert and several other leading researchers in the field set out to pinpoint the reasons that adopting a 'one-language-immersion-program-fits-all' approach in North American public education was grossly misguided (Campbell, 1984). Among the reasons identified were substantive program design differences: Canadian foreign language immersion programs were optional language enrichment programs that suspended instruction in English for a relatively short period of time during which the child's family and community continued to support development of the first language. In contrast, so-called 'structured immersion' programs in the US were publicly-funded, compensatory programs designed for minority language children whose L1 did not carry majority language status or whole community support for maintenance in public schools.

Therefore, language program practices that are not consistent with the label 'immersion' education as discussed in this volume include:

- using only the L2 to communicate while teaching explicitly about the language and offering limited to no long-term support for maintenance of the learner's L1;
- offering less than 50% of content instruction in an L2 during the

school day at the elementary (preK–5/6) level and offering fewer than two content areas to students in a secondary continuation program;
- providing intensive short-term (a few days to a few weeks) residential experiences that focus on developing communicative language skills and cultural understanding by using the L2 exclusively; and
- offering intensive in-country learning abroad opportunities where students live with families and attend classes to develop language proficiency.

By clearly delimiting its use, it is our intention to avoid potential miscommunication regarding research findings in language immersion education. As Torres-Guzmán *et al.* (2005) caution, when program labels are adopted without fully understanding and implementing the program's essential characteristics, program comparison research becomes highly problematic – nothing more than a meaningless comparison of apples and oranges. In the end, labels do not make a program model, within-program practices do.

Immersion Education: A Call for 'Cross-Fertilization"

In our work over a number of years with a range of immersion language programs and educators, we remain consistently impressed by the passion and commitment expressed by these practitioners and researchers. It has also become increasingly apparent that a relationship often exists between type of program, be it one-way, two-way or indigenous, and the predominant focus of this passion. Foreign language immersion teachers, for example, ardently argue for the importance of giving monolingual, majority language children L2 proficiency and an appreciation for other cultures. With a similar degree of conviction, two-way immersion teachers express a profound commitment to the education and well-being of minority language learners whose academic and linguistic needs have been poorly met for decades in US schools. Indigenous immersion teachers as well are deeply dedicated to breathing life back into an endangered language and culture, and rebuilding a positive sense of Native identity by passing on language and Native ways to children.

As truly inspiring as each group's impassioned focal point of purpose is, such singular focus holds the potential for unnecessarily narrowing one's vision and attention to a single group of learners. However, 21st century immersion classrooms are increasing in diversity both linguistically and culturally. Spanish-speaking children are enrolling in 'one-way' Spanish immersion programs (Fortune & Tedick, 2006), non-Hawaiian background,

English-speaking children are attending Hawaiian-medium schools (Kauanoe Kamanā, personal communication, December 5, 2006), Canadian French immersion programs are finding a greater number of third language children among their students (Dagenais, Chapter 10 this volume), and two-way immersion programs report difficulty in fulfilling the recommended one-third minimum guideline for both language groups (e.g. Torres-Guzmán *et al.*, 2005). As choice-based educational options, this is not surprising. It is parents, not educators, who largely determine the make up of program populations.

Given the range of linguistically and culturally diverse students enrolled in many immersion programs, we see a number of benefits in coming together as professional colleagues at conferences and for professional development. Professional exchange of findings and practices across immersion contexts can be mutually enriching. While each branch's primary purpose and learner audience are unique, immersion education's guiding principles, end goals and main curricular and instructional practices overlap and thus lend themselves to a variety of immersion contexts. Further, we suggest that to function as more or less isolated entities and limit our knowledge and understanding to research and practice in but one variety of immersion education is to remain uninformed about potentially enlightening findings emerging from another. In so doing, we also risk under-attending to the full range of diverse learning needs that exist in many immersion classrooms.

In sum, as language immersion teacher educators and researchers it is our experience that there is a great deal to be gained through exchange of research findings across program contexts such as those found in this publication. To increase understanding of effective immersion pedagogy, reflecting on teacher discourse practices, language and content integration and interrelationships between language and literacy development is important work. To increase understanding of issues in learners' immersion language development, considering the notion of instructional counterbalance, the productive role of repetition in language learning, and elicitation and feedback strategies makes a difference. To increase understanding of how local context shapes program evolution, giving consideration to the ways local agendas impact program potential, the more effectual teaching and learning practices in Native communities, the potential benefit of incorporating language awareness activities, and the need for systematic assessment of academic and linguistic development in both languages challenges all immersion educators.

We suggest that much will be gained by drawing upon research carried out in different program contexts to inform curricular and instructional practice. Each program has its unique situational dynamics to address, and such dynamics must be carefully considered particularly in the interpretation of research findings. Nevertheless, there is much to be learned from research and practices carried out in closely related immersion settings. This volume presents an opportunity to do just this.

Overview of the Volume

The volume begins with a chapter by Fred Genesee that addresses the importance of bi- and multilingual competence in this era of globalization of the world's economies and describes the important role that schools must play in developing bi- and multilingual citizens. Genesee's chapter sets the stage for the remainder of the book as it provides a research synthesis that highlights the critical issues underlying all dual language programs including topics such as additive bilingualism, content-based instruction, age and length of exposure. Drawing on research from the three dual language program models originally identified by Cloud *et al.* (2000), Genesee speaks to lessons learned about effective programs and challenges that remain in the fields of immersion and bilingual education, such as the need to further explore questions related to special needs populations, in particular those that are also minority language learners.

The next ten chapters are organized into three sections, each of which demonstrates different ways that the field of immersion education continues to evolve around the world. Part 1, *Evolving Perspectives on Immersion Pedagogy*, shows the evolution of our understanding of what it takes to provide effective instruction in immersion contexts. Part 2, *Evolving Perspectives on Language Development in Immersion Contexts*, speaks to the evolution of our responses to issues related to learner language development. The evolution of contexts in which immersion occurs and how context impacts programs are showcased in Part 3, *Evolving Perspectives on Social Context and Its Impact on Immersion Programs*.

Consisting of three chapters, Part 1 offers *Evolving Perspectives on Immersion Pedagogy*. Myriam Met opens this section with an exploration of the mutual interdependence of language, literacy, and academic achievement. She highlights our evolving understanding of and need to address the academic language and literacy demands in immersion contexts. Met concludes with a description of strategies for promoting language learning through content instruction that will benefit all immersion education program models.

In the next chapter, Tara Fortune, Diane Tedick and Constance Walker report on an interpretive study that examined the content and language teaching behaviors of five practicing immersion teachers representing both one-way and two-way contexts. Relying on the voices of the participating teachers, the co-authors describe six themes that emerged from the data and conclude with implications for teacher professional development.

By highlighting the role that equitable discourse in immersion class-room interaction plays in the development of cross-cultural under-standing, in the final chapter of this section Deborah Palmer contributes to our understanding of this core goal of all immersion programs. She summarizes her year-long ethnographic discourse analysis of a second grade classroom in a two-way immersion program where minority and majority language learners participate together, and illustrates how one immersion teacher, through skillfully managed classroom talk, creates opportunities for more equitable talk patterns among students. Doing so, Palmer argues, allows minority language students to develop academi-cally-oriented identities and find success in school.

The second section of the volume, *Evolving Perspectives on Language Development in Immersion Classrooms*, showcases research on language development in one-way, foreign language immersion programs. The first chapter is co-authored by Merrill Swain and Sharon Lapkin and reports on a study involving the use of multitask activities with Grade 8 French immersion students in Canada. They focus on the language learned through the task stages and share insights from the learners themselves.

In the second chapter of this section, Roy Lyster and Hirohide Mori draw on a number of studies to outline a rationale for 'instructional counterbal-ance,' or a balance of both form-oriented and meaning-oriented instruc-tional approaches to improve the language proficiency of immersion students. Lyster and Mori rely on data from French and Japanese immer-sion programs to illustrate their points.

This section concludes with a chapter by Margareta Södergård, who describes her ethnographic case study of a Swedish kindergarten class-room teacher in Finland. She identifies two categories of strategies that the teacher used to encourage and aid students in their production of the immersion language: strategies to elicit immersion language use and feed-back strategies that followed students' utterances.

Part 3, *Evolving Perspectives on Social Context and Its Impact on Immersion Programs*, contains four chapters that in turn provide examples of how immersion programs evolve responsively depending upon a particular social context. A unique US example of how immersion has evolved in response to the changing demographics of US schools and the ever-changing sociopolitical landscape is the focus of the first chapter in this section. In a synthesis of the research on two-way immersion programs in the US, co-authors Kathryn Lindholm-Leary and Elizabeth Howard draw on well-replicated research that highlights the language development and academic achievement of late elementary and middle school students. They conclude with instructional implications and suggestions for future research. As movement of people around the globe escalates, demographics continue to shift and other countries are now looking to the two-way model as one they might embrace.

In Chapter 10, Diane Dagenais shows how classic French immersion programs in Canada are evolving in response to demographic shifts. She describes her ethnographic research on critical language awareness activities in a one-way, early, total French immersion program that serves majority language (the L1 is English) children as well as third language learners. The sociocultural context of the school where the study was conducted is the highly diverse, multilingual region of Vancouver, Canada. Dagenais discusses how language awareness activities may foster more inclusive learning environments by having students systematically attend to the range of languages and cultures represented in their classmates and their communities.

Chapter 11 continues with the social context of Canada and highlights efforts to revitalize Canadian Aboriginal languages through immersion and other language intensive program models. Often turning to the voices of Aboriginal language speakers themselves, Merle Richards and Barbara Burnaby explore some of the unique challenges that face immersion education when the focus is revitalization of endangered Aboriginal languages and cultures. The authors share some of the successes that language intensive programs for adults in particular have brought to the country's revitalization efforts.

The sociocultural context of the final chapter in this section is Hong Kong, where Philip Hoare and Stella Kong review the continued evolution of English late immersion programs, which target Chinese speakers and provide them with access to a language of power. Hoare and Kong synthesize a wealth of research on these programs that has been conducted in the past decade and analyze the sociopolitical factors in the region that continue to weigh against English immersion.

The volume concludes with a synthesis chapter by G. Richard Tucker and Deborah Dubiner, who identify six overarching themes they found reflected in the volume's chapters. Tucker and Dubiner also discuss three areas of research in which, they argue, additional attention is needed. They conclude with a call for more longitudinal research in the field and find, in concurrence with other contributing authors and the editors of this volume, that language immersion education provides an excellent pathway to multilingualism.

Conclusion

In considering the title for this volume we purposefully chose to use pathways to 'multilingualism,' rather than 'bilingualism.' We did this for a variety of reasons. First, the linguistic landscape, as presently experienced in Canada and the US, is reflected in many parts of the world. More and more immersion programs enroll children who speak a home language not used at school. Secondly, we are beginning to see some immersion programs that systematically introduce all students to a third language as early as kindergarten – for example, Alicia Chacón International School in El Paso, Texas.[5] Thirdly, we are aware that a number of former immersion students choose to study a third language by the time they enter high school or university. We suggest that language immersion students, whether in foreign language, two-way, or indigenous language programs, may be uniquely primed for acquiring additional languages and propose this as an important area for future research.

It is increasingly clear that in the economically and politically interdependent world of today, realizing effective educational pathways to multilingualism and intercultural competencies is essential. Further, given the highly diverse social and cultural contexts in which immersion programs exist throughout the world, and the variety of purposes for implementing an immersion program, the challenge of identifying and consistently implementing program characteristics, whether at the macro- or micro-level, is significant. Still, we argue for the importance of delineating essential parameters that define the term 'language immersion' and for the need to come together as professionals to learn from and with one another and improve immersion program efficacy.

Notes

1. A minority language speaker speaks a minority or non-dominant language given a particular national context, for example, Spanish in the US or French in British Columbia, Canada. In contrast, a majority language speaker is an individual who is proficient in the majority or dominant language of the country, for example, English in the US and Japanese in Japan.
2. Thomas and Collier (2002) use the terms 'one-way' and 'two-way' to describe developmental bilingual education programs that may comprise either a linguistically homogeneous or a linguistically heterogeneous student group. Other researchers have also adopted this use (see for example, Freeman *et al.*, 2005; Gómez *et al.*, 2005).
3. The National Dual Language Consortium (NDLC) is a new collective of dual language supportive organizations and centers. Founding members include: the Center for Advanced Research on Language Acquisition (CARLA), the Center for Applied Linguistics (CAL), Dual Language Education of New Mexico, the Illinois Resource Center (IRC), and Two-Way California Association for

Bilingual Education (2-way CABE) and two-way immersion researcher Kathryn Lindholm-Leary. This consortium seeks to coordinate, consolidate and disseminate resources and research in support of dual language education.
4. Measuring academic success on English-medium tests only is typical of one-way programs. In contrast, many two-way immersion programs assess student achievement in both languages of instruction. This is viewed as necessary, since students enter the program with different native languages.
5. Alicia Chacón International School is a two-way Spanish/English program where the K–8 student body is subdivided into four third-language families. Through culture-specific activities and 30-minute language lessons, all students are introduced to either Mandarin Chinese, German, Japanese or Russian. This is referred to as an 80-10-10 model, and it is reported that students are successfully acquiring good communication skills in a third language in addition to Spanish and English (Calderón & Minaya-Rowe, 2003).

References

Baker, C. (2001) *Foundations of Bilingual Education and Bilingualism* (3rd edn). Clevedon: Multilingual Matters.

CAL (2006) *Directory of Two-Way Bilingual Immersion Programs in the US*. Online at http://www.cal.org/twi/directory. Accessed 25.05.07.

Calderón, M.E. and Minaya-Rowe, L. (2003) *Designing and Implementing Two-Way Bilingual Programs*. Thousand Oaks, CA: Corwin Press, Inc.

Campbell, R.N. (1984) *Studies on Immersion Education: A Collection for U S Educators*. Sacramento, CA: California State Department of Education.

CARLA (2006) *Frequently Asked Questions About Immersion Education*. Online at http://www.carla.umn.edu/immersion/FAQs.html. Accessed 9.11.07.

Christian, D. (1994) *Two-Way Bilingual Education: Students Learning through Two Languages* (Educational Practice Report No. 12). Washington, DC: National Center for Research on Cultural Diversity and Second Language Learning.

Christian, D. (1996) Two-way immersion education: Students learning through two languages. *The Modern Language Journal* 80, 66–76.

Cloud, N., Genesee, F. and Hamayan, E. (2000) *Dual Language Instruction: A Handbook for Enriched Education*. Boston, MA: Heinle & Heinle.

Cohen, A.D. and Swain, M. (1976) Bilingual education: The 'immersion' model in the North American context. *TESOL Quarterly* 10 (1), 45–54.

CPF (2003) *Canadian Parents for French Report: The State of French Second Language Education in Canada 2003*. Canada: Canadian Parents for French. Available online at http://www.cpf.ca/English/resources/FSL2003/FSL%20200303. htm. Accessed 9.8.07.

CPF (2006) *Canadian Parents for French Report: The State of French Second Language Education in Canada 2006*. Canada: Canadian Parents for French. Available online at http://www.cpf.ca/english/resources/FSL2006/2006%20Index.htm. Accessed 9.8.07.

Fortune, T.W. and Tedick, D.J. (2006) Foreign language immersion and Hispanic learners: Match or mismatch? Paper presented at the annual meeting of the American Educational Research Association, San Francisco, CA, April.

Freeman, Y., Freeman, D. and Mercuri, S. (2005) *Dual Language Essentials for Teachers and Administrators*. Portsmouth, NH: Heinemann.

Genesee, F. (1999) *Program Alternatives for Linguistically Diverse Students* (Educational Practice Report #1). Washington, DC: Center for Research on Education Diversity and Excellence. Online at http://www.cal.org/crede/pubs/edpractice/EPR1. htm. Accessed 9.8.07.

Genesee, F., Paradis, J. and Crago, M. (2004) Schooling in a second language. In F. Genesee, J. Paradis and M. Crago (eds) *Dual Language Development and Disorders: A Handbook on Bilingualism and Second Language Learning* (pp. 155–189). Baltimore, MD: Brookes Publishing Co.

Gómez, L., Freeman, D. and Freeman, Y. (2005) Dual language education: A promising 50–50 model. *Bilingual Research Journal* 29 (1), 145–164.

Hernandez-Chavez, E. (1984) The inadequacy of English immersion as an educational approach for language minority students. In R. Campbell (ed.) *Studies on Immersion Education: A Collection for US Educators* (pp. 144–183). Sacramento, CA: California State Department of Education.

Howard, E., Lindholm-Leary, K., Sugarman, J., Christian, D. and Rogers, D. (2005) *Guiding Principles for Dual Language Education*. Washington, DC: Center for Applied Linguistics.

Lambert, W.E. (1984) An overview of issues in immersion education. In R. Campbell (ed.) *Studies on Immersion Education: A Collection for United States Educators* (pp. 8–30). Sacramento, CA: California State Department of Education.

Lambert, W.E. (1995) Keynote address presented at the conference entitled Research and Practice in Immersion Education: Looking Back and Looking Forward, co-sponsored by the Center for Advanced Research on Language Acquisition and the Minnesota Council on the Teaching of Foreign Language. Minneapolis, MN: University of Minnesota.

Lambert, W.E. and Tucker, G.R. (1972) *The Bilingual Education of Children: The St Lambert Experiment*. Rowley, MA: Newbury House.

Lenker, A. and Rhodes, N. (2007) Foreign language immersion programs: Features and trends over 35 years. *The ACIE Newsletter* 10 (2), 1–8.

Lindholm, K.J. (1990) Bilingual immersion education: Criteria for program development. In A. Padilla, H. Fairchild and C. Valadez (eds) *Bilingual Education: Issues and Strategies* (pp. 91–105). Newbury Park, CA: Sage Publications.

Lindholm-Leary, K. (2001) *Dual Language Education*. Clevedon: Multilingual Matters.

Mora, J.K., Wink, J. and Wink, D. (2001) Dueling models of dual language instruction: A critical review of the literature and program implementation guide. *Bilingual Research Journal* 25 (4), 435–460.

Ovando, C.J. (2003) Bilingual education in the United States: Historical development and current issues. *Bilingual Research Journal* 27 (1), 1–24.

Peritz, I. (March, 2006) 'Language bath' parents earn a merci beaucoup. *The Globe and Main*. Available online at http://fanset4.blogspot.com/2006/03/language-bath-parents-earn-merci.html. Accessed 9.8.07.

Swain, M. and Johnson, R.K. (1997) Immersion education: A category within bilingual education. In R.K. Johnson and M. Swain (eds) *Immersion Education: International Perspectives* (pp. 1–16). New York, NY: Cambridge University Press.

Swain, M. and Lapkin, S. (2005) The evolving sociopolitical context of immersion education in Canada: Some implications for program development. *International Journal of Applied Linguistics* 15 (2), 169–186.

Thomas, W.P. and Collier, V. (2002) A national study of school effectiveness for language minority students' long-term academic achievement. Online at document: http://www.berkeley.edu/research/llaa/1.1_final.html. Accessed 9.8.07.

Torres-Guzmán, M.E., Kleyn, T., Morales-Rodríguez, S. and Han, A. (2005) Self-designated dual-language programs: Is there a gap between labeling and implementation? *Bilingual Research Journal* 29 (2), 453–474.

Wilson, W.H. and Kamanā, K. (2001) The movement to revitalize Hawaiian language and culture. In L. Hinton and K. Hale (eds) *The Green Book of Language Revitalization in Practice* (pp. 133–146). Cambridge, MA: Academic Press.

Wink, J. (1991) Immersion confusion. *TESOL Matters* 1 (6), 10.

Chapter 2
Dual Language in the Global Village

FRED GENESEE

The need to acquire two or more languages is not new. Historical documents indicate that individuals and whole communities around the world have been compelled to learn additional languages during the preceding two millennia for a variety of reasons – colonization, trade and intermarriage. We also know that promoting second language acquisition through education is itself not new or revolutionary and, indeed, we know that education through a non-native language was widespread during certain periods of history. For example, during the Roman Empire, education was available to colonies only through the medium of Latin, a non-indigenous language for many areas of the empire (Lewis, 1976). This practice continued into modern times and was only slowly replaced by use of local languages for instructional purposes.

Notwithstanding historical patterns, we are facing growing needs to learn other languages and unprecedented reasons for doing so as we move into the new millennium (Tucker, 1998). Some of the most salient, recent reasons for increased demand for bi- and multilingualism include the following:

(1) There is growing globalization of business and commerce. During the last 10 to 15 years we have witnessed extensive internationalization of industry and business. For example, in the automotive industry, head offices are located in one country (e.g. Japan), manufacture of automobiles takes place in another country (e.g. Brazil) and clients are in a third country (e.g. Canada). Even in North America, where English is clearly dominant, we are challenged to learn other languages to remain competitive; for example, in response to the Spanish-speaking markets in Mexico and the French-speaking market in Quebec. While globalization of the market place often provokes images of English domination, it also increases the demand to do business in local or regional languages.
(2) Voluntary movement of people from country to country is taking place on an expanding scale. Economic reasons for this have already been

mentioned, but there are also educational, political and personal reasons.

(3) The revolution in telecommunications has also created a need for proficiency in multiple languages. The Internet makes global communication available and easy, whether it be for personal, professional, commercial or other reasons. On the one hand, this has created a particular need for proficiency in English, which is widespread on the Internet. On the other hand, as with globalization of the economy, it also creates a need for proficiency in regional languages since Internet communication is not restricted to world languages. Indeed, the current domination of the Internet by English may give way to a much stronger presence of regional and local languages as e-commerce takes hold and begins to commit resources to communicating with local and regional markets.

With respect to the growing importance of English, while there is no doubt that English is growing in importance, there are reasons to believe that the situation will be more complex than the doomsayers predict, and recent evidence suggests that the domination of English does not lead to the replacement of local languages and, moreover, it does not eradicate cultural differences (Wallraff, 2000). Recent statistics indicate that there are more web sites in languages other than English (Global Reach, 2000). The spread of English as a world language does not reduce the importance of knowing other languages. Indeed, individuals and communities who know English *and* other languages will have the real advantages (economic, political, etc.) in the future in comparison to those who know only English.

The Role of Schools

Many children around the world are fortunate because they live in communities that afford them opportunities to acquire bilingual or even multilingual competence by virtue of the co-existence of two or more languages in the community. In many regions of Europe (such as Alsace, the Basque Country and Northern Italy), Asia, South America and Africa, two or more languages are used on a daily basis in the media, in stores, and on the street as people go about their daily business. The opportunities and incentives for dual language learning in these communities are great, and it is not uncommon for children to acquire these languages *on the street*. In other communities, however, such as many regions of North America, a single language dominates and, thus, the opportunity and need to learn other languages are limited. Schools have a particularly important role to play in providing opportunities for children in these communities to become competent in additional languages. Schools are important vehicles for dual language learning in all communities, however, even those that are naturally bi- or multilingual, because it is in school that children learn critical literacy skills. It is biliteracy, not just oral bilingualism, that is important if young people are to thrive in and take advantage of global realities. The value of knowing other languages is intimately linked to the ability to read and write, be it related to business, personal or cultural reasons and be it related to Internet or interpersonal communication.

There has been a long and productive history of research on dual language education in North America, and indeed worldwide (see Christian & Genesee, 2001; Johnson & Swain, 1997, for compendia of case studies of bilingual and immersion education around the world). As a result, we are fortunate to have acquired important insights into dual language teaching and learning and empirically-based information that we can draw on in creating dual language school programs. Studies of strong forms of bilingual education indicate clearly that dual language education is a feasible and effective form of education. Most significantly, they reveal that school-age children in dual language programs have the capacity to advance academically at the same rate and levels as children educated in monolingual programs at the same time, as they maintain age-appropriate levels of native language proficiency and acquire advanced levels of functional proficiency in a second language. Many of these points will be substantiated in the sections that follow.

In the remainder of this chapter, I aim to briefly describe three foundational models of dual language education in the US and Canada that have been tried and tested. I then review and discuss research findings pertinent to a number of important issues in dual language education; specifically, issues related to (1) additive bilingualism, (2) content-based language instruction, (3) age and (4) length of exposure. Finally, I consider the appropriateness of dual language education for all students and, in particular, for those students who are at-risk for academic difficulty or failure.

Three Models of Dual Language Education

I use the term *dual language education/programs* to refer collectively to three forms of bilingual education that can be found in Canada and the US:

(1) *one-way immersion programs* for majority language students (Genesee, 2004);
(2) *developmental bilingual education* for minority language students (Genesee *et al.*, 2004; Lindholm-Leary & Borsato, 2006);

(3) *two-way immersion programs* for majority and minority language students (Howard *et al.*, 2003; Lindholm-Leary, 2001).

It is not possible to provide detailed or comprehensive descriptions of these programs, but brief overviews of each are warranted in order to context-ualize the comments later in this chapter and to frame the program models highlighted in the other chapters in this volume. The descriptions that follow are prototypical, and there is considerable variation in how each type of program is actually implemented in specific schools.

In *one-way immersion programs* for majority language students (also referred to as foreign language immersion programs), students are taught academic subjects and literacy skills through a second language as well as through their native language. The amount of instruction through the second language varies. Figures 2.1 to 2.3 provide schematic representa-tions of alternative forms of one-way immersion. These are prototypical schema of one-way immersion options, and there is considerable variation in the exact allocation of time devoted to each language in actual programs. Minimally, 50% of instruction in immersion programs is provided in the second language (*partial immersion*), including instruction in language arts and other academic subjects. Yet other programs provide up to 100% of instruction during certain grades through the second language (*total immersion*). The grade levels during which the second language is used for general instruction vary, with some programs starting immersion in kindergarten or grade 1 (*early immersion*), and others delaying use of the second language for academic instruction until the middle elementary (*delayed immersion*) or early high school grades (*late immersion*). The grade level in which the L1 (English in North America, for example) is introduced also varies, with some programs introducing English as early as grade 2 and others not until grade 5. All students in one-way immersion programs are speakers of the societally-dominant language (English in North America, for example). Increasingly, third-language learners who are profi-cient in English but who have native languages other than English are attending immersion programs. In Chapter 10 of this volume, Dagenais describes her research in such a program context. Other chapters in this book that describe research studies or syntheses of research done in one-way immersion programs include those by Hoare and Kong (Chapter 12), Lyster and Mori (Chapter 7), Södergård (Chapter 8) and Swain and Lapkin (Chapter 6).

In *developmental bilingual education*, all students are native speakers of a minority language (e.g. Spanish in the US), and the native language along with the majority language (English in the case of the US) are used for

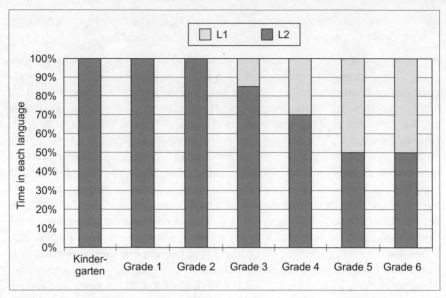

Figure 2.1 Early total immersion

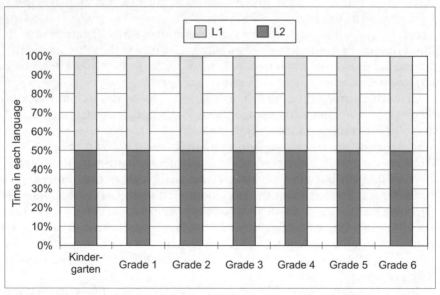

Figure 2.2 Early partial immersion

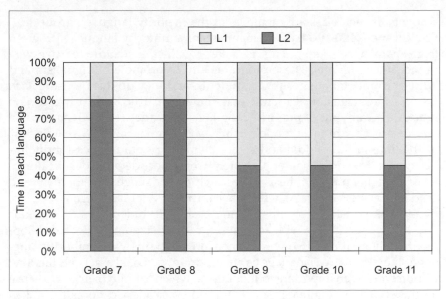

Figure 2.3 Late immersion

instructional purposes, both academic and literacy instruction. There are alternative models of bilingual programs; the main ones are transitional and developmental (see Genesee, 1999, for detailed descriptions of these programs). The focus of attention in this chapter is on developmental bilingual programs in which both languages are used for academic and literacy instruction, beginning in kindergarten and continuing until the end of elementary school and sometimes into secondary school. Typically, the minority language is used for 90% or 50% of general instruction in kindergarten and, in the case of the 90% programs, is reduced to 50% in grade 3 and beyond. These programs, like immersion programs, aim for proficiency in both oral and written forms of both languages. In contrast, transitional bilingual programs discontinue use of the minority language during the primary grades, usually in grade 2 or 3 and, unlike developmental programs, aim for full proficiency only in English. I do not consider these programs further because they do not aim for full bilingual proficiency. Bilingual education for minority language students has been implemented and evaluated most extensively in the US.

Two-way immersion programs are an amalgam of one-way immersion programs for majority language students and developmental bilingual programs for minority language students in that, ideally, half of the students in each class are members of the majority language group (e.g. English speakers) and half are members of a minority language program (e.g. Spanish speakers). This is a key distinctive feature of two-way immersion programs. These programs aim to promote bilingualism and biliteracy among both groups of students, and they do this by using each group's language for academic and literacy instruction during certain grades. The amount of minority language use varies from 90% to 50% in kindergarten, with most models using each language approximately 50% of the time in the middle and senior elementary grades. See Lindholm-Leary and Howard's chapter (Chapter 9) for a more detailed description of these models and a synthesis of research on language development and academic achievement. As with other forms of dual language education, two-way immersion programs aim to develop all students' academic skills and knowledge in line with school and district standards. Both developmental bilingual and two-way immersion programs view minority language students' native language as an important personal asset and life-long resource and as an important foundation on which to build their competence in the societally-dominant language and in academic domains. Taken together, all dual language programs view bilingualism as a feasible and desirable goal for all students, a point I return to in the next section.

Before leaving this section, it is useful to point out that trilingual school programs also exist in North America and elsewhere (Christian & Genesee, 2001). For example, some English-speaking Jewish students living in Montreal attend Hebrew/French/English immersion programs (Figure 2.4) in which each language is used for both academic and literacy instruction during specific grades (Genesee & Lambert, 1983). Also in the Montreal area, students of Mohawk origin can participate in a Mohawk/English/French program in which Mohawk and English are used for academic as well as literacy instruction while French is taught as a second language (Jacobs & Cross, 2001). Trilingual programs are interesting for ethnolinguistic groups living in Canada who speak a language other than English or French and wish to maintain the home language while learning Canada's two official languages. They are useful forms of education for any community whose parents want their children to learn multiple languages (Cenoz & Genesee, 1998a; Genesee, 2002).

Critical Issues

Research on the foundational programs described in the preceding section has afforded us opportunities to learn much about effective dual language education. In this section, I focus on issues that pertain specifi-

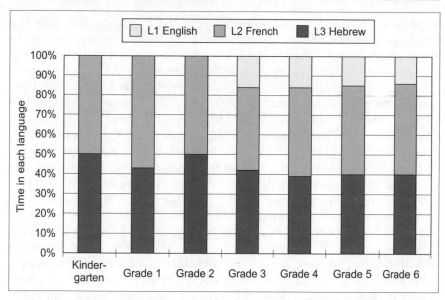

Figure 2.4 Example of an early double immersion program in Hebrew/French/ English

cally to dual language education because these are not always well understood in the general education profession and, indeed, some of them are counterintuitive. I do not consider issues that pertain to effective general education (e.g. the importance of appropriate and timely teacher education, appropriate and high quality instructional materials, systematic assessment, and so on). The issues I consider are: (1) additive bilingualism, (2) content-based language instruction, (3) age, and (4) length of language exposure.

Additive bilingualism

Critical to the successful implementation of any and all dual language programs is the concept of additive bilingualism. First and foremost, additive bilingualism is the belief that all students are capable of fully acquiring two, or more, languages. Viewed from the perspective of majority language students, additive bilingualism is the belief that acquisition of a second language does not interfere with or retard development of the native language. Additive bilingualism underpins all immersion programs for majority language students. For example, in French immersion programs in Canada, it is assumed that students' acquisition of French will not detract from their acquisition of English and, indeed, research confirms this expectation (Genesee, 1987). Viewed from the perspective of minority language students, additive bilingualism is the belief that maintenance of the students' native language will not detract from the full acquisition of the societally-dominant language. To the contrary, it is believed that maintenance of minority language students' native language will facilitate their acquisition of English (Cummins, 2000), and indeed research supports this expectation (Lindholm-Leary & Borsato, 2006; Lindholm-Leary & Howard, Chapter 9, this volume). Additive bilingualism is more than a set of beliefs. It is also an educational plan that fully supports students in the acquisition of two languages at the same time as they master the other academic and cognitive skills and knowledge that all school programs aim to achieve. Additive bilingualism is of particular importance in the development of programs for minority language students because special efforts to maintain and promote the students' native language must be made; otherwise, proficiency in the first language is likely to be lost as students inexorably acquire English, leading to a situation of subtractive bilingualism. Indeed, there are some who argue that use and development of minority language students' native language in school will retard and impede their full acquisition of English because it detracts from the amount of time spent in English (Rossell & Baker, 1996). However, the evidence does not support this claim (see, for example, Chapter 7 in Genesee *et al.*, 2004; and Lindholm-Leary & Borsato, 2006). Of importance for the present discussion, additive bilingualism has curricular and pedagogical implications that are essential for the attainment of full bilingualism.

The beneficial effects of additive bilingualism are linked to social psychological, psycholinguistic and educational issues. Social psychologically, programs that aim for additive bilingualism create supportive learning environments in which students acquire a second language while they maintain and continue to develop native language skills along with the cultural heritage that is a fundamental part of their social identities. Students, thus, have nothing to lose, and lots to gain. Programs that focus on students' second language to the detriment of their native language create subtractive learning environments in which students are expected to give up their native language in order to learn the societally-dominant language. Such programs create pedagogical *double binds* for young learners. We know from many years of research that programs that include the students' native language are just as or more successful at promoting competence in a second language than programs that do not (Genesee, 1987). This is equally true for students from majority language backgrounds (Genesee *et al.*, 2004) and those from minority language backgrounds (Lindholm-Leary & Borsato, 2006).

Psycholinguistically, additive dual language programs take advantage of linguistic transfer (Cenoz & Genesee, 1998b; Riches & Genesee, 2006). Transfer occurs when acquisition of one language facilitates acquisition of another language. This can occur either because specific features of the two languages are similar or because dual language learners acquire language learning strategies that facilitate acquisition of additional languages (Riches & Genesee, 2006). Research in the Basque Country, for example, has shown that acquisition of English was enhanced in the case of students who were already bilingual (in Spanish and Basque) in comparison to students who were monolingual in Spanish only or Basque only (Cenoz & Valencia, 1994). Research on immersion programs in Canada has shown that native English-speaking students in total French immersion programs need only one year in most cases to achieve parity in English development with other English-speaking students (Genesee, 1983). This short catch-up time is probably due to the transfer of critical skills from their French to English, and vice versa. Literacy skills are most likely to transfer. Evidence from Canada indicates that transfer from French to English is more likely when students have acquired advanced levels of proficiency in French (Genesee *et al.*, 1989). Indeed, transfer is most likely to occur when students have some relatively high level of competence in one of the languages; otherwise, there is insufficient competence to transfer.

Educationally, additive bilingualism is critical for successful dual language education because it establishes high standards of achievement. While important for educating all students, high expectations can be especially important for students from minority language and cultural backgrounds who may be thought to be disadvantaged and, thus, held to lower standards because they speak a language and come from cultural milieus that differ from those of mainstream schooling and society. It is not uncommon for educators as well as laypersons to believe that dual language learning poses a hardship and even a disadvantage for young learners because it exceeds their learning capacity. Programs that advocate English-only for minority language students in the US, for example, often do so on the assumption that the students' language learning capacity is limited and, thus, they should spend all their time in school focusing on English. While there is no evidence to support this assumption and, indeed, most research contradicts it, such a belief can result in subtractive learning environments that jeopardize the education of minority language students. Of importance to the present discussion, a belief that students have limited language learning ability and that instruction through two languages exceeds their capacity can result in lowered expectations and, ultimately, to impoverished educational programs (Cloud *et al.*, 2000).

Content-based language instruction

A distinctive feature of dual language education is the integration of language learning with content learning and instruction (Cloud *et al.*, 2000; Echevarria *et al.*, 2000; Met, 1998, and Chapter 3 this volume; Fortune, Tedick & Walker, Chapter 4 this volume). More specifically, in dual language programs, language instruction is integrated with academic instruction so that students are taught academic subjects through the target language, taking into account their language needs. In effect, content is the vehicle for teaching the second language, and content instruction provides opportunities for students to acquire the target language, much like native speakers learn their first language as a result of meaningful, significant and sustained communication with others. As a result, second language learning in dual language programs is often incidental to the learning of academic skills and knowledge and is said to occur naturally. The second language is also used for social interaction in class and elsewhere in the school so that additional opportunities are created for students to learn the language by using it for interpersonal social reasons.

Integration of language with academic/content instruction (especially in the case of young school-age children) takes advantage of young learners' natural language learning abilities because, in effect, it simulates the conditions that characterize first language acquisition. It also promotes the acquisition of authentic language skills – skills needed for success in school. Teaching second languages in isolation, as in more traditional approaches, risks teaching language skills that are not useful in other contexts. Integration of second language instruction with academic instruction has the added pedagogical benefit of efficiency because significant blocks of time do not need to be set aside for the sole purpose of direct teaching of the second language (Genesee, 1987). In support of the effectiveness of content-based second language instruction, extensive research on one-way immersion programs for majority language students (see Genesee, 2004, and Johnson & Swain, 1997, for reviews), developmental bilingual programs for minority language students (see Lindholm-Leary & Borsato, 2006) and two-way immersion programs (Howard *et al.*, 2003; Lindholm-Leary, 2001) has shown that students participating in these programs acquire high levels of functional proficiency in the second language that is significantly superior to that achieved by students in more conventional second/foreign language programs while acquiring grade-appropriate competence in academic subject matter.

Notwithstanding evidence in support of content-based language instruction, there are signs that an exclusive focus on meaning or functional use in dual language programs may not be optimal for developing students' competence in the target language. For example, research on the language skills of French immersion students in Canada has revealed that despite participation in immersion programs for many years, immersion students often fail to master important aspects of the target language, such as verb tense, pronouns, prepositions and sociolinguistic forms (Adiv, 1980; Harley & Swain, 1984; Lyster, 1994). There is additional evidence that students in dual language programs with extended exposure to the target language do not always outperform students with less exposure (findings that will be discussed later) on tests of linguistic competence, suggesting that extended exposure on its own and functional use of the second language do not necessarily lead to increased linguistic competence (Genesee, 1987). Students in dual language programs that emphasize functional use may fail to exhibit continuous growth in both their repertoire of communicative skills and the accuracy with which they use the language because they are able to get by in school using a limited set of functional and structural skills and they are not compelled by teachers to extend their linguistic competencies (Genesee, 1987; Swain, 1998). Arguably, more systematic and explicit language instruction that is linked to students' communicative needs in the classroom along with more explicit focus on the linguistic forms that students have difficulty acquiring would advance students' linguistic competence (Day & Shapson, 1991; Lyster, 1990; Swain, 1998). See Chapter 7 by Lyster and Mori for a discussion of approaches to form-focused instruction in immersion programs.

There is evidence that instruction on the formal properties of the target language within the context of content-based language teaching can enhance students' second language competence (Norris & Ortega, 2000). Explicit language instruction that draws learners' attention to problematic forms and gives them opportunities to self-correct appears to be especially effective in this regard (e.g. see Lyster, 2004; and the chapters by Lyster & Mori and Swain & Lapkin in this volume). Educators are now challenged to develop curricula for dual language programs that optimize language acquisition through a balanced approach that focuses on form and function. In short, while content-based language instruction is effective as a basic approach to dual language education, researchers and educators are calling for more direct and explicit language instruction in order to extend dual language learners' competence. Thus, in the same way that we must provide formal language arts instruction in general education programs for native speakers, we must also do so in dual language programs for second language learners. However, this should be done taking into account dual language students' specific needs to acquire L2 skills that are linked to the academic curriculum. See Chapter 3 for Met's discussion on the interdependence of language, literacy and academic achievement and description of strategies to address the instructional demands of immersion contexts.

Age

Perhaps one of the most controversial issues in second language education is the question of age (Marinova-Todd *et al.*, 2000; Singleton & Ryan, 2004). It is widely believed that *younger is better* when it comes to second language learning. Indeed, an early start to second language instruction has much to recommend. Early exposure to a second language takes advantage of young children's natural language learning ability (Genesee, 2003), and it also takes advantage of young children's openness to new experiences, including new languages and cultures. Moreover, the integrated approach to second language instruction that was discussed in the preceding section is particularly appropriate and feasible in the early grades when education is often experiential and student-centered. It can be much harder to achieve such integration in the higher grades when advanced, sophisticated language skills are needed to master academic content and skills that themselves are complex and abstract. In a related vein, elementary school teachers are more likely to be familiar with and prepared to integrate language instruction with content instruction (so-called *language-across-the-curriculum*) than high school teachers who specialize in specific content areas and seldom see themselves as language teachers. An added advantage to starting second language learning early in school is that it affords more time outside school for second language use and, thus, learning. Extra-curricular language learning affords students opportunities to broaden their repertoire of language skills beyond those that can be achieved in school settings. This is particularly useful when the target language is used in the community at large.

Notwithstanding some clear advantages to starting second language learning early, the issue of age is more complex, since research shows that older students often make faster initial progress than younger students. Let me illustrate this by reference to some Canadian studies on one-way immersion programs for majority English-speaking students. Evaluations of two-year (grade 7–8) *late* French immersion programs in comparison to *early* total French immersion programs for Anglophone students in Montreal (which begin in kindergarten) indicate that late immersion students can achieve the same or almost the same levels of second language proficiency as early immersion students in some domains of language even though early immersion students may have had two to three times more total exposure to French than late immersion students (Genesee, 1981; see also Figures 2.1 and 2.3 for schematic representations of early and late immersion programs in Canada). The advantage that older students have when it comes to second language acquisition is not limited to immersion-type programs, since this has also been reported in evaluations of other forms of second language education (see Burstall *et al.*, 1974).

There are a number of reasons why older students can make such rapid progress in acquiring a second language in school. First, older students have the benefit of a well-developed first language and, in particular, they have fully developed, or well developed, first language literacy skills. Literacy skills acquired in one language can facilitate literacy development in a second language (Riches & Genesee, 2006); this is especially true for languages that are typologically similar and/or have similar orthographies (French, Spanish and English, for example). The interdependence in language development that is evident in older learners is probably one explanation for why minority language students in developmental bilin-gual and two-way immersion programs in the US often exhibit the same or even higher levels of achievement in English than other minority language students who have been educated entirely in English. Students in dual language programs are able to transfer to English skills (and especially skills related to literacy) acquired in their native language. Older students may be faster second language learners than younger students in school settings also because language teaching and learning in school settings are generally abstract and context-reduced, to use Cummins' terminology (Cummins, 1981), and thus probably call on acquisitional strategies that are better developed in older learners. It is important to point out that an early start to second language learning is more likely than a later start to result in native-like proficiency in a second language *in the long run* if learners are given exposure to the second language in naturalistic settings outside school. The advantages that young language learners have in acquiring languages outside school probably result from language being highly contextualized, relatively concrete and simplified. This is not the case for language use in higher grades in school.

That older students can be effective second language learners is a decided advantage when it comes to planning dual language programs because it means that educators and parents can choose an early or delayed start to immersion in the second language and still expect success. It also means that parents and educators could choose to introduce a third language in the higher grades with considerable success. For example, Hebrew/French/English immersion schools in Montreal use Hebrew and French as languages of instruction during the first three grades and introduce English as a medium of instruction in grade 4; English is the students' native language. These programs have been shown to be very effective (Genesee & Lambert, 1983).

It might be questioned whether academic subjects can be taught through a second language in higher grades without diminishing the students' academic achievement. Studies in Canada on late immersion programs that provide 80% of instruction through the medium of French (the students' second language) in grades 7 and 8 have found that the participating students demonstrate the same levels of academic achievement as similar students who receive academic instruction through English in the same grades (Genesee, 1981). This is true for below-average, as well as for average and above-average students (Genesee, 1976, 1987). Academic achievement was assessed in these studies using different kinds of tests: (1) standardized tests in math and science, (2) state/provincial high school examinations and (3) local achievement tests. The late immersion students in these evaluations had studied French as a second language in the elementary grades for short 45- minute periods each day so that they were not immersed in French in grades 7 and 8 with absolutely no prior experience in French. In contrast, in Hong Kong recent subject matter achievement studies of late English immersion programs have not produced similar findings to those in Canada. In Chapter 12 Hoare and Kong offer a synthesis of research findings on late English immersion in Hong Kong, which show that Chinese-speaking students schooled in their first language significantly outperform English immersion peers in subjects other than English and Chinese. As Hoare and Kong suggest, these findings highlight the importance of understanding and responding to context-specific program implementation challenges.

Length of exposure

Another controversial issue in discussions of second language acquisition and dual language education is the matter of time. It is often assumed that *more exposure is better* when it comes to second language learning in school; this is often referred to as *time on task*. Indeed, one of the reasons we begin instruction early (be it in second languages, mathematics or other school subjects) is to provide more time for students to learn. Time is clearly important and often, although not always, students learn more when they have more exposure. This is true for second language learning as well – we know that students in total immersion programs generally perform better on second language tests than students who have been in partial immersion programs (Swain & Lapkin, 1982). But, there are upper and lower limits to the importance of time. At the lower limits, variations in exposure to a second language probably make little difference – 20 versus 30 minutes per day, for example, is probably an unimportant difference. Likewise, at the upper limits, there may be diminishing returns for extended exposure. As noted earlier, late immersion students in Canada perform as well or almost as well as early total immersion students in some domains, despite the fact that they have had significantly less exposure to their second language (Genesee, 1981).

Time alone cannot always account for achievement differences in different programs. Research in Montreal that compared two groups of grade 7 students, both in late immersion programs, illustrates this point well (Stevens, 1983). In one case, the students spent 80% of their school day immersed in French – all regular academic subjects were taught through French. The other group, in contrast, spent only half as much time – approximately 40% of their school day in French. Despite the time advantage of the first group, they did not score higher than the second group on a variety of second language tests. An explanation for the impressive performance of the students who received less exposure can be found in the pedagogical approach used in their program. The half-day immersion students participated in a student-centered, activity-based program that gave students certain choices about what they would study and how they would meet curricular objectives. In contrast, the other program was characterized by a decidedly more teacher-centered approach where all students studied the same topics according to the same timeline. Clearly, the nature and quality of curriculum and instruction are equally as important as, if not more important than, length of exposure in accounting for second language learner outcomes.

The importance of second language exposure can also be influenced by the status of the languages in question. Studies carried out in Canada on second language immersion programs for majority group students as well as those on developmental bilingual and two-way immersion programs in the US for minority language students both indicate that there is no consistent relationship between amount of exposure to English and English learning outcomes; but there is when it comes to acquisition of the minority language – Spanish in the US and French in Canada. In a summary of evaluative research on two-way immersion programs in California, Lindholm-Leary (2001) reports that both majority group English-speaking and minority group Spanish-speaking students participating in either developmental bilingual or two-way immersion programs achieve higher levels of proficiency in Spanish in programs with relatively high levels of exposure to Spanish (e.g. 90% of curriculum instruction) than do similar students in programs that provide less exposure to Spanish (e.g. 50%). In contrast, on English and academic achievement tests, both groups of students do as well as similar students in English-only programs. In fact, in some instances, students in developmental bilingual and two-way programs outperform control students on measures of English language and academic achievement even though the latter groups have had more instruction in and through English than the former groups. For further discussion, see Lindholm-Leary and Howard's synthesis of research findings on two-way immersion in Chapter 9. That time is less important when it comes to learning English is probably linked to its high status and extensive availability in the community at large. In effect, reduced exposure to English in school is offset by its availability outside school. In contrast, length of exposure to Spanish, French or other minority languages in North American schools is relatively more consequential because it has lower status and is less common outside school.

That time is not directly linked to level of learning should not be surprising since time is not a psycholinguistic variable. Time must be translated into effective learning opportunities. Indeed, as Stevens' (1983) study of the activity-centred late immersion program in Montreal discussed earlier illustrates, effective pedagogy can compensate for reduced exposure. Dual language programs must use time efficiently since students and teachers must cover the same standard curriculum as monolingual programs *and* an additional language within the same number of school hours. To use time effectively, educators in dual language programs must have a long term, as well as a short term, plan that links language and academic instruction. The foundations for the advanced language skills that students need in higher grades of dual language programs are built up during the early grades. However, without a plan that identifies what those advanced language skills are, it is likely that important foundational work will not take place in the primary grades.

There is another important aspect of time that deserves consideration here: the acquisition of competence in language takes time. Evaluations of early total French immersion programs have indicated consistently that students generally score lower than control students in all-English programs on tests of English language development when the evaluations are conducted during the primary grades. However, evaluations carried out in the upper elementary grades reveal no statistically significant differences between one-way immersion and control students on tests of English language proficiency (Genesee, 2004). The same has been reported in evaluations of developmental bilingual and two-way immersion programs in the US (Lindholm-Leary & Borsato, 2006; Lindholm-Leary & Howard, Chapter 9 this volume). Thus, the effectiveness of dual language programs can be judged properly only after several years (Collier & Thomas, 2004). Judgments of the effectiveness of dual language programs based on results during the primary grades lack critical information about long-term outcomes.

Dual Language Education for All?

A practical and ethical issue for educators and parents is whether dual language education is suitable for students who are disadvantaged in school owing to home background, cognitive, linguistic or other developmental factors. The concern behind this issue is whether students who struggle to cope with literacy and academic subjects in school should be included in programs in which two languages are used. The concern takes a slightly different form depending on whether we are talking about majority or minority language students. In the case of majority language English-speaking students, the concern is that they will be held back in their educational development if they are taught through a language they do not know. Since dual language programs are often optional and, moreover, they run counter to some commonsense notions about language learning, it is often thought that students with learning difficulties should be discouraged from participating in such programs and should enroll in native language English-only programs. In the case of minority language students (e.g. Spanish-speaking students in the US), the concern is that, since it is critical that they learn the societally-dominant language, minority language students with learning difficulties should be educated exclusively through the medium of English to expedite their acquisition of English. To educate them in dual language programs, it might be argued, will slow down and perhaps even jeopardize their acquisition of English and their integration into an English-dominant community.

In both cases, the concerns are predicated on the assumption that dual language learning is a linguistic, cognitive and educational burden, and students with academic learning difficulties will be at even greater risk in dual language than in monolingual programs. It could be considered unethical to admit students with special learning needs into dual language programs if they are not likely to benefit from them or if the experience is likely to exacerbate their educational difficulties. In contrast, it could be considered unethical to exclude students with special learning needs from dual language education since to do so would, arguably, deprive them of the opportunity to acquire valuable language and cultural skills that would benefit them in their current personal and future professional lives. The latter perspective takes on particular relevance in communities where the additional languages are used and, indeed, are necessary for future economic success (e.g. in Quebec where French is dominant) or for personal well-being (Spanish-speaking communities in the US). With increased globalization, it could be argued that competence in other languages and exposure to other cultures is important for all students and that we are doing all students a disservice if we do not provide them with opportunities to learn additional languages in school.

This section reviews research on the performance of students with personal or background characteristics that put them at a disadvantage in school (Genesee, 2004). Findings with respect to majority language and minority language students are summarized separately. With respect to majority language students (i.e., English speakers in Canada and the US), the following learner characteristics, which are generally associated with underachievement in school, have been examined:

(1) low academic ability or intelligence (Genesee, 1976);
(2) low socio-economic background (Bruck *et al.*, 1975; Genesee, 2004);
(3) poor first language ability (Bruck, 1978, 1982);
(4) minority ethnic group status (Caldas & Boudreaux, 1999; Genesee, 1992; Holobow *et al.*, 1991).

Research indicates quite consistently that majority language students (or students who speak a non-standard variety of a majority language) and have learner or background characteristics that put them at-risk for academic difficulty or failure can attain the same levels of first language competence and academic achievement in dual language programs as comparable students in programs that use only the native language. Students with learning difficulties in dual language programs generally perform less well than students in the same program who are without such difficulties, but their progress is not differentially impeded in comparison to comparable students in native language programs. This has been shown to be the case for all of the learner characteristics identified in the preceding paragraph, although the evidence for students with language impairment is limited. It is also important to point out that research on the performance of students from minority cultural groups (such as African American, Hawaiian, Mohawk) was carried out with students who speak a standard or non-standard variety of English (e.g. native English-speaking students who are of African American or Mohawk background). At the same time, research has shown that at-risk students can benefit from dual language education by acquiring advanced levels of functional proficiency in a second language. Unfortunately, there is no published research that I am aware of on the performance of students with severe sensory-perceptual, cognitive, or socio-affective disorders. This considerably limits our understanding of the suitability of dual language education for these students and poses real practical difficulties for school authorities that seek to integrate special-needs students in the same classrooms. This is clearly an issue that requires much more investigation.

Practically speaking, the available evidence does not justify arbitrary exclusion of majority language students who face special learning challenges from dual language programs on the assumption that they are incapable of benefiting from academic instruction through a second language, or that they will be held back in native language and academic development as a result of such instruction. At this time, decisions to exclude individual students can be justified only by well-documented difficulties for individual students and a sound rationale for why and how these difficulties are likely to be remedied or avoided if they participate in monolingual native language programs. This is not to say that dual language education is recommended for all students regardless of their learner profile since, as was pointed out earlier, the effectiveness of dual language instruction for students with severe sensory-perceptual, cognitive or socio-affective problems has not been investigated systematically.

When it comes to minority language students with special learning needs, the picture is much less clear, owing to a general lack of research on such learners. There is very limited evidence concerning the performance of minority language students with language or reading impairments in dual language programs. See Lindholm-Leary and Howard's chapter in this volume for discussion of preliminary evidence in this area. There is some, limited, evidence that minority language students from low socio-economic staus backgrounds who are participating in Spanish/English two-way immersion programs achieve lower reading and writing scores in grade 5 than do minority language students from more advantaged backgrounds in the same programs. However, this is equally true of English-speaking students in the same programs and in English-only programs (Howard, 2003). The same research also indicates that minority language students with special education needs had lower achievement scores in English than minority language students without special education needs, but that the former had faster rates of development, suggesting that they were actually closing the gap with the typically-developing students. This was also true for native English-speaking students in the same two-way immersion programs. Despite the paucity of research on minority language students in dual language programs, to date, the emerging evidence suggests a similar pattern of results to that found in one-way immersion programs for majority language students. However, caution is called for at this time, pending more extensive and in-depth studies of minority language at-risk students.

Conclusions

In the 1960s, the Canadian writer Marshall McLuhan coined the term *the global village* to describe the consequences that would result from emerging forms of electronic communication that would shrink our world (McLuhan, 1964). McLuhan could not have been more prescient – the global village is here. At the same time, our neighborhoods have become *globalized* as they come to reflect the multiple languages and cultures of the diverse groups that populate them. This is a form of globalization that McLuhan did not consider. Preparing students for globalization, around the world and in our own backyards, calls for educational opportunities to learn additional languages and become familiar with and used to living with diverse cultures. Dual language education offers these possibilities. I have attempted to show that dual language education, in a variety of forms, can and does work. Perhaps the most important lesson we have learned from past experience with dual language education is that most school-age children are able to acquire two, or more, languages successfully in these programs while mastering the academic skills and knowledge we expect of all students. The effectiveness of dual language education is not guaranteed, however. It depends on a variety of factors, some of which I have reviewed in this chapter. Both the challenges and rewards of globalization and the evolving multilingual/multicultural realties of our own neighborhoods are enormous. We are very fortunate because we can face these challenges using the results of our experiences and research on dual language education in North America and worldwide during the last 40 years.

References

Adiv, E. (1980) An analysis of second language performance in two types of immersion programs. Unpublished doctoral dissertation, McGill University.

Bruck, M. (1978) The suitability of early French immersion programs for the language disabled child. *Canadian Journal of Education* 3, 51–72.

Bruck, M. (1982) Language disabled children: Performance in an additive bilingual education program. *Applied Psycholinguistics* 3, 45–60.

Bruck, M., Tucker, G.R. and Jakimik, J. (1975) Are French immersion programs suitable for working class children? *Word* 27, 311–341.

Burstall, C., Jamieson, M., Cohen, S. and Hargreaves, M. (1974) *Primary French in the Balance*. Slough: National Foundation for Educational Research Publishing.

Caldas, S.J. and Boudreaux, N. (1999) Poverty, race, and foreign language immersion: Predictors of academic achievement. *Learning Languages* 5, 4–15.

Cenoz, J. and Genesee, F. (eds) (1998a) *Beyond Bilingualism: Multilingualism and Multilingual Education*. Clevedon: Multilingual Matters.

Cenoz, J. and Genesee, F. (1998b) Psycholinguistic perspectives on multilingualism and multilingual education. In J. Cenoz and F. Genesee (eds) *Beyond Bilingualism: Multilingualism and Multilingual Education* (pp. 16–32). Clevedon: Multilingual Matters.

Cenoz, J. and Valencia, J.F. (1994) Additive trilingualism: Evidence from the Basque Country. *Applied Psycholinguistics* 15, 195–207.

Christian, D. and Genesee, F. (2001) *Bilingual Education*. Alexandria, VA: Teachers of English to Speakers of Other Languages.

Cloud, N., Genesee, F. and Hamayan, E. (2000) *Dual Language Instruction: A Handbook for Enriched Education*. Boston: Heinle & Heinle.

Collier, V. and Thomas, W. (2004) The astounding effectiveness of dual language education for all. *NABE Journal of Research and Practice* 2, 1–20.

Cummins, J. (1981) The role of primary language development in promoting educational success for language minority students. In C.F. Leyba (ed.) *Schooling and Language Minority Students: A Theoretical Framework* (pp. 1–50). Los Angeles, CA: Evaluation, Dissemination and Assessment Center.

Cummins, J. (2000). *Language, Power and Pedagogy: Bilingual Children in the Crossfire*. Clevedon: Multilingual Matters.

Day, E. and Shapson, S. (1991) Integrating formal and functional approaches to language teaching in French immersion: An experimental study. *Language Learning* 41, 25–58.

Echevarria, J., Vogt, M.E. and Short, D.J. (2000) *Making Content Comprehensible for English Language Learners*. Boston: Allyn & Bacon.

Genesee, F. (1976) The role of intelligence in second language learning. *Language Learning* 26, 267–280.

Genesee, F. (1981) A comparison of early and late second language learning. *Canadian Journal of Behavioral Science* 13, 115–127.

Genesee, F. (1983) Bilingual education of majority-language children: The immersion experiments in review. *Applied Psycholinguistics* 4, 1–49.

Genesee, F. (1987) *Learning through Two Languages: Studies of Immersion and Bilingual Education*. Rowley, MA: Newbury House.

Genesee, F. (1992) Second/foreign language immersion and at-risk English-speaking children. *Foreign Language Annals* 25, 199–213.

Genesee, F. (1999) *Program Alternatives for Linguistically Diverse Students*. Santa Cruz, CA: University of California, Center for Research on Education, Diversity and Excellence.

Genesee, F. (2002) Multilingual education in the new millennium. In D.W.C. So and B.M. Jones (eds) *Education and Society in Plurilingual Contexts* (pp. 17–36). Brussels: VUB Brussels University Press.

Genesee, F. (2003) Rethinking bilingual acquisition. In J.M. deWaele (ed.) *Bilingualism: Challenges and Directions for Future Research* (pp. 158–182). Clevedon: Multilingual Matters.

Genesee, F. (2004) What do we know about bilingual education for majority language students. In T.K. Bhatia and W. Ritchie (eds) *Handbook of Bilingualism and Multiculturalism* (pp. 547–576). Malden, MA: Blackwell.

Genesee, F., Holobow, N., Lambert, W.E. and Chartrand, L. (1989) Three elementary school alternatives for learning through a second language. *Modern Language Journal* 73, 250–263.

Genesee, F. and Lambert, W.E. (1983) Trilingual education for majority language children. *Child Development* 54, 105–114.

Genesee, F., Paradis, J. and Crago, M. (2004) *Dual Language Development and Disorders: A Handbook on Bilingualism and Second Language Learning*. Baltimore, MD: Brookes Publishing.

Global Reach (2000) Global internet statistics: Sources and references. Online document: www.glreach.com/globstats/refs.php3. Accessed 13.8.07.

Harley, B. and Swain, M. (1984) An analysis of verb form and function in the speech of French immersion pupils. *Working Papers in Bilingualism* 14, 31–46.

Holobow, N.E., Genesee, F. and Lambert, W.E. (1991) The effectiveness of a foreign language immersion program for children from different ethnic and social class backgrounds: Report 2. *Applied Psycholinguistics* 12, 179–198.

Howard, E.R. (2003) Biliteracy development in two-way immersion education programs: A multilevel analysis of the effects of native language and home language use on the development of narrative writing ability in English and Spanish. Unpublished doctoral dissertation. Harvard University.

Howard, E., Sugarman, J. and Christian, D. (2003) *Trends in Two-Way Immersion: A Review of Research*. Santa Cruz, CA: University of California, Center for Research on Education, Diversity and Excellence.

Jacobs, K. and Cross, A. (2001) The seventh generation of Kahnawà:ke: Phoenix or Dinosaur. In D. Christian and F. Genesee (eds) *Bilingual Education* (pp. 109–121). Alexandria, VA: Teachers of English to Speakers of Other Languages.

Johnson, R.K. and Swain, M. (1997) *Immersion Education: International Perspectives*. Cambridge: Cambridge University Press.

Lewis, E.G. (1976) Bilingualism and bilingual education: The ancient world to the Renaissance. In J. Fishman (ed.) *Bilingual Education: An International Sociological Perspective* (pp. 150–200). Rowley, MA: Newbury House.

Lindholm-Leary, K. (2001) *Dual Language Education*. Clevedon: Multilingual Matters.

Lindholm-Leary, K. and Borsato, G. (2006) Academic achievement. In F. Genesee, K. Lindholm-Leary, W. Saunders and D. Christian (eds) *Educating English Language Learners: A Synthesis of Empirical Evidence*. New York: Cambridge University Press.

Lyster, R. (1990) The role of analytic language teaching in French immersion programs. *The Canadian Modern Language Review* 47, 159–176.

Lyster, R. (1994) The effect of functional-analytic teaching on aspects of French immersion students' sociolinguistic competence. *Applied Linguistics* 15, 263–287.

Lyster, R. (2004) Research on form-focused instruction in immersion classrooms: Implications for theory and practice. *French Language Studies* 14, 1–21.

Marinova-Todd, S.H., Marshall, D.B. and Snow, C.E. (2000). Three misconceptions about age and L2 learning. *TESOL Quarterly* 34, 1, 9–34.

McLuhan, M. (1964) *Understanding Media: The Extensions of Man*. New York: McGraw-Hill.

Met. M. (1998) Curriculum decision-making in content-based language teaching. In J. Cenoz and F. Genesee (eds) *Beyond Bilingualism: Multilingualism and Multilingual Education* (pp. 35–63). Clevedon: Multilingual Matters.

Norris, J. and Ortega, L. (2000) Effectiveness of L2 instruction: A research synthesis and quantitative meta-analysis. *Language Learning* 50, 417–528.

Riches, C. and Genesee, F. (2006) Literacy: Crosslinguistic and crossmodal issues. In F. Genesee, K. Lindholm-Leary, W. Saunders and D. Christian (eds) *Educating English Language Learners: A Synthesis of Empirical Evidence*. (pp. 64–108). New York: Cambridge University Press.

Rossell, C.H. and Baker, K. (1996) The educational effectiveness of bilingual education. *Research in the Teaching of English* 30, 7–74.

Singleton, D. and Ryan, L. (2004) *Language Acquisition: The Age Factor* (2nd edn). Clevedon: Multilingual Matters.

Stevens, F. (1983) Activities to promote learning and communication in the second language classroom. *TESOL Quarterly* 17, 259–272.

Swain, M. (1998) Focus on form through conscious reflection. In C. Doughty and J. Williams (eds) *Focus on Form in Classroom Second Language Acquisition* (pp. 64–81). New York: Cambridge University Press.

Swain, M. and Lapkin, S. (1982) *Evaluating Bilingual Education: A Canadian Case Study.* Clevedon: Multilingual Matters.

Tucker, G.R. (1998) A global perspective on multilingualism and multilingual education. In J. Cenoz and F. Genesee (eds) *Beyond Bilingualism: Multilingualism and Multilingual Education* (pp. 3–15). Clevedon: Multilingual Matters.

Wallraff, B. (2000) What global language? *The Atlantic Monthly* 286, 52–66.

Part 1

Evolving Perspectives on Immersion Pedagogy

Chapter 3

Paying Attention to Language: Literacy, Language and Academic Achievement

MYRIAM MET

Language, literacy and academic achievement are the fundamentals of schooling. Teacher sensitivity to learner diversity and, in particular, student ability to use language for academic tasks such as literacy, requires thoughtful planning, monitoring of instruction and formative assessment. In immersion programs – whether one-way (foreign language) immersion or two-way immersion – attention to learner diversity becomes even more significant, since teachers are continually challenged to provide content instruction to students learning through the medium of a new language. Because language is at the heart of schooling and, because in immersion, language plays an even greater role than in other classrooms, immersion educators must be ever mindful of language, its role in the development of literacy and its influence on academic achievement.

Language and Literacy

Language and literacy go hand in hand. Readers need to know language in order to make meaning from the words they decode, and to make connections among the strings of words to create larger chunks of meaning. Oral language, and, in particular, vocabulary knowledge, is a cornerstone of literacy. Decoding words, matching sounds with their symbols, is an important first step in literacy, but ultimately, reading comprehension rests on the ability to make an accurate construction of meaning from text. To read for meaning, students need to know the meanings of the words they encounter (Anderson & Freebody, 1981; Stahl, 2003; Stahl & Nagy, 2006). Vocabulary knowledge has been shown to be a strong predictor of successful literacy development. As student proficiency improves, performance requires the ability to link meanings with forms; linking meanings with forms both results from and contributes to higher level oral competence. The ability to construct meaning from syntax and grammar is also required for high level reading and for effective writing.

Language is linked to literacy in other ways as well. Literacy is a primary vehicle for language development beyond childhood, and most literate adults have a large vocabulary gained through their encounters with text. Good readers learn the meanings of new words and phrases from multiple encounters in context, while good writers recognize the gaps between what they want to say and what they are able to say, seek the language required to fill the gaps, and therefore grow in language as they engage in literacy tasks.

In immersion, literacy skills in a second language (L2) are expected to transfer to the first language (L1), particularly in languages that share a writing system. Since one of the goals of immersion education is the attainment of L1 literacy at or above expectation, development of L2 language and literacy must be a priority in immersion settings.

Language, Literacy and Academics

As we have seen, language is the cornerstone of literacy. Literacy, in turn, is a tool for gaining, storing, interpreting, and retrieving information. As such, literacy is a critical element in academic success, becoming increasingly important as students become autonomous, independent learners.

Once they have gained the fundamental skills of reading, students are expected to use their literacy as a tool for learning. They read for information; they store information by writing or keyboarding; they interpret what they read, and report through speaking or writing; they retrieve stored information by reading notes they have made; they display and report their academic learning by writing summaries or reports; they give oral reports based on what they have learned.

Language and inner thought are inextricably linked, as are language and learning (Vygotsky, 1986). As students progress through the grades, and as the curriculum becomes increasingly abstract, decontextualized language takes on an expanded role, while the use of concrete materials, hands-on experiences or manipulatives diminishes. By the upper elementary grades, the conceptual abstractions of the curriculum are less amenable to instruction and demonstration of learning through blocks, pictures and objects, and instead, require language and the ability to verbalize thought. For example, students will need a great deal of language to explain the motivations of Europeans who chose to settle in the Americas during the 18th and 19th centuries, or to explain the system of checks and balances in the three branches of US Government.

Verbalizing thought is critical for revealing and addressing incomplete knowledge, fuzzy thinking or poorly formed ideas. Expressing complex concepts through words often reveals gaps in language as well as knowledge. As immersion students are expected to demonstrate their learning verbally, through talk and through writing, they can be challenged by their limited linguistic repertoire. This challenge can actually promote both language and content development as teachers enable immersion students to put complex ideas into words.

At the point in their academic career where they are expected to read and write in order to learn, students need greater proficiency in language and literacy in order to succeed in internalizing academically rigorous curriculum. Academic knowledge is acquired and expressed through language and literacy. 'In school, students are expected to demonstrate what they have learned and what they think in ways that can be shared, evaluated, further challenged or supported' (Schleppegrell, 2004: 2). Clearly, students with lower levels of literacy and language proficiency will have difficulty carrying out the academic tasks required to meet high standards. In immersion education, where students are learning language while learning academic content, and where students have less than full command of the language of instruction, attention to language development is a key to ensuring that students meet the goals and objectives of schooling, and meet the expectations of parents and school leaders.

The Language of Academics

Immersion students must learn both the language of the curriculum and how to identify important information when reading or listening. They also need to be able to convey their learning in ways consistent with the discourse style particular to a given discipline. For immersion students, the ability to use academic language in both languages is important for their intellectual development; it is even more critical in performing at expectation on the standardized measures of academic learning through which both students and program effectiveness are assessed.

Academic language differs from day-to-day informal language in a number of ways. It is organized differently, has specific discourse styles and has a lexicon not normally found in social interactions. The structure of oral and written academic discourse has specific expectations for how information is formatted, where it is to be found and how language is used. Spoken social language is highly contextualized; spoken academic language is highly decontextualized. Where everyday social spoken language relies on the immediate context and shared assumptions between speaker and listener, and is heavily laden with anaphoric references (e.g. this, that, it), academic language relies on words, assumes less shared knowledge between speaker and listener and therefore specifies the subject and uses the noun in places where social language might use pronouns (Schleppegrell, 2003; Stahl & Nagy, 2006).

Immersion students must read academic texts, and these texts also differ from the day-to-day oral interactions of classrooms. Even when hands-on activities are an effective way of enabling students to access abstract concepts, students need extended opportunities to read as well as to do. Written academic language is best acquired through extensive reading and writing, primarily because many aspects of academic language occur infrequently in oral language but with regularity in written text.

Vocabulary knowledge, topic knowledge and academic achievement interact and are interdependent. Knowledge of technical vocabulary is associated with the topic knowledge (knowing the meaning of *chrysalis* entails knowledge of the life cycle of a butterfly). The more students know about a topic, the more they are likely to have acquired the corresponding terminology for their knowledge, and the more likely they are to comprehend direct instruction and texts on that topic, which in turn extend topic knowledge and expand vocabulary.

Among the texts students encounter in school, there are significant differences between narrative and expository texts. Narrative texts are organized around sequences of events; expository texts are organized around logical relationships among ideas. It is possible to get the main idea and even many supporting details from narrative text even when the text contains a number of unknown words. In contrast, deep understanding of the terminology of academic disciplines is necessary for understanding expository text because such terminology labels important and complex concepts. Further, these terms and concepts are often critical as they undergird continued understanding of curriculum concepts to be encountered in subsequent lessons and units (Harmon *et al.*, 2005).

Language, reading and academics are powerfully connected once students have mastered the fundamentals of reading. Language is a vital key to accessing learning: texts in the social sciences are heavily laden with abstract concepts to which the primary access is language. These texts may use familiar words in new ways, and immersion students must come to identify the specialized meanings of words when used in academic contexts (e.g. in English: labor, strike, house, seat). Students must be able to read social studies texts (history, civics, geography) that have relatively few contextual supports for meaning. A cursory review of textbooks reveals that they are often inconsiderate of the reader in numerous ways: illustrations are used to add new information or to provide interesting side notes, rather than to provide visual clues to the meaning of the text; heads and subheads do not always capture main ideas with supporting details; important information may be buried in the captions for illustrations; academic vocabulary is frequently assumed to be known to the reader; and sentences are dense, long and complex.

Mathematics texts, particularly story problems, also present challenges to immersion learners. Mathematics texts are not structured like other forms of expository text. Skimming for the main idea is unlikely to be productive. It is usually not possible to guess the meanings of words from context, and skipping unknown words in the hope that their meanings will be clarified later rarely works. Often, the text is too short to provide the necessary multiple encounters that allow for contextual guessing to be successful. Further, story problems tend to be parsimonious, with few of the natural redundancies found in narrative texts. Decoding skills can also be problematic since symbols used in texts are not amenable to decoding. Reading strategies that are useful in constructing meaning from narrative text may not be applicable to story problems. Although a story problem looks like a short paragraph, it does not function like a paragraph. The relationship among sentences in story problems tends to be coordinate (each sentence having co-equal significance) as opposed to paragraphs where the topic sentence has a super-ordinate relationship with the following subordinate sentences containing supporting details as usually found in informational text. Specific vocabulary (e.g. quotient, denominator), frequent use of abbreviations (e.g. in., cm.) as well as the way in which language is used in mathematics (e.g. Let $x = ...$) are not common to social interaction or other kinds of text and may be confusing to L2 learners.

Reading and writing science pose challenges to immersion students as well. Science texts are replete with academic language that may not be known to students (variable, notwithstanding) and with technical vocabulary that must be understood to comprehend the connected ideas. Harmon *et al.* (2005) observe that this heavy load of academic and technical vocabulary makes reading comprehension more challenging for students who then resort to memorizing facts in lieu of understanding concepts. Fathman *et al.* (1992) suggest that second language learners struggle with science texts that use a depersonalized style that distances the writer from the reader. They suggest that a personalized style might be more accessible (e.g. 'Blood circulates through the body through the veins and arteries' versus 'Your blood travels through your body through your veins and arteries'). For L2 readers, complex sentences and passive voice are more difficult to understand than simple sentences in active voice: 'All living things need nutrients. A good diet contains the proper nutrients' versus

'Nutrients are needed by living things; therefore one's daily diet should contain the proper nutrients.' (Examples are from Fathman *et al.*, 1992.)

Academic texts are a genre with differing text types, structures and organization and different ways of using language. Relationships among ideas are expressed using connectors that occur infrequently in social language: as a result of, arise from, characteristic of, be considered (Harmon *et al.*, 2005). Schleppegrell (2003, 2004) has examined academic genres, drawing on functional linguistics to identify their characteristic grammatical features, and to identify pathways that can lead students into successful academic writing by developing the linguistic resources they will need to control. She notes, for example, that narration relies heavily on the past tense (although present and future occur as well), whereas expository text more frequently employs the simple present. Narration may be personalized whereas expository writing is decontextualized, where language is used to distance the writer from the reader by employing a 'more authoritative voice, using third person and technical language' (Schleppegrell, 2003: 17). Schleppegrell suggests that successful L2 writers need to develop the grammatical tools to elaborate concrete details in narration, to elaborate noun phrases in expository texts, to develop clause-linking strategies and to use the kinds of relative clauses found in academic writing.

Academic writing requires an appropriate vocabulary, not just the technical words that label curriculum concepts, but the types of words found most frequently in academic, rather than social, language. Nation (2001) summarizes a number of research studies that conclude that L2 writers use a far more restricted corpus of vocabulary than do native speakers, and that assessment of the quality of L2 writing can be significantly influenced by vocabulary use. Because academic language is far more decontextualized than social language, L2 writers must struggle to meet the same challenge that native speakers do: 'Students need to develop an understanding of how written language works – and in particular, how well-chosen words are one of the most powerful tools available for making your meaning clear to someone who doesn't already know what you are going to say' (Stahl & Nagy, 2006: 41).

The Role of Vocabulary

It may overstate the case to say that vocabulary knowledge is central to children's and adults' success in school and in life, but not by much. (Stahl & Nagy, 2006: 4)

Vocabulary is a critical element in language and literacy. Vocabulary is defined as knowing the meanings of words – not just nouns, and not just dictionary definitions, but also the contexts in which words are used, how they are similar to and different from synonymous words, their syntactic relationships with other words, and the words with which they often co-occur. Vocabulary knowledge is a significant positive correlate of reading comprehension (Anderson & Freebody, 1981; Baker *et al.*, 1995a; Stahl & Nagy, 2006). Clearly, knowing the meanings of words affects how well both L1 and L2 learners understand what they hear or read. Stahl (2003), citing Wixson and Lipson (1996), reports that it is estimated that comprehension is diminished if readers encounter more than 5–10% of unknown words in a text. Similarly, Nation (2001) suggests that readers need to know the meanings of about 95% of the words they encounter to make an accurate construction meaning of oral or written text, and 97% or more to deduce the meanings of unknown words from context. While learners may be able to get the big ideas or gist with lower levels of vocabulary knowledge, deep understanding relies on knowing what the words mean.

If vocabulary is key to reading success, then it is also important for the growth of literacy. Children with limited vocabularies are not only struggling readers, they are also likely to be reluctant readers. They read less simply because reading is hard for them. And because reading is hard, they do not gain the fluency or vocabulary needed to become better readers. They avoid the kinds of challenging texts that are precisely those that could lead to expanded word knowledge and topic knowledge. Thus, these children know less, and know fewer words. The less they know, the less they learn what they need to know, setting in motion a self-sustaining cycle, a cycle in which the rich get richer while the poor get poorer, termed the Matthew Effect (Stanovich, 1986). Pulido (2003: 264) found the same Matthew Effect in L2 readers: 'In this present study, the rich indeed got richer ... in the acquisition of explicit semantic knowledge pertaining to targeted lexical items ... With increases in L2 reading proficiency, readers also had correspondingly larger passage sight vocabularies ....'

The research on the role of vocabulary in making meaning has significant impact for immersion programs. One reason is that immersion students in one-way programs enter the program with close to zero knowledge of the new language. Another reason is that immersion programs enroll students from a range of linguistic and socio-economic backgrounds, and one way in which this range manifests itself is in the L1 linguistic repertoire of children upon entering school.

Researchers have compared the vocabulary size of children from welfare families, working class families and professional families (Hart & Risley, 1995). Exposure to words varied significantly among the three categories of socio-economic status (SES), children in welfare families heard about one-third the number of words per hour than did children in professional families. The cumulative effects of this exposure and other variables in communication patterns in the home resulted in substantial differences in vocabulary development – by age 3, children in professional families knew almost twice as many words as children in welfare families. By kindergarten entry, the gap in vocabulary development among children from differing backgrounds impacts their readiness to learn to read, and subsequently, to learn by reading. These differences persist as students move through the elementary school grades. Studies have shown that subsequent to school entry, students from low socio-economic status learned about 60% of the number of words learned by students from middle SES backgrounds (Baker *et al.*, 1995a). In addition to differences in vocabulary size among pre-school children, different ways of using language in the home and different parenting styles affect student preparation for the kinds of academic tasks and interactions typical of classrooms. The language that is privileged in school settings may be more familiar to those students whose parents use language in parallel ways in the home, such as in interactions in which children are encouraged to talk about stories and books, interpreting, evaluating, focusing on key text features (Schleppegrell, 2004).

Given these data, it is clear that immersion programs that serve children from diverse socio-economic backgrounds must build proficiency in a new language on fundamentally different bases, while simultaneously developing academic content knowledge and skills. Even more complex are two-way immersion programs, since they serve two groups of students, each of which has a different dominant language, and each of which typically demonstrates a range of proficiency levels in the two primary languages of instruction, and often, comes from a range of socio-economic backgrounds.

Language, Literacy and Academics: Meeting the Challenge in Immersion

The implications of the critical interplay of language, literacy and academic achievement make it paramount that immersion teachers pay conscientious attention to language development. Every content lesson must be a language lesson as well, with particular attention to expanding students' repertoire of word knowledge, word families and word use.

Immersion teachers are accountable to school leaders, parents, and students for ensuring that students develop prescribed academic standards. As a result, it is not surprising that immersion teachers must be certified as elementary school teachers or in a secondary subject matter area and see themselves as responsible for the curriculum. Developing proficiency in the immersion language is often viewed as a natural by-product of content instruction, rather than a separate-but-equal content area to be addressed. Immersion teachers recognize the importance of ensuring that students develop the vocabulary critical to mastering a specific content unit, and almost always attend to student development of the language required to understand, and demonstrate knowledge of, a curriculum topic. Thus, students studying the climate in regions of the world are quite likely to learn terms such as tundra, desert, rain forest, wet, dry, hot and cold. These indispensable terms are part of the *content-obligatory* vocabulary for this unit. That is, there simply is no way to deal with the content without this vocabulary. In contrast, *content-compatible* vocabulary is not required for content mastery, but can be included in a unit to expand students' linguistic repertoire (Met, 1994; Snow, *et al.*, 1989). Content-compatible language is opportunistic – it is included whenever and however teachers can find a natural fit with the content they are already teaching. For example, content-compatible vocabulary for the unit on climate in world regions could be a range of terms to describe gradations of hot/cold/wet/dry: scorching, humid, frigid, arid, etc.

Developing Vocabulary in Immersion Settings

Incidental vocabulary learning

As previously noted, most of the vocabulary known by mature L1 language users is acquired incidentally, rather than through direct instruction. New words are learned through context and life experiences. Few readers of this paper were ever explicitly taught the meanings of *hip-hop*, *hard drive* or *vegan*. Mature readers substantially increase their vocabularies incidentally through multiple encounters with new words used in context.

Incidental vocabulary learning results primarily from volume reading (Cunningham & Stanovich, 2003). The more children read, the more new words they encounter, the more often they are likely to encounter those new words in new contexts, refining their knowledge of what words mean, when and how they are used, with what other words they are likely to co-occur. For vocabulary learning to result from extensive reading, students need to read texts that have enough known vocabulary to make it possible to infer the meaning of unknown words; at the same time, texts also need to include words unknown to the learner so vocabulary growth can take place.

For immersion students, incidental vocabulary development will most likely occur when students are engaged in reading extensively in their new language. In two-way programs, incidental vocabulary learning is more likely to take place in English than in the other language. For speakers of English as well as for learners of English, volume reading in the non-English language is not common as, by the upper grades, most students are reading English outside the school day. Even in school, incidental vocabulary development in the target language may be limited, since, given the scarcity of useful academic texts in the target language, students learn content primarily through oral classroom experiences or from brief texts. These texts may be excerpted from authentic sources or created by their teachers, thus limiting the volume of academic reading in the non-English language. The volume of reading required for vocabulary growth in the non-English language is thus constrained by time and material resources.

Explicit vocabulary instruction

Most researchers agree that while incidental vocabulary development is desirable and possible, it is best complemented by explicit instruction as well (Baker *et al.*, 1995a, 1995b; Beck *et al.*, 2002; Carlo *et al.*, 2004; Cunningham & Stanovich, 2003; Nation, 2001; Stahl & Nagy, 2006). Nagy and Anderson (1984) argue that any program of direct vocabulary instruction can cover only a small proportion of the words students need to know, and propose that explicit vocabulary instruction focus on the skills and strategies that facilitate learning new words from context. Their recommendation is echoed by other researchers (Baker, Simmons & Kameenui 1995a, 1995b; Carlo et al., 2004; Nation, 2001).

Explicit instruction in technical vocabulary may be necessary because of its very low frequency (Harmon *et al.*, 2005), restricting the multiple encounters needed to learn word meanings and uses. For immersion students whose contact with their new language may be limited to a few hours per school day, there simply may not be enough time for a large number of new words to be heard, understood, processed, internalized and produced.

Students can also be taught new words in the context of reading instruction or in subject matter instruction. As teachers begin to pay closer attention to teaching vocabulary in a consistent and systematic way, the first step will be to decide which words to teach.

There are several ways to categorize words. Nation (2001) suggests four categories: high-frequency words, academic words, technical words and low-frequency words. The first and last categories are self-explanatory. Academic words are those regularly encountered in academic text but not necessarily associated with a specific discipline or subject. Some examples of academic words are: academic, mutual, perpetual, integrate. Technical words, in contrast, are specific to a topic or discipline, and knowledge of the word implies some content knowledge as well. Some examples of technical words are: tundra, integer, volt, democracy. Beck *et al.*, (2002) suggest teachers consider three tiers of words:

(1) *Tier One* words are high-frequency words that a student at a particular age or grade level is likely to know (e.g. happy, sad, baby);
(2) *Tier Two* words are important words to know because of their frequency in age-appropriate texts, their relevance to becoming a mature language user, or their importance to understanding a particular text at hand;
(3) *Tier Three* words are all other words, primarily low-frequency words, words not necessary to teach at this point in time.

Clearly, Tier Two words represent the core of what teachers should consider teaching explicitly.

Choosing words to teach

While there are no right or wrong choices for Tier Two words, Beck *et al.* (2002) recommend that teachers select words that provide more precise, complex, or mature ways to express known concepts and words that are: (1) critical to making meaning from a given text; (2) high frequency at the student's age level/literacy level; (3) highly useful (especially for second language learners); and (4) closely tied to an important aspect of the text (e.g. setting, character development, mood).

Beck *et al.* (2002: 19) emphasize three criteria in selecting words to teach:

(1) *importance and utility*: words that are characteristic of mature language users and appear frequently across a variety of domains;
(2) *instructional potential*: words that can be worked with in a variety of ways so that students can build rich representations of them and of their connections to other words and concepts;
(3) *conceptual understanding*: words for which students understand the general concept but which provide precision and specificity in describing the concept.

Immersion teachers may find these criteria a useful guide in selecting content-compatible vocabulary to incorporate into reading and other content area lessons. The challenge, however, is distinguishing Tier One from Tier Two words for L2 learners. Beck *et al.* (2002) classify words as Tier One if teachers can readily assume that most, if not all, students already know these words. Tier One words are the high-frequency words that constitute part of every day life for even those children with less than optimal exposure to language in their home. Despite controlling a limited lexicon in their L2, most immersion students know far fewer words in their L2 than does a native-speaker peer. In two-way immersion programs, the complexity of classifying words as Tier One or Tier Two is intensified by the nature of the student population. Obviously, one factor is that at least half the class has proficiency in the language of instruction, whether the school day is divided equally between English and the immersion language, or with 90% target language and 10% English. Further, the population of English language learners (ELLs) in a two-way classroom will present a wide range of English language proficiency upon school entry. The vocabulary inherent in new academic content is content-obligatory, and is probably new vocabulary needed by all students. In contrast, Tier Two words constitute content-compatible vocabulary, the selection of which will rely on teachers' extensive informal vocabulary assessment in order to determine which words may be already known to most students.

Another factor teachers will want to consider is the number of words to be taught. In immersion settings the number of unknown words in a text or new words needed for concept attainment may exceed the number that would need to be learned by native speakers of the language who, it is estimated, increase their vocabularies by approximately 3000 words per year (Baker *et al.*, 1995a; Stahl & Nagy, 2006). Too many words unknown to an immersion student will render oral language or written text incomprehensible.

Teaching vocabulary in immersion classrooms

Once teachers have decided which words to teach, they need to decide when and how to teach them. Explicit instruction in vocabulary does not mean providing students with lists of words and their definitions. Rather, explicit vocabulary instruction is a considered approach that leads students to a deeper understanding of what words mean and how they are used.

Nation (2001) suggests that we learn new words through noticing, retrieval and generative use. Beck *et al.* (2002) describe explicit vocabulary instruction as a series of well thought out activities that, in many ways, parallel Nation's description of vocabulary development. Others, such as Carlo *et al.* (2004) have also developed thoughtful and effective approaches to vocabulary instruction in L2 settings. These approaches, like others, focus on providing rich experiences for students with new words and their meanings.

The first step in learning new words is matching meaning with form (how a word sounds or is spelled), consistent with Krashen's (1982) notion of *comprehensible input*. One of the most common strategies used by immersion teachers is to support language with visuals, such as body language, pictures, diagrams, manipulatives, illustrations, overhead transparencies, graphic organizers (including charts or timelines) and concrete objects. This strategy has the benefit of making the larger meaning of discourse transparent as well as giving students the opportunity to learn new words in context, facilitating deducing a match between what they see or experience with what they hear. Particular words within a lesson or text can be singled out for explicit instruction.

While comprehension is clearly a vital step, students must notice the new words in the input. Student noticing can be facilitated in a number ways such as teacher voice used for emphasis, pausing and repetition (or boldface/highlights in text), calling attention to specific words, or using visuals to emphasize particular words. Even simple techniques such as writing the word on the board, stopping to define a word, or paraphrasing a key word in the context of telling a story can promote noticing. Students may also notice words in the input because they have heard the word before. Frequently, words or expressions are noticed because they fill a gap perceived by the learner. Experienced language learners report that they frequently notice novel words or expressions in the input when they encounter a felicitous word or phrase, particularly when they have been searching for a means of expressing that very idea (the '*oh that's how you say it*' phenomenon). In Chapter 6 of this volume Swain and Lapkin provide an example of giving students a specific noticing task wherein they compare a draft of their work with a reformulation or rewriting of their work by a native speaker. Such noticing tasks serve not only as strong research tools but also as valuable pedagogical tools.

After students have noticed a word in the input, they must repeatedly retrieve it from memory (Nation, 2001). Retrieval can be receptive or productive. *Receptive* retrieval is occasioned by hearing or reading the word used in context many times. *Productive* retrieval occurs when students use the word when speaking or writing. Teachers promote retrieval by structuring classroom activities that require repeated retrieval of meaning from storage. Research indicates that retention of new vocabulary and incidental vocabulary learning are enhanced by class discussion (Harmon *et al.*, 2005). Teacher questions should use the new vocabulary and be structured to elicit use of the vocabulary in student responses. It is helpful at this stage for teachers to avoid substituting pronouns for new terminology (e.g. 'Hurricanes and tornadoes share some things in common. ~~They~~ Hurricanes and tornadoes both ...').

Complex or challenging texts for which comprehension of new vocabulary is required can be re-written in parallel forms that use simple sentences that not only include new vocabulary, but embed multiple ways of defining the new vocabulary. There are a number of ways of defining new words in the context of a lesson or text: paraphrasing (in other words, ...); defining by example (mountains, plateaus and buttes are landforms); defining through explanation (evaporation is the process by which...); definition (one foot equals 12 inches); synonymy (a letter carrier is sometimes called a mailman); or context of use (in this case, *the people* refers to those represented by the government). These definitional strategies result in multiple exposures to new language in a more comprehensible fashion. They also scaffold access as students work through the original, more complex version of the text. Texts written collaboratively by the whole class give students opportunities to hear and produce new terms related to a content lesson (We learned that cotyledon provides food to the plant. The cotyledon ...).

Extensive reading on a given topic promotes retrieval as a particular corpus of vocabulary is likely to be encountered in multiple texts on the same subject. Focused extensive reading on a given topic also allows readers to encounter the same key words in many contexts, allowing students to gain a deeper understanding of what the word means, how it is used, with what other words it is likely to co-occur. Similar to focused reading on a topic, author study can enhance retrieval as well. Reading extensively works produced by a given author is likely to result in multiple encounters with a corpus of vocabulary, given that author style results in some word choices over others.

Productive retrieval requires students to recall words and their meanings from storage and use them in their output. When new words occur in narration, repeated storytelling, re-tellings with minor variations, paraphrasing and summarizing are ways in which both receptive and productive retrieval can be encouraged. These same strategies – paraphrasing and summarizing – are effective for retrieval of new vocabulary from oral and written informational texts.

Beck *et al*. (2002) have researched strategies that deepen students' understandings of word meanings and their appropriate contexts of use, all of which align well with Nation's (2001) assertion that repeated opportunities for receptive and productive retrieval is essential to acquiring new vocabulary. Among the strategies that Beck *et al*. recommend are word associations, sentence completions that require students to attend to word meaning (The *turbulence* caused the airplane to ...); questions/answers focused on new word meanings (What are some reasons a person might be *livid*?); making choices (Which of the following places do you think has *scorching* temperatures?); and eliciting examples from students (If there were an *urgent* message for you from your mom, what might it say?).

As we have seen, internalizing new words and using them appropriately requires multiple encounters with them used in meaningful contexts.

These encounters help refine what the word means (and sometimes, what it does not mean), how it is used in context, the words that frequently accompany it, and reinforce multiple meanings (polysemy) when students encounter known words in new contexts. For immersion students, this is a challenging aspect of word knowledge.

As mentioned earlier, students learning a language other than English in immersion settings have far more restricted contact with their new language than do ELLs. Their exposure to the new language is usually limited to several hours a day; even ELLs in two-way programs may have considerably less contact with their L1 than do peers living in the target culture. Because their understanding of words in the non-English language may not be sufficiently well developed, they may miss subtleties of meaning inherent in narrative text, and may have difficulty dealing with notions of author craft, style and stance. For example, skilled authors imply character traits and feelings through word choice, such as the differences implied by a character who *said*, *murmured*, *demanded* or *argued*. They may miss the imagery inherent in describing a character who *walked*, *lumbered* or *scampered*. In academic informational text, technical vocabulary occurs with low frequency beyond the parameters of a specific lesson or topic. Repeated opportunities to encounter these new words in multiple contexts need to be created in the immersion classroom to provide the multiple encounters required to learn a new word.

One strategy teachers might find useful is to have students keep a journal or index cards with new words, particularly those they meet in narrative texts, and record the sentence in which the new word occurs. Subsequent encounters yield additional sentences that begin to give students a clearer picture of the word in use. As students learn words related in meanings, teachers may ask students to go beyond identifying antonyms and synonyms by sorting related words or developing continua of meanings. For example, students can classify social studies vocabulary according to their referents (e.g. people, event, place) (Harmon *et al.*, 2005). Other words can be sorted by their context of use: the words *scorching*, *scalding* and *sweltering* are all adjectives that indicate high temperature, but they can be sorted according to the kinds of nouns they can modify (objects, liquids, air). Using additional words (*chilly, frigid, tepid*) students can make a continuum of meanings from hot to cold. These types of activities, like those suggested by Beck *et al.* (2002), force students to interact with word meanings and deepen their knowledge of word use.

Second language learners can access the meanings of many new words simply because they have already learned their native language. For students whose native and new languages are related, cognates can be a ready source of new vocabulary. However, some research has shown that teachers need to call student attention explicitly to cognates (Garcia & Nagy, 1993). Students may not recognize cognates because the sounds in the two languages are quite dissimilar (e.g. triangle/*triángulo*); sometimes the spellings of the words in the two languages only hint at their relationship (e.g. *homerun/jonrón*).

Students may also need to be explicitly taught the relationships between spellings or affixes in L1 and L2: *ph* in English is *f* in Spanish; the suffix *-tion* in English is *-ción* in Spanish; *-ty* in English is *-tad* or *-dad* in Spanish and *-te* in French. Understanding and recognizing affixes can help students significantly expand their vocabulary in L1 and L2. In fact, for some language pairs, there are many shared affixes with shared meanings (bi-, mono-, -tion). Learning the meanings of prefixes and suffixes means that students are not just learning words, but word families. This knowledge is also a powerful strategy for dealing with unknown words in text.

Because processing words at the meaning level is useful for internalizing new words, semantic mapping (in which students create word webs) can deepen student understanding of what words mean, how they are used and words associated with the same topic domain. Deep processing also is required as students identify the semantic features of known words. For example, the words *pew, stool* and *sofa* are all things people can sit on, but differ in some ways. Table 3.1 illustrates a semantic features analysis for these and other related words.

Table 3.1 Semantic features

Name	Special features	Found in a house?	Special location?
Stool	no back; 3 or 4 legs	yes	sometimes (classroom, kitchen)
Sofa	seats more than one person; 4 or more legs	yes	yes (also lobbies, waiting areas)
Pew	seats more than one person; 4 or more legs	no	yes (church)
Throne	ornate; seats one person; used by royalty	no	yes (palace, castle)

Using Words in Context

Nation (2001) explains that generative processing may be receptive or productive. Receptive generative processing occurs when students encounter a known word used differently from previous encounters, resulting in a restructuring of their knowledge of the word. New information about the word can be anything from its syntactic function (a word that can serve as a noun or a verb), its metaphorical use (*shelf life*), to a collocation (e.g. tea bag, bag lady, in the bag). Productive generative processing involves using vocabulary in new ways or new contexts, or defining the word in one's own words.

Ultimately, increased vocabulary size is only part of the picture. Students need to use vocabulary in larger contexts: phrases, sentences and extended discourse. As students encounter increasingly abstract curriculum concepts that rely on language as a primary means of learning and for demonstrating learning, the ability to read and produce extended texts is a key element of the instructional program. As students come to use reading to learn, they must also use writing and speaking to learn.

Classrooms tend to be places where teachers do most of the talking and students do most of the listening. Swain's (1985) research on immersion classrooms revealed that not only do teachers talk far more than students do, but that the types of responses elicited from students tended to be words or brief phrases. Swain suggests that the preponderance of teacher talk and the limited output generated by students contributes to the less-than-native-like productive skills of immersion students. Swain's research, along with other studies that have shown the importance of output, provides a strong rationale for increasing student language use in immersion classrooms. In addition to the contribution that output makes to language proficiency, output promotes cognitive development. The need to verbalize one's thinking pushes learners to a deeper understanding of concepts as they are forced to confront and address gaps in their knowledge, to clarify fuzzy thinking or concretize incompletely formed ideas. And again, given the intricate relationship between language and content learning in general, and given that immersion classrooms are venues where the intersection of language and content are paramount, attention to producing extended discourse that embeds new vocabulary and concepts needs to be a core feature of instructional experiences once student utterances have progressed beyond the word level.

Opportunities for output and in particular, extended discourse are easily overlooked in the tightly scheduled world of immersion classrooms. Time is a precious commodity in all classrooms because there is so much to learn. In immersion settings, where learning content in a new language often involves instructional experiences that are time-intensive, teachers often report that they are pressed to fit everything into the time available. When time for teaching literacy in two languages (not just one) is added to the mix, it can be challenging to find the time required for engaging students in extended language output.

Graphic organizers

Extended output needs to be nurtured and scaffolded. In many K–12 classrooms, graphic organizers are commonly used as a means of organizing, classifying, and displaying information. In immersion classrooms, graphic organizers can provide an opportunity for meaningful vocabulary retrieval activities, as students enter information in their graphic organizer they are forced to interact with the meanings of new vocabulary. Harmon *et al.* (2005: 268) report that 'the use of graphic organizers accompanied by in-depth discussions can effectively impact the mathematical vocabulary of fourth-grade students.' For immersion students, discussion provides the opportunities for extended output noted by Swain. Completing graphic organizers also provides an excellent scaffold for immersion students, providing the think time needed to formulate the content of what they want to say, to retrieve the language needed to convey that content, and to organize their thoughts prior to speaking.

Student-to-student collaboration

Collaborative pairs and groups are a common means of increasing student opportunities to speak. Pair and group work not only increases air time for immersion students, it provides repeated opportunities for students to notice, retrieve and generate new language. Grouping students of varying proficiency levels facilitates the negotiation of meaning, while giving lower-proficiency students an opportunity to fill the gaps as they hear the language they need to complete the assigned task. In two-way immersion, consideration of who is paired with whom, and for what, can help language learners learn from native speakers. How pairs and groups are structured is critical; as Palmer illustrates in Chapter 5, teachers must carefully and skillfully create equitable discourse patterns among learners in two-way contexts. Grouping students by dominant language also allows native speakers to improve and expand the range of proficiency in their L1, since students are likely to have differing levels of L1 proficiency. Whenever students are working in pairs and groups their interactions must be clearly and carefully structured. Students need to understand how each and every one of them individually will be held accountable for task completion and learning. Without such clear guidelines, some students will dominate while others will be observers. Unfortunately, in such situations, it is often the case that the students who need the practice the most are those that get the least, and vice versa.

Scaffolding output

Scaffolding output tasks can enable students to produce richer and more extensive language. For example, *Think-Pair-Share* is a student-to-student collaborative structure used extensively in elementary school classrooms. In three steps, students first think independently, they pair with a partner to discuss their ideas, and then pairs share with the whole class. For L2 learners, insertion of additional steps that involve writing provides a scaffold for more extensive and complex language. Figure 3.1 gives an overview of Think-Pair-Share Modified. In this modified *Think-Pair-Share*, students write during the *Think* phase. In response to a teacher prompt, students jot down key words or phrases, or begin to complete a graphic organizer. Advocates of *Think-Pair-Share* point out that this thinking time is akin to wait-time (Rowe, 1974), which has been shown to increase the quality and quantity of student responses. In L2 settings, the *Think* phase allows all students opportunities to think about the response, formulate it linguistically as well as conceptually, and engage in written output. Asking students to write as part of the thinking process scaffolds oral output by allowing students time to retrieve the linguistic resources needed for quality participation in the *Pair* phase.

During the *Pair* phase, students exchange ideas, using their written work as a resource. Either during, or immediately after, listening to a partner, students return to their notes or graphic organizer, recording information gained from their partner. Groups of four students (two pairs) then take turns, each student contributing to the discussion using his/her written notes or graphic organizer as a resource, and adding to it as new ideas emerge. As the discussion proceeds, students will have numerous opportunities to expand their knowledge of the topic and accompanying language, and to negotiate meaning, working to ensure that they understand one another and are being understood. At the end of this phase, students may summarize the discussion in a sentence or more (depending on the proficiency level and the topic), and/or prepare to give an oral summary during the *Share* phase.

The third phase, *Share*, is a whole class discussion. At this point, students have had several opportunities to rehearse their output in the sheltered environment of a small group, to verbalize and refine their ideas and to retrieve needed language and to formulate it into comprehensible responses. Teachers may request a written summary, oral report or completed graphic organizer to provide additional opportunities for verbalizing concepts, for encouraging extended output and for providing data for informal or formal assessment.

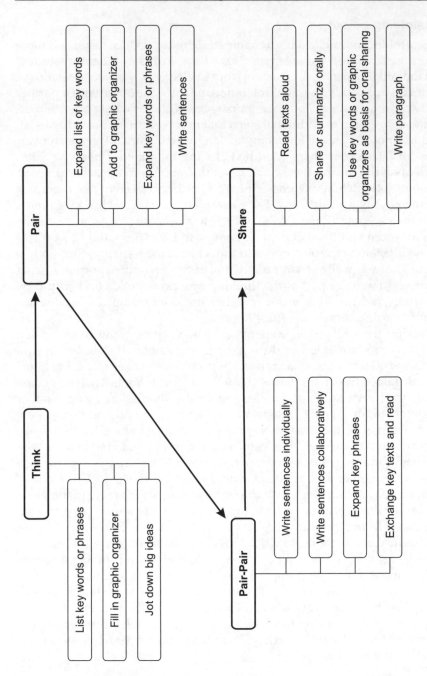

Figure 3.1 Think-Pair-Share Modified

Conclusion

The voluminous research base on language, literacy and school success is compelling: the language children know when they enter school, and the language they learn while they are in school, affects their ability to read with comprehension, to learn rigorous academic content and to attain the growth required to meet high academic standards. This research base, conducted primarily in L1 settings, has significant implications for immersion classrooms in which students are expected to maintain and extend the range of their proficiencies in their home language while simultaneously learning a new language and learning new content through that language. Enabling immersion students to attain high academic standards is a humbling and formidable challenge, but also a moral, ethical and professional obligation.

Immersion teachers and administrators cannot overlook the need to plan carefully and thoughtfully for language growth as carefully and as thoughtfully as they plan for growth in subject matter such as mathematics, science and social studies. Every content lesson needs to be a language lesson as well. Vocabulary development in both the L1 and L2 is the key that allows students to enter the world of literacy and information. Knowing language helps students learn ideas and the words that go with them; the more words and ideas students know, the more successful they will be in learning more words and ideas. The complexity of learning content through a new language makes it imperative that language learning be a central focus of instructional planning and delivery. We can do no less. We must do so much more.

References

Anderson, R.C. and Freebody, P. (1981) Vocabulary knowledge. In J. Guthrie (ed.) *Comprehension and Teaching: Research Reviews* (pp. 77–117). Newark, DE: International Reading Association.

Baker, S.K., Simmons, D.C. and Kameenui, E.J. (1995a) Vocabulary acquisition: Synthesis of the research. Online at http://idea.uoregon.edu/~ncite/documents/techrep/tech13.html. Accessed 14.08.07.

Baker, S.K., Simmons, D.C. and Kameenui, E.J. (1995b) Vocabulary acquisition: Curricular and instructional implications for diverse learners. Online at http://idea.uoregon.edu/~ncite/documents/techrep/tech14.html. Accessed 14.08.07.

Beck, I.L., McKeown, M.G. and Kucan, L. (2002) *Bringing Words to Life*. New York: Guilford Press.

Carlo, M.S., August, D., McLaughlin, B., Snow, C.E., Dressler, C., Lippman D.N. and others (2004) Closing the gap: Addressing the vocabulary needs of English-language learners in bilingual and mainstream classrooms. *Reading Research Quarterly* 39 (2), 188–215.

Cunningham, A. and Stanovich, K. (2003) What principals need to know about reading. *Principal* 83 (2), 34–39.

Fathman, A.K., Quinn, M.E. and Kessler, C. (1992) Teaching science to English learners, grades 4–8. NCBE Program Information Guide Series, Number 11. Online at http://ncela.gwu.edu/pubs/pigs/pig11.htm. Accessed 14.08.07.

Garcia, G.E. and Nagy, W.E. (1993) Latino students' concept of cognates. In D.J. Leu and C.K. Kinzer (eds) *Examining Central Issues in Literacy Research, Theory and Practice* (pp. 367–373). Chicago, IL: National Reading Conference.

Harmon, J.M., Hedrick, W.B. and Wood, K.D. (2005) Research on vocabulary instruction in the content areas: Implications for struggling readers. *Reading & Writing Quarterly* 21, 261–280.

Hart, B. and Risley, T. (1995) *Meaningful Differences in Everyday Parenting and Intellectual Development in Young American Children*. Baltimore, MD: Brookes.

Krashen, S. (1982) *Principles and Practice in Second Language Acquisition*. Oxford: Pergamon Press.

Met, M. (1994) Teaching content through a second language. In F. Genesee (ed.) *Educating Second Language Children* (pp. 159–182). Cambridge: Cambridge University Press.

Nagy, W. and Anderson, R.C. (1984) How many words are there in printed school English? *Reading Research Quarterly* 19, 304–330.

Nation, I.S.P. (2001) *Learning Vocabulary in Another Language*. Cambridge: Cambridge University Press.

Pulido, D. (2003) Modeling the role of second language proficiency and topic familiarity in second language incidental vocabulary acquisition through reading. *Language Learning* 53 (2), 233–284.

Rowe, M.B. (1974) Wait-time and rewards as instructional variables, their influence in language, logic and fate control. *Journal of Research in Science Teaching* 11, 81–94.

Schleppegrell, M.J. (2003) Grammar for writing: Academic language and the ELD Standards. Report for University of California Linguistic Minority Research Institute.

Schleppegrell, M.J. (2004) *The Language of Schooling*. Mahwah, NJ: Lawrence Erlbaum Associates.

Snow, M.A., Met, M. and Genesee, F. (1989) A conceptual framework for the integration of language and content in second/foreign language programs. *TESOL Quarterly* 23 (2), 201–217.

Stahl, S.A. (2003) Vocabulary and readability: How knowing word meanings affects comprehension. *Topics in Language Disorders* 23 (3), 241–247.

Stahl, S.A. and Nagy, W.E. (2006*) Teaching Word Meanings*. Mahwah, NJ: Lawrence Erlbaum.

Stanovich, K.E. (1986) Matthew effects in reading: Some consequences of individual differences in the acquisition of literacy. *Reading Research Quarterly* 21, 360–407.

Swain, M. (1985) Communicative competence: Some roles of comprehensible input and comprehensible output in its development. In S. Gass and C. Madden (eds) *Input in Second Language Acquisition* (pp. 235–253). Rowley, MA: Newbury House.

Vygotsky, L. (1986) *Thought and Language*. Cambridge, MA: MIT Press.

Wixson, K.K. and Lipson, M.Y. (1996) *Reading Disability*. New York: Harper Collins.

Chapter 4

Integrated Language and Content Teaching: Insights from the Immersion Classroom

TARA WILLIAMS FORTUNE, DIANE J. TEDICK and CONSTANCE L. WALKER

Introduction

Early in the history of foreign language immersion education in Canada and the US there was an assumption that second language skills developed *naturally*; proficiency in a second language just seemed to spring from the experience of content study within a richly interactive environment involving language proficient adults and language learning peers. Over time, students' actual proficiency after years of immersion schooling, together with teacher and researcher insight has proven such beliefs to be naive. Research conducted in one-way Canadian immersion programs since the late 1970s has firmly established that students do not attain native-like proficiency in speaking and writing the immersion language (Genesee, 1987; Harley, 1992; Lyster, 1987; Pawley, 1985; Spilka, 1976).

The primacy of subject matter achievement (a legitimate concern of parents and educators and often measured exclusively in English), and a lack of systematic approaches for attending to language development contribute to less-than-optimal levels of immersion language proficiency (e.g. Chaudron, 1986; Harley, 1989; Lyster & Ranta, 1997; Salomone, 1992; Swain, 1988). How can higher levels of proficiency be attained while engaging students in complex learning tasks required for successful academic achievement? The integration of language and content, in particular the kind of teaching that has to occur for such integration to take place, is the 21st century focus in second language education, most especially in contexts where a second language is the medium of teaching and learning (Björklund *et al.*, 2006; Calderón & Minaya-Rowe, 2003; Cloud *et al.*, 2000; Echevarria *et al.*, 2004; Evans *et al.*, 2001; Freeman *et al.*, 2005; Gibbons, 2002; Met, Chapter 3 this volume; Snow & Brinton, 1997; Snow *et al.*, 1989). It is our plan to have the immersion setting and immersion teachers, both one-way and two-way, serve as major contributors to the discussion of how to make such integration possible.

This study aims to engage language immersion teachers in the process of examining their own experiences integrating language and content, and asks them to reflect on specific experiences by reviewing videotapes of their practice.[1] It was our intent to have these teachers articulate their thinking and beliefs about how they attend to language within content. In this way, we hoped their insights might inform current understanding of the practices and processes involved in this complex interplay.

Review of the Literature

There is still much to learn about the knowledge, thinking and teaching practices of immersion teachers, in both one-way and two-way contexts. A review of the literature exposes the lack of attention paid to immersion pedagogy as a topic of inquiry, in particular inquiry from a classroom-based, teacher-informed perspective. A few studies have sought to define the *what* and *how* of effective immersion teaching by surveying experienced practitioners, classifying specific teacher behaviors into broad areas such as *content comprehension techniques*, *negotiation of meaning strategies* and *building redundancy into lessons* (Boutin, 1993; Lindholm-Leary, 2001; Snow, 1990). Other investigations have sought to describe specific teaching behaviors through direct teacher observation (Boutin, 1993; Hoare, 2001; Lapkin & Swain, 1996; Peregoy, 1991; Pérez, 2004; Salomone & Palma, 1995; Södergård, 2001). For example, in Chapter 8 of this volume, Södergård shares findings from her ethnographic work in a Swedish immersion kindergarten classroom and reveals strategies the teacher used to elicit language from learners and to give feedback following children's utterances.

Still other classroom-based research has examined whether specific form-focused instructional adaptations positively impact the language development of students (Day & Shapson, 1991; Harley, 1989, 1998; Kowal & Swain, 1997; Lyster, 1994, 2004). Collectively, this research offers practitioners a base of core immersion teaching strategies and underscores the language development potential of focus-on-form within otherwise communicative activities.

Beyond descriptive and quasi-experimental intervention research targeting pedagogical practices in immersion classrooms, studies that investigate the nature of language use *as it relates to content* teaching and learning in the grade-level classroom are also offering greater insight into both teaching processes and student learning. A most interesting part of the equation is the relationship between teacher talk and students' second language acquisition, including how teachers provide corrective feedback to students and may inadvertently delimit student exposure to a more authentic range of linguistic forms and registers within the confines of classroom interaction (Lyster & Ranta, 1997; Netten & Spain, 1989; Salomone, 1992; Södergård, Chapter 8 this volume; Swain, 1996; Swain & Carroll, 1987; Takahashi-Breines, 2002; Tardif, 1994).

Recently researchers have argued that the way in which language and content are co-structured within the immersion classroom may well be the determining factor in reaching high expectations for language production as well as quality academic experiences (Swain, 1996; Walker & Tedick, 2000). In Chapter 12 of this volume, Hoare and Kong argue that for a variety of reasons late English immersion teachers in Hong Kong do not integrate language and content in ways that result in student learning of both. Much remains to be explored concerning the ways in which teachers act (1) to fashion the language input students receive, (2) to embed a language development agenda into content-driven curricula and (3) to shape activities to promote meaningful output – the kind of verbal production that facilitates learning.[2] How does the teacher construct the classroom day so that optimal opportunities for content and language learning can occur, while remaining conscious of producing meaningful input, developing language and content knowledge, and eliciting more native-like language from students? How do teachers understand their classroom behaviors as they consider the intricate relationship between language and content as well as teacher and student interaction?

The voices of teachers have been more audible in research studies over the past few decades (e.g. Clark & Peterson, 1986; Cochran-Smith & Lytle, 1993), and the quantity of systematic research as well as anecdotal and reflective work from teachers has been substantial. In second language education, teacher thinking and the process of teacher decision-making have formed the basis for exploration of classroom processes in bilingual, English as a second language, and foreign language classrooms (e.g. Bailey & Nunan, 1996; Calderón, 1999; Freeman & Richards, 1996; Johnson, 1999; Richards & Nunan, 1990; Smith & Rawley, 1998). However, studies that explore immersion teacher thinking specifically are rare (Arnau, 2001; Jackson, 2001). With direct attention placed on the language and content connection, this study attempts to dig deeper into that unique teaching process by structuring an opportunity for teachers to speak about their practice.

The Study

Research questions

The questions driving the study include:

- How do six practicing immersion teachers (both one-way and two-way) understand the complex phenomenon of integrated language and content teaching?
- What particular beliefs, knowledge and behaviors do these teachers identify as guiding immersion teacher practice?

Study participants

A total of six teachers were invited to participate: a native English-speaking (NES) and a native Spanish-speaking (NSS) teacher from each of three Spanish immersion schools in a large metropolitan area in the US Midwest. This study reports on five of the six teachers, as one dropped out before data collection was complete. Two of the schools are K–6 full, one-way immersion sites (one urban, one suburban) and one is a K–8 two-way immersion setting (urban).

Data sources

The study drew upon four data sources.

(1) _Individual teacher interviews_ were held, in which each teacher discussed her ongoing issues with students' language development and content learning and constructed a question that she wished to explore related to her teaching. This question (see below) would determine the teaching activities that would be videotaped.

(2) _Four classroom sessions_, which teachers believed would best illustrate their focal concern, were videotaped for each teacher. A project assistant scheduled the sessions with the teachers and made all arrangements to videotape.

(3) Teachers watched videotapes of four episodes of their teaching and afterward created _audio-taped reflections_. They were asked to reflect on their observations of both their own and students' use of language and classroom behavior related to the focal issue identified.

(4) Finally, after all teachers had completed the reflections, a _focus group meeting_ of approximately 90 minutes in length was held with all members of the research team and participating teachers present. During the focus group, teachers engaged in discussion about integrating language and content instruction while able to refer specifi-

cally to their own videotaped lessons, and they shared insights gained during the process.

The data were triangulated in three ways. We used several methods of data collection (interviews, focus groups, reflections, videotapes of classroom sessions), several sources of data (researchers interpreted videotapes and identified themes from interviews, focus groups and reflections; teachers offered retrospective reflections on the videotapes individually and shared issues across the group in focus groups), and a team approach to data analysis involving three researchers who examined the data independently to confirm emerging findings.

Table 4.1 profiles the study participants along with the various types of data provided by each. It is important to note that there were some challenges with data collection due to (1) equipment failure (leading to loss of interview transcripts), (2) one study participant's lost videotapes and reflections, and (3) one participant not completing the study. Despite the missing data pieces, we collected a large amount of very rich data from a majority of the participants, including one hour of interviews, approximately 11 hours of videotaped classroom teaching, over three hours of reflections, and lastly, one 90-minute focus group.

Table 4.1 Overview of study participants and data sources

School	Teacher (Grade level)	Native language	Initial interview transcripts	Videotaped sessions	Transcripts of reflections	Focus group
Hughes (2-way, urban)	Claire[3] (Grade 6)	English	X	X (4)	X	X
Pierce (1-way, urban)	Deborah (Grade 3)	English		X (4)	X	X
	Cristina (Grade 5)	Spanish		X (4)	X	X
Marshfield (1-way, suburban)	Susan (Grade 3)	English		X (4)	X	X
	Maria (Grade 3)	Spanish				X

Note: Although self-described a one-way program, Pierce had approximately 25% students from Spanish-speaking homes at the time of the study.

Teacher focus questions

The following teacher-constructed questions were used to facilitate a more focused exploration of the overarching research questions.

- *Content area: Spanish language arts/literature.* How can the two-way immersion teacher improve student access to reading, listening to and writing about literature in the immersion language? (Claire, NES)
- *Content area: math.* What is the nature of teacher talk during math instruction? (Susan, NES) How can an immersion teacher expand student use of verb tenses beyond the present tense during math instruction? (Maria, NSS)
- *Content area: social studies.* What are ways an immersion teacher can attend to language growth within the research paper writing process during social studies instruction? (Deborah, NES) How can an immersion teacher maintain balance between content and language development within the social studies curriculum? (Cristina, NSS)

Data Analysis

We independently viewed videotapes and read transcripts focusing specifically on each individual teacher's identified issue with language and content, and examining the data for common themes across the teachers. The constant comparative method of analysis (Merriam, 1998) was used to uncover themes, particularly with an eye toward *cross-case* analysis – parallel themes that emerged in the data from all five teachers. Because each of the five teachers posed her own question, in essence, this study involved five distinct lenses. However, the analysis for this chapter focuses on the big picture addressed by the two main research questions: the understandings and behaviors identified by all of the teachers around the question of integrating language and content instruction.

After independent analysis, the research team gathered together to share preliminary findings, and then came to mutual agreement about particular and recurrent themes that emerged from issues the teachers addressed in their reflections and during the focus group.[4] Data analysis thus involved a two-fold process. During our initial review of the data we came independently to an understanding of what we observed in the videotapes and read in the teachers' video reflections. After this occurred, we came together to discuss and develop a sense of shared understandings through interaction about the data. The research questions served as guideposts for these discussions. Through the process of independent analysis and comparison of preliminary analyses among the three researchers, we refined impressions and conclusions. Finally, we distributed a draft of this paper to participating teachers and held an informal 'member check' meeting (Merriam, 1998) to ensure that our interpretation of these data accurately reflected the teachers' understandings and experiences.

Study Findings

Theme 1: 'Always teaching language'

When engaged in non-reading and writing activities and subject matter areas such as math, teachers still readily identified and described their behaviors as teaching language. One of the teachers reflected on an interaction with a student in which she suggested that the learner consider a possible English cognate for the unknown Spanish word as a strategy for guessing at word meaning. She said, 'Always teaching language, even during math' (Susan, NES, VR3).[5] Throughout the video reflections are references to the multiple ways these teachers attend to the immersion language development of their students. On a macro-level, teachers described the activities of developing students' reading comprehension skills or engaging students in a process approach to writing as well-suited to teaching language. Not surprisingly, the three teachers who chose to look at their teaching within the Spanish Language Arts or Social Studies curriculum focused mainly on reading and writing activities. The teacher-scaffolded task of writing a report, for example, allowed one teacher to attend to language growth at the micro-level by calling attention to pronoun referents of singular versus plural nouns, making explicit the rules of good writing mechanics and encouraging self-editing (Deborah, NES, VR3). A structured creative writing activity provided a second teacher with the opportunity to force student use of more sophisticated vocabulary as well as more difficult and complex sentence structures and verb forms (Cristina, NSS, VR2&4). Teachers were clearly aware that asking students to produce written text created multiple and varied ways to focus on language specifically.

The 'Vs' of language teaching: Vocabulary and verbs

While the above-named examples of attending to language growth stand out as exemplary, the components of language that the teachers typically targeted can be summed up in two words: vocabulary and verbs. Specific word-focused behaviors teachers named repeatedly when describing their *language teaching* included supplying students with vocabulary as needed, asking questions or structuring activities in such a way as to purposefully and repeatedly elicit the focal vocabulary from the students, pushing students to reference persons, places and things with greater lexical specificity, expanding students' breadth of word knowledge by finding and listing synonyms, or collectively brainstorming possibilities for connectors for use in a writing project. Most of the teachers' commentary on teaching language included some reference to vocabulary development. Yet these references emphasized the semantic aspects of vocabulary development only, and the vocabulary selection was largely restricted to nouns serving as key content concepts.

There were many observed instances in which the teachers acted as living dictionaries for the students as they required a particular term, a common event in the immersion language classroom. The following excerpt from the videotaped data is an example of a frequently observed teacher-student interaction:

Student: *¿Cómo se dice* shelf? [How do you say *shelf*?]
Teacher: *Estante*. [shelf]

At times students explicitly requested assistance with specific vocabulary words; other times the teacher responded to a perceived need and quickly supplied the necessary terminology. As a third grade teacher reflecting on a math lesson indicated:

> Later on, David, in the demonstration there, David is called to explain his thinking and he starts using ordinal numbers, *primero, segundo*, [first, second] and he gets stuck on number seven. I think he just said, '*Siete*.' [seven] So I supply, '*Séptima*,' [seventh] and then he said, '*Ocho*,' [eight] and I supply, '*Octavo*' [eighth]. So again, me supplying the student's vocabulary when they make a mistake or when they don't know the word. (Susan, NES, VR3)[6]

As aware as these teachers seemed to be of their students' basic word needs, they voiced an even greater consciousness about their desire to push learners towards a more lexically accurate use of the immersion language. In the context of a lesson in which students were working in groups to fill in a graphic organizer used to organize information and new vocabulary from the textbook reading, one 5th grade immersion teacher noted:

> And one objective that I have in mind is to draw from vocabulary that is more complex, that really explains and defines what they're talking about. One example you see on the tape is: 'indigenous people live in houses.' I asked them to define what type of houses. I want them to have the vocabulary to come out and really define what kind of settings they

live in because that is, that's what is necessary here. So I'm asking them to go to the next level of proficiency in their vocabulary. (Cristina, NSS, VR1)

Getting students to this *next level of proficiency* with vocabulary occurred in a variety of ways. For example, the teacher might expand on a students' response to a teacher question:

Student: *Pelotas.* [balls]
Teacher: *Pelotas de tenis.* [tennis balls] (Susan, NES, VR1)

Alternatively, teachers were conscious of wanting to provide their students with more native-like complexity in their word repertoires and thus sought to introduce words that would allow the students to be more exact in their communications. Instead of accepting the more generic *juego* [game], the teacher offered *damas* [checkers] (Susan, NES, VR1). Continuous *pushing* of more complex and specific vocabulary is a theme that appeared often with this group of immersion teachers, as they sought to build students' language skills beyond the basic terms that would satisfy meaning making within a context-embedded situation.

Besides talking a lot about vocabulary development, teachers saw themselves as attending to language by focusing on student use of verbs, as an excerpt from the focus group illustrates.

DT: So talk a little bit about your questions and the questions that you started to explore and videotape, and what has this process been like to go through, as you have focused on something in particular in your teaching? The question was the math, the role of the math teacher?
Maria (NSS): No... Like what's the, how to expand verb tenses and that.
Deborah (NES): Oh, interesting. I was doing verb tenses in social studies. (FG)

These teachers were aware that their students struggled with using verb endings accurately as well as understanding and using a variety of tenses. In response, one of the teachers attempted to clarify student understanding of the nuanced difference between the imperfect and the preterit verb tenses when talking and writing about the past. Another designed a task that created a real need to use the subjunctive form in student writing following a specific group of conjunctives so that student awareness of this under-utilized aspect of the verb system might increase. As part of this focus on developing language, this teacher felt it important to explicitly use the term *subjunctive* with her students so that they were aware on a metalinguistic level of what they were doing with language.

In sum, these teachers were able to pinpoint several behaviors as evidence that they regularly address the language development of their students. Such references to their language teaching were typically limited to some aspect of vocabulary expansion or verb usage.

Theme 2: Content takes center stage

After viewing the videotape of a given lesson, the teacher reflections typically contained a description of what occurred in the lesson as well as the teacher's identification of the main learning objectives for that lesson:

Lesson description 1. The lesson was for students to start looking for things that come in groups, particularly rows. We're getting ready to look at and use matrices for multiplication. Vocabulary I want the kids to be using are the words like *grupo* [group], *fila* [row] and possibly *matriz* [matrix] if they get to that point. (Susan, NES, VR1)

Lesson description 2. Actually, I divided the activity into four groups taking into account the way the textbook is divided. So they really need to read what's in the book, understand the concept, then decide what is the most important information they need to share. So that will be the content. Regarding the vocabulary, I don't want to see any spelling mistakes. (Cristina, NSS, VR2)

As the two excerpts above exemplify, the teachers consistently began by naming the content objectives. Reference to language objectives, if at all, was frequently reduced to the listing of content-specific vocabulary. While this tendency to view the content goals as primary was clear in the way teachers talked about their lessons, it was not frequently discussed in their reflections. However, during the final focus group discussion (see excerpt below) one of the teachers did express her awareness of the way content takes precedence over language. She took particular pains to develop a lesson in which language *was* a specific focus, recognizing that for the most part she is so busy addressing content learning that language is often an afterthought:

It was very interesting for me as a teacher because my first lesson was basically focusing on vocabulary production and being more specific about the language they use. And realizing that I am so concerned about them learning the content that I just didn't have any objective, language objectives in mind, more than do as correct as possible. (Cristina, NSS, FG)

Interestingly, this same teacher made great strides over the course of this research project with integrating a systematically planned language component into her content-focused lessons. She was completing course-work for her Masters degree in second language education at a local university. During this time she wrestled with how she might more thoughtfully plan for students' language development within the context of her social studies curriculum. This led to the development of the Bill of Rights activity – a creative writing task carried out by small groups of students which, while furthering understanding of a right, incorporated a complex sentence structure requiring use of the subjunctive mood. Students were asked to generate 13 rights targeting perceived needs of a focal group of choice, for example, 5th grade girls. Each right followed a pre-determined format, demonstrating their conceptual understanding of what constitutes a right. The right needed to comprise two components: (1) a basic right and (2) the possible limiting factor for the particular group requesting the right. To express these two ideas in one complex sentence, students were expected to use specific connectives such as *aunque* [although] and *a pesar de que* [in spite of; despite]. These connectives, in turn, forced use of verbs in the subjunctive, an aspect of Spanish verb morphosyntax rarely used by immersion students. The final two of this teacher's four videotapes focused on this newly developed creative writing task. The following is an excerpt from her reflection on the fourth videotape:

> In this session, I decided to focus on individual help for each student. It is a continuation of Session 3 where each student wrote their own Bill of Rights. I'm basically editing with them. When I'm doing this, I have a couple of things in mind. I want them to understand that what really matters here is the content. I really want good ideas. I want to under-stand what they mean. I want them to be able to explain why they wrote what they did. At the same time, we're going to focus on the form I want. I want to make sure that whatever they want to say can be understood through the language they understand. Another goal I have in mind is the verb endings... (Cristina, NSS, VR4)

Once again one notes the teacher's focus on ensuring that her content area objective, to provide students an opportunity to demonstrate their comprehension of a *Bill of Rights*, was met. However, of equal importance were the language forms produced by the students, in particular, accurate use of verbs.

It is interesting to note that Cristina was the only teacher who made overt mention of the importance of planning for a specific grammatical structure in the context of content. It is possible that her enrollment in a Master's course on second language curriculum development, which focused on language and content integration and the writing of both content and language objectives, influenced her lesson preparation and thinking on this issue. In fact, Cristina corroborated this hunch during the member check gathering and added that she believed that her educational background in English philology also contributed to her ability to identify and address the language component so successfully.

Theme 3: 'Am I getting it right?': Teachers' internal language monitor

Immersion teachers act as language models for their students. In one-way programs, particularly in the initial years of the program, teachers may be the sole language model in the classroom. Because of these teachers' awareness of this important role, they stated a desire to provide the best example possible for the students. In their reflections, the teachers whose native language was not Spanish described the constant and cognitively-draining language monitor that posed questions and raised concerns about the accuracy of their language use:

> Emily then starts talking about the connect four game and I want her to show the class and I say, '*Muestra a ellos*' [Show them]. And again, here the articles [*sic* – here Susan is referring to direct/indirect object pronouns] come up for me, *le, lo, les* [him/her, it, them], you know, what, was that right? I don't know. So sometimes I just keep going but that self-monitoring of my Spanish is always going on. (Susan, NES, VR1)

> As I watched the videotape, I'm embarrassed to realize that I never quite figure out the word for mural. I use the word *pintura*, which is really a painting and I don't think that's quite the right word for mural. And I also, you know, I noticed a few other things with my Spanish when I kind of get stuck. (Claire, NES, VR1)

As they described themselves questioning their own language use, the tone was that of self-confident insecurity. In other words, these professionals were confident enough in their command of the language to be using it exclusively in the classroom and to be pinpointing the particular areas where they were unsure. They were also confident enough to talk directly about their language monitoring among a group of immersion teaching peers. One interesting and telling interaction during the focus group revealed that modeling incorrect usage of the immersion language is not exclusively the domain of those teachers for whom Spanish is a second language:

Susan (NES):	Some of the mistakes I made were kind-of embarrassing, you know, and then the questions I'm left with. And it's not like something I will remember, and then when I see Maria [NSS colleague] I might ask, 'Now how do you say this or that?' It's just in the moment and then it's gone so...
Deborah (NES):	You realize you don't know.
Susan (NES):	It's not really a learning opportunity for me. It's just like, 'Okay, let's highlight all the errors,' but then they never get corrected. You know, so that, that's a little frustrating.
Maria (NSS):	But I was telling her because she was like, 'Oh, my Spanish.' I said, 'I'm native, and let me tell you, I make a lot of mistakes... ' (FG)

In addition to the non-native Spanish-speaking teachers being aware of the effort expended in self-monitoring their use of Spanish, another of the native Spanish-speaking teachers (Cristina) was struck by how she occasionally found her classroom use of Spanish being adapted in ways that later sounded unnatural and non-native-like.

Consistent across the reflections was an awareness of the pressure these teachers feel as language models for their students. And for the non-native speakers there was an awareness of the additional cognitive energy expended on consciously producing accurate Spanish.

Theme 4: Questions, commands and cues – the core of immersion teacher talk

One of the six study participants opted to focus specifically on her language use during the course of classroom instruction. This focused attention led to an increased awareness of the number of teacher utterances involving questions, commands and cues for familiar instructional routines. In addition to this individual teacher's commentary on the prevalence of imperatives and cues to routines in her talk, the teachers as a group were conscious of their questioning strategies.

Teacher questions served a variety of important purposes. Study participants expressed awareness of using questions to elicit student ideas, encourage student language use, hold students accountable for the task at hand, guide students to new understandings, demonstrate multiple ways of expressing similar ideas and check to ensure current understandings of a given concept.

I'm trying to question them in such a way that will elicit ideas from them for the note cards. (Deborah, NES, VR1)

I walk around to make sure they're on task. Then I ask the specific questions that each group has. (Cristina, NSS, VR3)

And then later I say again, 'How can we say it in terms of groups?' trying to direct their language. And then, 'Who has another way of saying it?' Often in math I'm always asking for different ways of saying it and describing it, trying to form different ways, but in this case directing them in a certain way. (Susan, NES, VR1)

Teachers described their use of questions as largely strategic, a means of getting students to participate in the classroom discourse and move their thinking from point A to point B. Questions served to encourage and gradually unveil or lead students to new understandings.

In addition to teachers commenting on their use of questions, they observed that teacher talk was also marked by frequent use of directives.

Another thing about teacher language I noticed is, it's not surprising, but I sure give a lot of commands, *piensan* [think], *comparan* [compare], *arréglalo* [fix it], *búscalo* [look for it], *pide ayuda* [ask for help], *cierra la puerta* [close the door], you know, constant commands and that may be the verb tense that the kids hear modeled an awful lot. (Susan, NES, VR2)

Many of these directives came in the form of commands as in the examples above. In addition to using imperatives, however, one teacher became aware that she made frequent use of routine cues – familiar patterned expressions that quickly communicate classroom procedures to the students.

I notice that lots of my expressions are patterns that I repeat, like *piensa* [think], *pareja* [partner], *palo* [stick, referencing a popsicle stick with a student's name written on it used for student selection], which are the key words I use for think, pair, share. So lots of times they're patterns or procedures that I cue with language ... .

Another phrase that cues a procedure is I say, '*Primero tres, a mí después,*' which means the kids are supposed to ask help from three different people in the class and then come to me. (Susan, NES, VR3)

Immersion teachers' use of language in the classroom often served to guide student behavior either directly through commands and cues or more indirectly through leading questions and task and comprehension check-ins.

Theme 5: Awareness of the 'over and above' nature of their work and lack of planning time[7]

Several times, as the teachers talked about the nature of their work, they referred to the additional issues that they are required to address because they are immersion teachers. Specifically, when school districts place new curriculum demands on the teachers, immersion teachers need not only to become familiar with the new curriculum, but also figure out how to do it in a second language.

One of the teachers repeatedly referenced the complexity of what she believes immersion teachers are asked to do as she interacted with her peers in the focus group discussion.

Susan (NES):   But the first thing, again I was reminded how complex it is, what we do. You know, the whole time I'm thinking about the kids' behavior, where they are, whose turn it is...

Deborah (NES): There's so many layers.

Susan (NES):   Yeah, and the, what the math lesson is, what they're supposed to do, the language, what time of day it is, what their energy level is, you know, the whole complexity. Then, plus my monitor of my own language... which is on all the time. (FG)

As the focus group discussion evolved and different teachers shared what they had learned during the year by targeting and reflecting on a particular issue in their teaching, Susan offered this insight after listening to Cristina talk about her language-focused activity:

> Something you said makes me think of, you know, often in immersion we say that the content is the vehicle, or the language is the vehicle for the content, you know, so there's no add-on. But when it comes to the planning, there is an add-on. ['Mmhm.'] There's the added-on, 'What am I going to do with language?' (Susan, NES, FG)

This formerly-professed principle that with immersion education a learner will learn language simply by being exposed to subject matter instruction in a second language is not the whole story. On the contrary, for immersion teaching to be effective in meeting the language and content learning goals of the program model, immersion teachers need to understand their roles as both content and language teachers. Herein lies the complexity or as one of the study participants described, the awareness that as an immersion teacher you are an exception among classroom teachers because 'nobody else has this extra issue of language and you're not doing anything like anybody else is doing' (Claire, NES, FG). During the final member check meeting one of the teachers summed it up well: 'We're still in the *language is the vehicle* mode – not the *language objective* mode. Now that we are asked to attend explicitly to language, immersion is being reinvented.' (Cristina, NES, MC)

At the same time that these teachers were acutely aware of the additional expectations inherent in being an immersion teacher, they lamented the lack of adequate planning time. With sufficient planning time they believed they would be far more able to succeed in designing quality curricular and instructional experiences for their learners and succeed with their complex, dual agenda as language and content teachers.

> You know, I always think here, just on the side, that if ideally I had lots of time to plan, I can always see how to do it differently. You know, where the kids would be acting this out and we'd have, you know, real kid examples, which is what I often do. But, um, there's so little time to prep, really, so it's just sort-of on the fly, as usual. (Susan, NES, VR2)

Theme 6: Assisting students in accessing the abstract

One of the key challenges identified by the teachers as they reflected on their teaching was the issue of how to effectively address more challenging texts and abstract concepts. For teachers this concern grew as immersion students progressed through the grade levels and encountered increasingly complex topics and texts. As the grade 6 teacher stated:

> ... but at the upper grade levels, we're getting really abstract. I mean, the question we want to talk about is, 'How would we compare our civil rights movement to South Africa's anti-apartheid movement?' Well, I can jump up and do all the antics I want. If they can't do the vocabulary, they can't do that. (Claire, NES, Inter.)

There were a number of different strategies that the teachers used to assist their students in accessing more abstract, challenging content. For example, on occasion teachers grouped students by ability to engage in more linguistically sophisticated tasks and topics. Teachers also encouraged students to focus more on getting the gist as opposed to needing to understand each and every word in the text, and used visuals and rich whole-class discussions to build foundational vocabulary and topic knowledge before launching into the actual text.

The development of the *Bill of Rights* activity began as a result of the teacher's desire to make her social studies curriculum and the demanding textbook readings on US history more meaningful for the students. Prior to engaging in the creative writing task, students orally presented information on select topics such as the distribution of power across legislative, judicial and executive branches of the government. These complex ideas were distilled down into brief student-led poster presentations to the whole class. The rationale behind designing such tasks was explained by the teacher in the following way:

> Things they need to learn are so abstract, so far away from their own reality that I decided that they will present it to the class, using illustrations and key words and key vocabulary to explain what the concept meant. (Cristina, NSS, VR2)

Discussion

In this study we put teachers in the position of driving the conversation about integrating language and content in the immersion classroom, by considering an aspect of their own teaching, videotaping four lessons that attend to that aspect and reflecting on observed behaviors. In this way experienced teacher insight is brought to bear on teaching and learning within the immersion setting. The teachers in this study co-created, in a sense, a mosaic of issues encountered daily in immersion teaching. As teacher educators considering these teacher-identified themes, we are led to at least three implications:

(1) the need for ongoing teacher development to expand teachers' knowledge of the immersion language;
(2) the need for continued professional development in areas of curriculum writing and instructional follow-through;
(3) the need for a redirection of teachers' self-focused internal language monitor towards a classroom-focused attentiveness to language development within the context of interaction.

Staff development related to the immersion language

Native English-speaking (NES) teachers in this study repeatedly spoke to their ongoing frustration with their own second language skills. Their internal language monitor hounded them, always ready to critique the degree of accuracy with which they spoke. In a similar vein, the native Spanish-speaking teachers expressed an awareness of a tendency to make inauthentic adaptations to their use of Spanish in an effort to make their meaning more easily understandable to the students. When considering the need for ongoing professional development for immersion teachers, it becomes clear that teachers will benefit from opportunities to further develop the immersion language and engage in sustained and sophisticated discourse. The language development need has previously been identified in surveys of two-way immersion teachers (Calderón, 2002; Carranza, 1995) as well as one-way immersion teachers (Day & Shapson, 1996). How might this occur?

Teacher language proficiency can benefit from a variety of experiences both within and outside of the school. Within the schools, when administration is bilingual, whole staff meetings and informal gatherings of immersion teachers can be conducted in the immersion language. We are aware of one administrator who encourages every teacher on staff to develop his/her own language goals for the academic year and joins the staff in this practice by taking advantage of summer travel to countries where the immersion language is used (U. Swanson, personal communication, March 5, 2004). Another way to address specific questions of language use that surface for teachers during instruction might be to make an Immersion Language Box available in the staff lounge. Any staff member could jot down their particular language use question (for example, Susan's questions about indirect and direct object pronouns) and place them in the box. At staff meetings the administrator could reserve a five-minute block of time during which questions from the language box would be anonymously addressed.

Grant-funded projects, such as the Fulbright Hays Group Studies Abroad, also offer unique opportunities to structure in-country immersion experiences with a small group of teachers (Tedick & Walker, 2002). In addition to study-abroad experiences like this, other outside-the-school opportunities might include enrolling in an upper-level language course at the local university, participating in an informal dinner group that meets monthly at a local restaurant specializing in the cuisine of the target culture, or starting a book group that reads and discusses literature in the immersion language.

Wong Fillmore and Snow (2002: 19) argue that today's English as a second language and bilingual teachers need 'better, more intensive, and more coherent preparation in educational linguistics.' They define educational linguistics as dealing with 'issues of language use in daily life, issues that require only a basic understanding of the descriptive work that linguists engage in and the concepts that they use' (Wong Fillmore & Snow, 2002: 19). Similarly, we suggest that before immersion teachers are likely to more effectively teach to the wide array of forms and functions that comprise the immersion language, they will need professional development experiences that introduce them to basic units of language and how these units fit together to create meaning and build discipline-specific knowledge.

Professional development for curriculum planning and instructional follow-through

In addition to professional development related to language issues, immersion teachers need learning experiences that will support their ability to design curriculum and learning activities that integrate language and content. Teachers in this study repeatedly acknowledged a strong tendency to focus on content, often at the expense of language. They cite a lack of planning time and realize that immersion teachers must address the immersion language as an *add on* or *extra*. Yet their discussions consistently demonstrate their belief that they already *do* attend to language. There is an apparent contradiction here. On the one hand, teachers see themselves as always attending to their students' language needs; on the other hand, they state that if they were to really address the language piece, it would require focused planning and more time. They fear that time spent on language may result in less attention to content. The pre-service English immersion teachers in Singapore who Silver studied expressed similar concerns and wondered whether attending to language might 'distort or diminish' their ability to teach content (Silver, 2003: 20). In Chapter 12 of this volume, Hoare and Kong report on an even more extreme lack of attention to language. Many of the late English immersion teachers assume that much of the student talk generated in the immersion classroom must be in their L1 (Chinese), not the immersion language, if they are to learn content. The importance of helping teachers learn how to integrate language and content teaching in immersion classrooms cannot be understated.

Professional development experiences that enhance teachers' skills in identifying the language implications of their content-focused lessons need to explicitly address ways that teachers can find, focus on and follow up on language issues at a micro-level. We find the most difficult aspect of planning to be the initial identification of which language features merit explicit attention. Harley (1993) posits that not all features are worthy of classroom teaching. She argues that immersion teachers would benefit from considering a number of principles that can guide their selection of language-specific features. For example, English-speaking students learning languages that differentiate nouns by gender will need to notice, name and pay attention to gender and its impact on language production. Preparing teachers to recognize and delimit attention to these principles in their teaching would go along way toward minimizing the sense that language and content is an either/or proposition in the immersion classroom.

In their ongoing work with immersion teachers Fortune and Tedick (2003) have developed a number of scaffolding tools and strategies that can assist the language-focused development of curriculum. One of the tools is a detailed written text analysis form that allows teachers to carry out an in-depth analysis of a particular text with an eye toward identifying the primary content of the text and the language structures, functions and vocabulary that are embedded within the text. Once language features are identified at a micro-level, teachers are able to construct specific language objectives that are linked to the content of a lesson. Such specificity in planning brings a new level of clarity to teachers, and results in more effective integration of language and content for the learner.

Professional development experiences for immersion teachers must also provide clear examples of how to attend to language by providing demonstration lessons and encouraging an analysis of transcripts based on model teacher–learner interactions in an immersion setting such as those found in Lapkin and Swain (1996) and Lyster (1998). In addition, as our understanding of effective immersion teaching and learning processes continues to mature, we are beginning to identify a need to consider important developmental nuances that make a one-size-fits-all approach to immersion teaching insufficient. For example, Hoare (2001) suggests that immersion teachers can at times over-rely on a graphic representation of a complex concept at the expense of a verbally rich depiction of this same concept. While use of graphics and visuals is well-known to be an essential teaching strategy early on in the program or at the outset of a new unit, if such a scaffold is never dismantled it may serve to inhibit continued language growth.

All of the above-mentioned suggestions for improved professional development experiences for immersion teachers will be effective only if they are sustained over time (Calderón & Minaya-Rowe, 2003). For this, schools need to provide regularly scheduled time for teacher planning and reflection. Reflection and planning time allows teachers to increase their own clarity about the language and content goals of the program, both as individuals and members of a school community. Structured professional time for planning and ongoing teacher development should also occur both within and across grade levels for program-level improvement.

Need for a new kind of internal language monitor oriented towards the classroom

Teachers in this study consistently reported on an internal language monitor – a kind of critical voice in their head – that challenged their use of the immersion language. The voice focused on self-critique of language accuracy and concern for appropriate modeling of native-like language use. As we reflected on the presence and persistence of this monitor, we came to believe that it did not serve a very useful purpose within the context of the immersion classroom. The teachers themselves acknowledged that this constant critique was frustrating for them and rarely helpful in that they were often unable to take the time to address their concerns about accuracy and authenticity or use the voice as a learning opportunity.

An implication that we would draw from this is to encourage teachers to embrace their internal language monitor but refocus its attention away from one of *self*-critique towards a more 'language-aware' (Hoare, 2001: 196) orientation to *all classroom participants'* use of language. In other words, teachers' questions would shift from 'Am I saying this right?' or 'Should it be *le* or *lo*?' to 'What language functions and structures might my students need to use to successfully engage in this next activity?' or 'How can I expand my students' word knowledge by drawing their attention to the various prefixes or suffixes one can use to make more words from this word stem?' What we're suggesting here is a change to monitoring language development within the interactional space of the classroom *not* monitoring the teacher's individual language accuracy. Such monitoring and attention might help teachers to develop in students the kinds of sophisticated word and language knowledge necessary for demanding literacy and academic tasks, as discussed by Met in Chapter 3.

While how teachers see themselves using the language is a concern of immersion educators, a shift in focus from *teachers'* language accuracy to *classroom* language use might well direct their attention to the more critical question of how *much* of language in the classroom is teacher versus student talk. This focus on the classroom's interactional environment might then involve a teacher's directed attention to how she creates a context that encourages students to see themselves as co-participants in classroom discourse. In this study we were especially impressed by Susan's ability to repeatedly invite dialogue among students and with the teacher through her purposeful use of questions and cues. A consistent theme in classroom research has been the limiting nature of excessive amounts of teacher talk on student engagement and learning (Sinclair & Coulthard, 1975; Swain & Carroll, 1987). To address this, the internal language monitor could serve to challenge teachers to consciously promote a more equitable distribution of teacher- and student-talk time. We understand that there are times where more teacher talk may be necessary and developmentally appropriate, for example, in the early stages of language development or at the beginning of a theme-based unit when new concepts and language are first being presented. However, to remain developmentally appropriate, the amount of teacher talk needs to decrease as students' proficiency levels advance across the grades, and within a curricular unit as students gain more content knowledge/concept familiarity and learn the language they need to interact with that content.

A final role for the immersion teachers' internal language monitor might be to give themselves permission to pause and reflect. Research has shown us the value of pausing long enough after posing a question for students to respond. We refer to this as making effective use of wait time (Rowe, 1974). The pause we are suggesting here, however, is intended to assist the teacher's response. Teachers can benefit from taking time to consciously let go of their tendency to act as the *knower*, or the *explainer*. Instead of immediately supplying students with the unknown word or phrase as teachers in this study described themselves doing, teachers might pause, and in that pause formulate the next best language-supportive question or comment to guide the student towards their next *ah-ha* moment with the language. In this way, teachers would employ their internal language monitor to help them take advantage of those teachable moments that regularly surface during the course of teaching and learning.

Conclusion

Immersion programs are engaged in ensuring additive bilingualism such that the cognitive-academic benefits of bilingualism can come to bear for learners. The daily work of immersion teachers is setting the stage for those cognitive-academic benefits to occur. With ongoing opportunities for professional development experiences that develop new understandings of how to design the immersion curriculum and encourage a more reflective, language-aware practitioner in the classroom, the field of immersion teaching will continue to move towards realizing the learner's full language and content learning potential.

Notes

1. The study was supported with funds through the US Department of Education Title VI National Language Resource Center grant, which is housed in the University of Minnesota's Center for Advanced Research on Language Acquisition. Earlier versions of this paper were presented at the American Educational Research Association (April, 2003), the third International Conference on Language Teacher Education (May, 2003), and *Pathways to Bilingualism: Evolving Perspectives on Immersion Education* (October, 2004).
2. We would like to acknowledge that some scholars have recently begun to question the continued use of the terms *input* and *output* as they relate to

language acquisition (e.g. Kramsch, 1995; van Lier, 2000). Swain has replaced *output* with terms such as 'speaking, writing, utterance, verbalization and collaborative dialogue,' although she considers this 'an interim solution ... [until] ... the appropriate terminology ... emerge[s]' (Swain, 2000: 103). Because of a lack of other, broadly accepted labels in the field, we maintain the use of *input* and *output* in this chapter.

3. Pseudonyms are used for both teachers and schools to protect anonymity.
4. We also identified additional themes that we found salient from our perspective as researcher-teacher educators. Researcher-identified themes comprise a second study focus and will be reported separately.
5. We use a number of codes to identify the specific data sources for quotes and examples. VR = video reflection (and with four reflections, specific numbers are noted); FG = focus group; Inter. = interview, MC = member check. Also NES is a native English speaker, and NSS is a native Spanish speaker.
6. Excerpts from transcripts have undergone minor editing (e.g. hesitation devices such as 'um' have been deleted).
7. Met (1989) described immersion teaching as 'over and above' regular elementary language teaching. We acknowledge her contribution to this theme title.

References

Arnau, J. (2001) Catalan immersion teachers: Reflecting on their roles. In S. Björklund (ed.) *Language as a Tool: Immersion Research and Practices: Proceedings of the 5th European Conference on Immersion Programmes* (pp. 9–41). Vaasa: University of Vaasa.

Bailey, K.M. and Nunan, D. (1996) *Voices from the Language Classroom*. Cambridge: Cambridge University Press.

Björklund, S., Mård-Miettinen, K., Bergstrom, M. and Södergård, M. (eds) (2006) *Exploring Dual-focused Education: Integrating Language and Content for Individual and Societal Needs*. Vaasan yliopiston julkaisuja, Selvityksia ja raportteja 132, Vaasa 2006. Vaasa: University of Vaasa, Centre for Immersion and Multilingualism.

Boutin, F. (1993) A study of early French immersion teachers as generators of knowledge. *Foreign Language Annals* 26 (4), 512–524.

Calderón, M. (1999) Teachers' learning communities for cooperation in diverse settings. *Theory into Practice* 38 (2), 94–99.

Calderón, M. (2002) *Teacher Training and Effective Pedagogy in the Context of Student Diversity*. Greenwich, CT: Information Age.

Calderón, M. and Minaya-Rowe, L. (2003) *Designing and Implementing Two-Way Bilingual Programs*. Thousand Oaks, CA: Corwin Press, Inc.

Carranza, I. (1995) Multilevel analysis of two-way immersion classroom discourse. In J.E. Alatis, C.A. Straehle, B. Gallenberger and M. Ronkin (eds) *Georgetown University Round Table on Languages and Linguistics* (pp. 169–187). Washington, DC: Georgetown University Press.

Chaudron, C. (1986) Teachers' priorities in correcting learners' errors in French immersion classes. In R. Day (ed.) *Talking to Learn: Conversation in Second Language Acquisition* (pp. 64–84). Rowley, MA: Newbury House.

Clark, C.M. and Peterson, P.L. (1986) Teachers' thought processes. In M.C. Wittrock (ed.) *Handbook of Research on Teaching* (3rd edn; pp. 255–296). New York: MacMillan.

Cloud, N., Genesee, F. and Hamayan, E. (2000) *Dual Language Instruction: A Handbook for Enriched Education*. Boston: Heinle & Heinle.

Cochran-Smith, M. and Lytle, S.L. (1993) *Inside/Outside Teacher Research and Knowledge*. New York: Teachers College Press.

Day, E.M. and Shapson, S. (1991) Integrating formal and functional approaches to language teaching in French immersion: An experimental study. *Language Learning* 41 (1), 25–58.

Day, E.M. and Shapson, S. (1996) *Studies in Immersion Education*. Clevedon: Multilingual Matters.

Echevarria, J., Vogt, M.E. and Short, D.J. (2004) *Making Content Comprehensible for English Language Learners: The SIOP Model* (2nd edn). Boston: Allyn & Bacon.

Evans, M., Hoare, P., Kong, S., O'Hallaron, S. and Walker, E. (2001) *Effective Strategies for English-Medium Classrooms: A Handbook for Teachers*. Hong Kong: Hong Kong Institute of Education.

Fortune, T.W. and Tedick, D.J. (2003) So where's the language in content-based instruction? Paper presented at the annual meeting of the American Council on the Teaching of Foreign Languages, Philadelphia, PA.

Freeman, D. and Richards, J.C. (eds) (1996) *Teacher Learning in Language Teaching*. New York: Cambridge University Press.

Freeman, Y., Freeman, D. and Mercuri, S. (2005) *Dual Language Essentials for Teachers and Administrators*. Portsmouth, NH: Heinemann.

Genesee, R. (1987) *Learning through Two Languages: Studies of Immersion and Bilingual Education*. Cambridge, MA: Newbury House.

Gibbons, P. (2002) *Scaffolding Language, Scaffolding Learning: Teaching Second Language Learners in the Mainstream Classroom*. Portsmouth, NH: Heinemann.

Harley, B. (1989) Functional grammar in French immersion: A classroom experiment. *Applied Linguistics* 10 (3), 331–359.

Harley, B. (1992) Patterns of second language development in French immersion. *Journal of French Language Studies* 2 (2), 159–183.

Harley, B. (1993) Instructional strategies and SLA in early French immersion. *Studies in Second Language Acquisition* 15, 245–259.

Harley, B. (1998) French immersion research in Canada: The 1990s in perspective. *Mosaic* 6 (1), 3–10.

Hoare, P. (2001) A comparison of the effectiveness of a 'language aware' and a 'non language aware' late immersion teacher. In S. Björklund (ed.) *Language as a Tool: Immersion Research and Practices* (pp. 196–210). Vaasa: University of Vaasa.

Jackson, J.E. (2001) Thoughts behind the work: Teacher thinking and the implementation of a complex curricular innovation. Unpublished doctoral dissertation, Harvard University.

Johnson, K. (1999) *Understanding Language Teaching: Reasoning in Action*. Boston: Heinle & Heinle.

Kowal, M. and Swain, M. (1997) From semantic to syntactic processing: How can we promote it in the immersion classroom? In R.K. Johnson and M. Swain (eds) *Immersion Education: International Perspectives* (pp. 284–309). New York: Cambridge University Press.

Kramsch, C. (1995) The applied linguist and the foreign language teacher: Can they talk to each other? *Australian Review of Applied Linguistics* 18 (1), 1–16.

Lapkin, S. and Swain, M. (1996) Vocabulary teaching in a grade 8 French immersion classroom: A descriptive case study. *Canadian Modern Language Review* 53 (1), 242–256.

Lindholm-Leary, K. (2001) *Dual Language Education.* Cleveland: Multilingual Matters.

Lyster, R. (1987) Speaking immersion. *Canadian Modern Language Review* 43 (4), 701–717.

Lyster, R. (1994) La négociation de la forme: Stratégie analytique en classe d'immersion. *Canadian Modern Language Review* 50 (3), 447–465.

Lyster, R. (1998) Immersion pedagogy and implications for language teaching. In J. Cenoz and F. Genesee (eds) *Beyond Bilingualism: Multilingualism and Multilingual Education* (pp. 64–95). Clevedon: Multilingual Matters.

Lyster, R. (2004) Research on form-focused instruction in immersion classrooms: Implications for theory and practice. *French Language Studies* 14, 321–341.

Lyster, R. and Ranta, L. (1997) Corrective feedback and learner uptake: Negotiation of form in communicative classrooms. *Studies in Second Language Acquisition* 19 (1), 37–66.

Merriam, S.B. (1998) *Qualitative Research and Case Study Applications in Education.* San Francisco, SA: Jossey-Bass.

Met, M. (1989) Walking on water and other characteristics of effective elementary school foreign language teachers. *Foreign Language Annals* 22 (2), 175–183.

Netten, J. and Spain, W. (1989) Student–teacher interaction patterns in the French immersion classroom: Implications for levels of achievement in French language proficiency. *The Canadian Modern Language Review* 45 (3), 485–501.

Pawley, C. (1985) How bilingual are French immersion students? *The Canadian Modern Language Review* 41 (5), 865–876.

Peregoy, S. (1991) Environmental scaffolds and learner responses in a two-way Spanish immersion kindergarten. *The Canadian Modern Language Review* 47 (3), 463–476.

Pérez, B. (2004) *Becoming Biliterate: A Study of Two-Way Bilingual Immersion Education.* Mahwah, NJ: Lawrence Erlbaum Associates.

Richards, J.C. and Nunan, D. (eds) (1990) *Second Language Teacher Education.* New York: Cambridge University Press.

Rowe, M.B. (1974) Wait time and rewards as instructional variables: Their influence on language, logic and fate control. Part 1: Fate control. *Journal of Research in Science Teaching* 11 (2), 81–94.

Salomone, A.M. (1992) Student–teacher interactions in selected French immersion classrooms. In E.B. Bernhardt (ed.) *Life in Language Immersion Classrooms* (pp. 97–109). Clevedon: Multilingual Matters.

Salomone, A.M. and Palma, E. (1995) Immersion grammar: A changing portrait of Glenwood school. *Foreign Language Annals* 28 (2), 223–232.

Silver, R.E. (2003) There isn't much English in a maths lesson: Training teachers to find the language in content-based instruction. Paper presented at the Third International Conference on Language Teacher Education, Minneapolis, MN.

Sinclair, J. and Coulthard, R. (1975) *Toward an Analysis of Discourse.* New York: Oxford University Press.

Smith, A.N. and Rawley, L.A. (1998) Teachers taking the lead: Self-inquiry as professional development. In J. Harper, M. Lively and M. Williams (eds) *The Coming of Age of the Profession: Issues and Emerging Ideas for the Teaching of Foreign Languages* (pp. 15–36). Boston: Heinle & Heinle.

Snow, M. (1990) Instructional methodology in immersion foreign language education. In A. Padilla, H. Fairchild and C. Valadez (eds) *Foreign Language Education: Issues and Strategies* (pp. 156–171). Newbury Park, CA: Sage.

Snow, M.A. and Brinton, D. (eds) (1997) *The Content-Based Classroom: Perspectives on Integrating Language and Content.* New York: Longman.

Snow, M.A., Met, M. and Genesee, F. (1989) A conceptual framework for the integration of language and content in second/foreign language education. *TESOL Quarterly* 23 (2), 201–217.

Södergård, M. (2001) Teacher strategies for second language production. In S. Björklund (ed.) *Language as a Tool: Immersion Research and Practices: Proceedings of the 5th European Conference on Immersion Programmes* (pp. 398–411). Vaasa, Finland: University of Vaasa.

Spilka, I. (1976) Assessment of second language performance in immersion programs. *The Canadian Modern Language Review* 32 (5), 543–561.

Swain, M. (1988) Manipulating and complementing content teaching to maximize second language learning. *TESOL Canada Journal* 6 (1), 68–83.

Swain, M. (1996) Integrating language and content in immersion classrooms: Research perspectives. *The Canadian Modern Language Review* 52 (4), 529–548.

Swain, M. (2000) The output hypothesis and beyond: Mediating acquisition through collaborative dialogue. In J. Lantolf (ed.) *Sociocultural Theory and Second Language Learning* (pp. 97–114). New York: Oxford University Press.

Swain, M. and Carroll, S. (1987) The immersion observation study. In B. Harley, P. Allen, J. Cummins and M. Swain (eds) *The Development of Bilingual Proficiency: Final Report. Volume II: Classroom Treatment* (pp. 190–341). Toronto: Modern Language Centre, Ontario Institute for Studies in Education.

Takahashi-Breines, H. (2002) The role of teacher-talk in a dual language immersion third grade classroom. *Bilingual Research Journal* 26 (2), 213–235.

Tardif, C. (1994) Classroom teacher talk in early immersion. *The Canadian Modern Language Review* 50 (3), 466–481.

Tedick, D.J. and Walker, C. (with Spanish immersion teachers) (2002) *Bringing the Biodiversity of Ecuador to Spanish Immersion Classrooms. CARLA Working Paper Series #22.* Minneapolis: University of Minnesota.

Van Lier, L. (2000) From input to affordance: Social-interactive learning from an ecological perspective. In J. Lantolf (ed.) *Sociocultural Theory and Second Language Learning* (pp. 245–259). New York: Oxford University Press.

Walker, C.L. and Tedick, D.J. (2000) The complexity of immersion education: Teachers address the issues. *Modern Language Journal* 84 (1), 5–27.

Wong Fillmore, L. and Snow, C. (2002) What teachers need to know about language. In C. Temple Adger, C.E. Snow and D. Christian (eds) *What Teachers Need to Know About Language* (pp. 7–53). McHenry, IL: Delta Systems Co, Inc.

Chapter 5

Diversity Up Close: Building Alternative Discourses in the Two-Way Immersion Classroom

DEBORAH K. PALMER

Overview

It is a Friday morning in mid-November in a two-way immersion second-grade classroom in Northern California. The children work in groups at their English Centers while their Friday English teacher, Ms Emma,[1] works with a small reading group. There are four children working with Ms Emma: James, Nancy and Aaron, all English speakers, and Marcos, a Spanish-speaker. They have just finished independently reading the first chapter of a mystery, and are discussing the story elements.

Ms E: Marcos, what's the setting of the story? Do you remember what setting means?
Marcos: No.
Ms E: Where does the story happen?
Marcos: Ummm,
Ms E: Do you have any clues?
Marcos: No.
Ms E: Well what do you think? Is it happening at school?
Marcos: No.
Ms E: No, is it happening at somebody's house?
James: In the forest.
Ms E: Are they in the forest yet?

This lesson is riddled with similar exchanges, in which Ms Emma invites thoughtful responses from Marcos and from low-skilled Aaron, while James jumps in with the answers, cuts off his classmates' thinking and diverts the teacher's attention. During the course of the lesson, the teacher moves away from trying to manage a conversation and instead asks the children to work independently on white boards. Yet James persists in interrupting her as she attempts to work one-on-one with other students. In the end, of all the students in Ms Emma's small group, the student who least appears to need her attention to succeed with the task, James, has managed to monopolize her the most.

In this chapter, I will explore the ways students' academic identities emerge in moments like these; and how a teacher can manage discourse to avoid some of the pitfalls we witness above. In a reading group with his Spanish teacher, Ms Melanie, James will hear himself stopped, hear the teacher reprimand him for interrupting, and find himself learning to value the contributions of his Spanish-speaking classmates. Students' construction of academic identities, which can lead directly to their success or failure in school contexts, occurs continually in the classroom as they engage in conversations around academic material with their peers and teachers. If teachers want to encourage healthy, equitable exchanges in linguistically diverse classrooms, they must learn how to effectively manage these micro-interactions (Cummins, 2000).

As Freeman (1998) points out, the construction of equity in a two-way immersion environment involves much more than just using the minority language (in this case Spanish) to instruct all students. Ms Melanie's classroom organization and management places often-marginalized students in the center of the action; she uses pedagogical strategies such as cooperative learning that challenge all students with rigorous content; she chooses and designs lessons and activities meant to teach students directly about empathy, conflict resolution and cross-cultural communication. In all of these ways, Ms Melanie's classroom is intentionally designed to open up more equitable learning spaces. Strategies such as these are well-documented in the literature on best practice in immersion classrooms (Cloud *et al.*, 2000; Lindholm-Leary, 2005).

Yet even with these various strategies in place in a strong two-way immersion classroom, inequity in discourse will persist. The children receive countless messages outside of the classroom, which tell them clearly what language is powerful and what achievers look like. According to Freeman (1998), skilled and successful immersion teachers see their roles as offering students 'alternative educational discourses,' helping students see themselves and their classmates in new, more powerful ways.

This chapter will explore some of the strategies involved in building those *alternative educational discourses* within the conversations that occur during class instruction. A skilled immersion teacher, the second grade Spanish teacher Ms Melanie, engages tactics such as selective error-correction, turn-taking management, re-voicing and careful listening, managing wait time, and thoughtfully questioning students, which enable less privileged students to participate more fully in academic lessons.

While power plays continue to occur in even the most skillfully managed classroom talk, the efforts of a skilled teacher to reshape discourse for equity can be witnessed at every turn. These efforts can help develop more equitable talk patterns and alternative discourses among students, thereby opening opportunities for linguistic minority students to develop academically-oriented identities and find success in school.

The Classroom, the Teachers and the Study

To better understand the classroom dynamics described above, I conducted an ethnographic discourse analysis, similar in methodology to that of Freeman's (1998) study. To deeply analyze the talk occurring in this classroom, I drew upon the ideas developed in the field of discourse analysis, and more particularly in the realms of conversational analysis (Sacks et al., 1974: Schegloff, 1991) and interactional sociolinguistics (Cazden, 2001; Gumperz & Hymes, 1972). Conversational analysis offered me a set of tools to examine the unspoken rules by which speakers accomplish things – such as obtaining a turn at talk, repairing damaged performance or showing themselves to be knowledgeable. Interactional sociolinguistics is more concerned with the ways that speakers draw on cultural practices and routines to make themselves understood, and the ways that speakers who have access to different sets of cultural practices may fail to understand one another. In my study, as I drew on these traditions for the tools to look in detail at talk, I also took a critical approach to my data: I was interested in questions of power and status and, therefore, my work falls under the broad umbrella of Critical Discourse Analysis (Fairclough, 1999). In this study, I also made extensive use of techniques of ethnography. Including participant observation and in-depth interviews, ethnography in education attempts to unveil what Mehan (1982) calls the *black box* of the classroom. Ethnographic observation allowed me to understand the context for talk that occurred in this setting.

This study was conducted at a diverse urban elementary school in Northern California. The school boasts a two-way immersion strand in Spanish and English. One classroom of three at each grade level is two-way, and the program follows the 90:10, or *minority language dominant* model of language division, in which children spend 90% of their K–1 day in Spanish and 10% in English (Lindholm-Leary, 2001). (See also Chapter 9 for a more detailed description of the 90:10 model.) I studied the second grade two-way classroom where the children received approximately 70% of their instruction in Spanish, and 30% in English. It was a self-contained classroom of 20 children. Eight children spoke only English at home, nine spoke mainly Spanish at home, and three came from bilingual households. A little under half of the students received free/reduced lunch, which is often used as an indicator of socioeconomic status.

The Spanish teacher, Ms Melanie, was a native English speaker whose Spanish was strong, but had a detectable accent. Having majored in ethnic studies in college and spent many hours thinking about the implications of diversity, Ms Melanie was very cognizant of inequities in her classroom and at the school. She cared deeply about fighting the linguistic dominance of English-speaking children and maintaining high expectations for academic performance for all children. This was her sixth year of teaching in bilingual elementary settings and her third year at this school in the two-way second grade classroom. Along with the other teachers in the two-way immersion program, Ms Melanie was involved in ongoing staff development on immersion pedagogy led by the school's former bilingual resource teacher, one of the founding members of Two-Way CABE (the Two-Way Immersion sub-organization of the California Association of Bilingual Education) and the writer of the grant that began the program at this school.[2]

The year of this study, Ms Melanie decided to work only four days a week, and so the class had a Friday English teacher, Ms Emma. Ms Emma was not bilingual, but did understand some Spanish. She was in her fifth year of teaching at this school but taking a year's leave from full-time teaching. Up until this year, Ms Emma had taught in English-medium *mainstream* classrooms, which at this school were still very diverse. Her need for leave emerged from a particularly challenging group she had the year before, in which issues of ethnic and linguistic diversity had over-whelmed her. Ms Emma was open and reflective about her practice. She worked very hard throughout the year of this study to make sense of the challenges that had driven her out of her classroom the year before and to improve her abilities to manage the two-way immersion environment.

Data collection

I audio-recorded two to three sessions per week in the classroom during October, December, and parts of February for a total of 22 sessions. I video-taped an average of twice per week during March and April for a total of 11 sessions. I balanced my visits between Spanish language instruction and English language instruction, taking detailed ethnographic field notes each time. Sessions lasted between twenty minutes and two hours. I recorded the children during varied times of day, and in varied settings.

I chose six focal children during the first month of observations. These students represented all three linguistic groups (Spanish-dominant, English-dominant, and bilingual), both genders, all three ethnicities (African

American, Latino, and White) and a wide range of social and communicative skills and styles. James, the focal student of the segment that opened this chapter, was one of these six, as were Aaron and Nancy, the other English speakers. In addition, there were Braulio, Oswaldo and Laura, who you will meet later in the chapter. While I generally focused my observations around the interactions of at least one of these six, I had permission to involve the entire class in the study. Thus, for the purposes of analysis, I focused not on individual students but on activities situated in a participation framework. Goodwin (1990) argues that individuals construct their social identities within the talk of specific activities, so if we want to understand identity construction we must look at the participation frameworks of the activities within which the construction takes place.

In addition to observing and recording classroom interactions, I served as a classroom volunteer (participant observer) generally once per week throughout the school year; I kept field notes of all experiences in the school. Finally, during the spring I conducted and audio-taped open-ended interviews with eight staff members at the school (including both classroom teachers) and with the parents of the six focal students.

Data analysis

As is common in qualitative studies of this nature, analysis of my data first began as I was collecting it (Bogdan & Biklen, 1998). Immediately following my visits to the classroom, I would sit down with the audio or videotape of a session and elaborate on my hand-written field notes, producing as 'thick' a description of the classroom and class-members' engagement as I could (Geertz, 1973). While I listened and typed field notes, I would also flag in my notes moments in which I noticed metalinguistic talk, code switching or some indication of either cooperation or conflict between or among focal students and other class members. As I was looking at as wide a variety of participation structures as possible, I periodically read through the data looking for larger themes and patterns to guide me, both as I continued to collect data and as I flagged episodes. From these coding sessions, I would return to data collection with renewed direction. One example of this was the way I began to look for small-group interactions with the teacher after having recorded the above interaction. I knew there were some exchanges of linguistic capital occurring, and while I still had only a nascent understanding of the dynamic, I wanted to ensure a quantity of data from a similar participation framework in order to improve the trustworthiness of anything I might notice in those interactions.

Once all data collection was complete, I conducted a full thematic analysis of all field notes and related data, which led me to flag a few additional segments. I transcribed the flagged segments in greater detail, and began to work on close discourse analysis. This cycle repeated numerous times, as I would then return to my field notes and interview data to check the validity of findings in the discourse data, and come back to the discourse segments with more perspective drawn from the context and larger themes. I shared my thoughts along the way, together with drafts of my findings, with the classroom teachers I was studying; they were able to confirm for me that my depiction of the classroom was accurate.

Theoretical Background

This study is primarily an examination of the discourses offered to students by two teachers trying their best within the confines of their classroom to counter the dominant discourses of society. Bourdieu (1991) defines discourse to mean a language or set of linguistic practices that communicate a certain set of values within or to a specific community or context. All human interchange, for Bourdieu, operates within a *linguistic market*, in which individuals strategically employ whatever discourses are most appropriate in the setting for gaining *linguistic capital*, in other words increasing their personal status (i.e. relative power). In this setting, the Spanish teacher, Ms Melanie, works to manipulate the parameters of the classroom's *linguistic market* in order to effect more equitable power balances among students. Freeman's (1998) *alternative educational discourses* emerges from this theoretical frame. She argues, as I will, that the teachers at the school she studied (a two-way immersion school in Washington, DC) worked hard to develop alternative ways of talking about and to minority language children, which communicated an alternative set of values that allowed these children to construct academic-oriented identities for themselves.

In her analysis of gender identities, linguist Deborah Cameron (1997: 48) asserts that 'discourse *constructs* (gender) differentiation'. Thus, through talk, individuals perform different scripts and thereby define themselves. The students in this classroom construct their academic identities as learners (or as non-learners) or as respectful listeners (or talk-controllers) in the atmosphere of the classroom discourse. Further, the scripts of expectations they take on for their identity performances come not only from the larger society in which this classroom is situated, but also from a very deliberate effort on the part of Ms Melanie to offer the students alternative scripts.

However, Cameron (1997) acknowledges that because gender identity is defined by its ongoing performance, it is unstable and variable. Similarly with academic identities, a student who performs as a learner in one context can be seen to abandon this script and behave as a non-learner in another; a student who listens respectfully to classmates when with his teacher is observed interrupting and dominating the talk of those same classmates when a substitute teacher is present.

In addition to their academic identities, bilingual students also construct their linguistic identities within the context of their family, school and peer relationships, as they choose which language to use for what purposes in what settings (Potowski, 2004). When specific attention is paid to developing equitable environments, constructing cross-cultural understandings and valuing minority languages, two-way immersion settings lend themselves to the study of the construction of academic and linguistic identities for minority language students – indeed, all students – in the classroom (Cummins, 2000).

A Program Designed to Open Communicative Spaces for Minority Language Speakers

The ideal

Latino children in California, and throughout the United States, are chronically underserved by the schools (August & Hakuta, 1997; Garcia, 2004). Mounting evidence is showing two-way immersion education to be an effective means for reversing the trend toward academic failure among Hispanic students (Lindholm-Leary, 2001; Thomas & Collier, 2002). In Chapter 9 Lindholm-Leary and Howard provide an extensive synthesis of research in support of two-way immersion and speak in particular of the way Hispanic learners benefit. The two-way immersion program at this elementary school was started to help reverse a negative trend in the education of the approximately 38% of students in the school who are Latino. It was the hope of the parents, teachers and administrator who originally formed the program that it would open more opportunities for learning for all students in the program than did the former Transitional Bilingual Education program it replaced. (See Chapter 2 by Genesee for a brief description of transitional bilingual education programs.)

Perhaps the best articulation of the ways the two-way immersion program is designed to provide an opportunity for Latino students to develop *alternative educational discourses* was offered by the school's principal:

Principal: We see it as a big advantage for [Latino] children to not only be successful academically but also provide the modeling to English-speaking [students] so that we sort of tip the scales a little bit. And so then our Spanish-speaking children become the power agents in the classroom. And English-speaking kids traditionally and

> historically ... learn to be power agents early on. Our
> Spanish-speaking children are not brought up that way.
> They're supposed to be submissive. They're supposed to
> be quiet ... And so for us to put them in the [two-way]
> immersion setting and say we want you to be the power
> agents because you're going to be able to communicate
> more to the English-speaking kids than ever before…

Researcher: It's almost like a manipulative game…

Principal: Yeah. But it's a good manipulation. Because we're
producing Spanish-speaking bilingual children that
become more confident in school. They are more assertive
and they state their needs. The same way that historically
English-speaking kids state them in middle class schools.

In her interview, Ms Melanie describes her thoughts about developing *alternative educational discourses* for Latino students by empowering children both culturally and linguistically, goals that she feels go hand in hand:

> On a cultural validation level, having their language prioritized from
> the onset of their education as being the dominant one, the one that's
> most important, I think is an empowering phenomenon rather than
> being pushed into an environment where you don't understand
> anything ... And definitely not congruent with what happens in your
> home. And so I think that there's that ... cultural validation aspect of dual
> immersion that it's difficult to measure through ... standard measures ...
> But I think it can be measured through things like their participation ...
> Or just their sense of self and their self-esteem and their confidence in
> taking risks in the classroom or offering up their ideas.

Ms Melanie also asserts that English-speaking students will benefit from seeing Latino classmates as strong, confident, academic learners, and the result will be beneficial both academically and linguistically for all of the children.

The reality

In February and March of the study year, Ms Emma was encountering mounting difficulties with the English-speaking students during English instruction days. As she described it, they were behaving arrogantly and disrespectfully towards her and towards the parent volunteers who helped with morning centers. The following excerpt was taken from a whole-class lesson on nouns, where students were working on a worksheet as Ms Emma talked them through it (note: all students participating in the interaction below are English first language (L1) speakers except Eduardo, who is a Spanish L1 speaker).

James:	I know!! (...)
Ms E:	*Ok.[3]
James:	*Look at, Level 2, Noun junction.
Ms E:	Ahh James. We're gonna look at the backside number one, I'm gonna read the sentence,
James:	I already did that.
Ms E:	As soon as you guys hear a noun I want you to raise your hand. *Is what I want to do.
James:	*There's two nouns.
Ms E:	... I'm waiting for better attention from red and white group and blue group (the three groups with strong English speakers). Green group is doing a great job. Perhaps because I'm standing right here, huh.
Aaron:	ehhehh!
Ms E:	Yellow group is doing a good job. Listen to – number one, and read it with me, and then let's fi... let's circle the nouns, let's find them. Trees shade our playground during recess. Raise your hand tell me one noun that you see. Nancy.
Nancy:	Trees
Ms E:	Trees everyone circle trees ... circle trees ... and now right away let's sort it. Should we put trees – here, in person, place or thing?
(many):	Thing! ...
Ms E:	Um, Eduardo one more *noun in that sentence.
Eduardo:	*Recess.
Ms E:	Recess! What is recess? A person, right? Hi recess *how are you?
Eduardo:	*Nooo!
Ms E:	What?
Child:	(general direction of red group): A thing!
Eduardo:	A thing
Ms E:	Ok. Recess. *Daniel. You were gonna say something.
Child:	*Hello recess!
Daniel:	Can I draw?
Ms E:	No, you may not. You need to check your work and make sure you've got all the nouns circled. (Excerpt from classroom session recorded February 21, 2003)

At the beginning of this passage, James is talking with his buddies, Nick, Daniel and Jonathan, all native English speakers, rather than paying attention to Ms Emma. When she reprimands him by embedding his name into her instruction, he responds, 'I already did that' (meaning, he has already found the nouns in the sentence). He follows this by immediately responding to her question with, 'There's two nouns,' ignoring (even interrupting) her request that students raise their hands when they hear a noun. In this way he attempts to take the floor without teacher authorization, and by giving the answers he sabotages the teacher's attempts to allow other students the opportunity to demonstrate their knowledge. Both comments appear to be an effort to demonstrate his quick mastery of the material (which for him is apparently lacking in challenge) and thereby justify his lack of attention.

The teacher responds to his comments (and to the general inattention of the three groups of English-dominant students) by pausing the lesson to state, I'm waiting for better attention 'from... .' Then she moves on with the lesson. Finishing up the first sentence, she calls on Eduardo, a Spanish-speaking child, to identify the next noun. He correctly identifies *recess*, so she asks him to categorize it: is it a person, place or thing? But before he can respond, another student (the data do not allow us to identify who, but the voice emerges from the general direction of the four native English-speaking boys) again jumps in with the answer, 'a thing!' usurping Eduardo's opportunity to respond as the knower. He repeats the answer anyway, but the teacher hardly acknowledges it before moving on to interact with English speaker Daniel, who raises his hand to ask, 'Can I draw?' This statement functions as a bald statement that he too feels he's mastered this material and does not need to pay attention to the lesson (which may in fact be true, as he is a strong English reader and writer and a lesson categorizing nouns is hardly difficult for him). Ms Emma responds, equally baldly, 'No you may not.' Ms Emma comments to me afterwards that she rarely conducts whole class lessons with the group because the lessons tend to be, as this one was, dominated by English speakers.

While these students appear to demonstrate a lack of respect for the teacher and for their fellow students, it could also be argued that they are not being challenged as they should be. This lesson is not the most exciting presentation of material. Ms Emma admits that she struggles to develop lessons that will both challenge the English speakers and 'meet the [language and literacy development] needs' of the English learners (Spanish L1 speakers) in English. The role of strong English-speaking students in the English portion of a two-way immersion program is to raise the level of challenge by presenting strong native models of English speech so that all students, including beginning English learners, have the opportunity to engage with challenging and (hopefully) interesting linguistic material.

Watching Ms Emma struggle with the class over these issues foregrounds for us the need for a different set of strategies when working with the strong middle-class English-speaking children that so often populate two-way immersion programs. Very often, these children already see themselves as strong academic achievers. To a great extent, because they have access at home to academic English through reading and interaction with their parents, they are already familiar with academic language and literacy experiences and classroom discourse routines that teachers work to offer to many Spanish-dominant students. And they, like everyone else, deserve to be treated respectfully and taught to excel. Yet their behaviors are not appropriate in diverse settings, because either by jumping to respond to the teacher or by setting a tone of disengagement, they inadvertently deny opportunities to their minority language classmates to participate in the academic life of the class. This in turn means they risk coming to see their Spanish-speaking classmates as less competent than themselves, and the cycle continues. These children have a right to be in this program; in fact, their membership and the ethnic, class and linguistic diversity it entails are exactly what the school's bilingual staff was trying to achieve when they turned their transitional bilingual program into an attractive enrichment two-way immersion program. Yet the teachers (particularly Ms Melanie) adamantly express their conviction that these English-dominant children must not be allowed to dominate their classroom to the exclusion of other children – for their own sake as well as the sake of their classmates.

In her interview, Ms Melanie expresses her goal for the English-dominant children in her class:

> There's already so much personal power that they have in their lives that my perspective is that their lesson to learn in life ... is to learn humility and to learn how you can learn from someone else. And also how to take pride in if you do know more in a certain area than someone else how to help teach someone else a concept in a compassionate, caring way rather than gloat about what you know.

Thus Ms Melanie feels her English-speaking students need to learn to share the power they bring with them.

Mitigating Inequities in the Physical and Interactional Environment

Ms Melanie has organized her classroom, employing best practices in immersion pedagogy and in pedagogy for minority language students, to work toward these goals. She deliberately places strong Spanish speakers at each table and spreads strong English speakers as far apart as possible, physically integrating her class linguistically and academically (Cloud *et al.*, 2000). She offers the bulk of her instruction in small groups, organized around rigorous, developmentally-appropriate academic tasks that involve communication and, as often as possible, interaction with an adult expert (Fillmore, 1992; Garcia, 1991). Ms Melanie's classroom is always very structured, and her behavioral expectations for students very high. In the interview, she explains her use of such structure because English-dominant students' families are more accustomed to unstructured schooling environments, and because there is a natural tendency in U.S. society to let English-speaking students control talk, 'in unstructured environments then the [English-speaking] kids dominate... structure also facilitates equity.' In addition, she chooses or develops curriculum that highlights aspects of Latino culture, includes the history of Mexico and the Mexican immigrant experience in California, and involves students' family/life experiences (Garcia, 1991). Both Ms Melanie and Ms Emma collaborate to offer the children instruction in conflict resolution, and to help students themselves learn to communicate effectively with one another.

These practices are all well-documented as contributing to effectively offering minority language students a chance at academic success. However, as can be seen in the classroom segments with Ms Emma, the devil is often in the details. Opening up communicative spaces in a diverse classroom has everything to do with how each conversation is managed. Whether in small group or whole class, Ms Melanie uses the considerable power available to her as the teacher to subtly tone down the students who are more willing to talk at every opportunity, while at the same time eliciting the talk of more reserved students by giving them more wait time and expecting strong, academically-rich contributions from them. During her interview, Ms Melanie explains her motives and actions:

> If you've internalized, if you believe that your job is to counteract this power dynamic because you want to have an equitable classroom then you just implicitly do things to make sure that comes about or that that is happening as much as possible. And by being conscious of who's talking. Making sure that kids aren't interrupting and dominating things.

Ms Emma, by her own report, learned a great deal during this school year about managing micro-interactions in the classroom. In an interview at the end of March, Ms Emma expresses that she struggles to keep the English speakers from 'jumping in, trampling on other kids' voices' or from disengaging because they feel they know it all; while one of her goals for

Latino students is to 'have them confident in English enough to speak it in front of their classmates in a safe environment.'

Sharing Linguistic Capital During Guided Reading

Ms Melanie employs various strategies to manage micro-interactions in her classroom, including increasing wait time after asking questions, re-voicing student contributions, and deliberately managing turn-taking – by randomizing the students she calls on, by keeping group sizes small, by running _sharing circles_ in which all students are expected to participate, or simply by paying close attention to who has spoken and who hasn't. She also appears to use the strategy of selective error correction, that is, baldly correcting language, content, or behavioral mis-steps, to communicate to certain students when they have trampled on the speaking rights of others.

It is difficult to imagine a setting more ripe for errors of all types than a two-way immersion classroom full of seven and eight-year-old children not only exploring a wide range of new content material, learning new skills in reading and mathematics and learning to behave in the environment of school, but also learning a second language. It has been generally seen as part of the instructor's role to lower students' affective filters, and build a classroom culture that is safe for students so that they may take the risks required, and commit the errors required, to learn content, skills (including language skills) and behavior (Snow, 1987; Thomas & Collier, 2002). So, every time a student commits an error, a teacher must make a decision about whether – and how – to address that error. In making these decisions, teachers weigh their desire to build students' confidence and sense of safety, against what they often see as their responsibility to teach by correcting students' misunderstandings and to maintain a certain standard of accuracy in the classroom. It is important to note that such correction is not a recommended practice in two-way contexts, as adherence to a standard form of correctness tends to undervalue minority language students' home language varieties and discourage English-dominant students' experimentation with the target language (McCollum, 1999; Pérez, 2004). Yet correction is still present as an option for teachers, whether they take it up or not. Moreover, corrective feedback (as discussed in Chapter 7 by Lyster and Mori) rather than overt correction, is another option, though precisely how corrective feedback strategies might play out in two-way rather than one-way immersion classrooms is unclear.

For Ms Melanie often there are many errors to choose from in the language, skills, behavior and content understandings of her students. The evidence in this study suggests that her choice to correct an error often appears to have

more to do with managing the overall conversation and the student's participation for equity than with the degree or type of error she notes.

The exchange below is taken from a transcribed session of a Spanish
Guided Reading group. The group contains English speakers James, Rose
and Jonathan, and Spanish speakers Braulio and Oswaldo. The students
have just finished reading a story about a little boy who writes a message,
puts it in a bottle and throws it into the sea. Much to the boy's chagrin, the
message bottle finds its way to a friend's house rather than to a faraway
place as the boy had hoped. The message bottle nevertheless captures the
imagination of his friends, and with his father's help, several children come
together to send message bottles into the sea.

In this passage, English speaker James is extremely anxious to share
what he knows about the story. He attempts to gain the floor several times,
inappropriately interrupting his teacher and trying to take turns from
classmates. Ms Melanie's reactions (whether direct or indirect) to James are
highlighted by underlining:

Ms M:	**Y...* [And ...]
James:	*Y, y donde *fuuee...* [And, and where it went]
Ms M:	*Pero *es-pera, no interrumpas*. So Rose, *¿qué fue lo que um ... qué fue lo que agarró el niño y que puso alrededor de lo que escribió en el papel?* [But wait, don't interrupt. So Rose, what was it that um ... what was it that the boy grabbed and put around what he had written on the paper.]
Rose:	*¿Qué?* [What?]
Ms M:	*¿El papel estaba dentro de qué?* [The paper was inside what?]
Rose:	*Un botella.* [A bottle.]
Ms M:	*Una botella. Mmhmm, una botella. Y umm, ¿y después qué pasó? ¿Braulio?* [A bottle. Mmhmm, a bottle. And um, and then what happened? Braulio?]
Braulio:	*Um, estaba esperando a ver quien le llamaba pero no le llamaba.* [Um, he was waiting to see who called him but they didn't call him.]
Ms M:	Ok. **Mmhmm...*
James:	**Oh! Y despues...* [Oh! And after..]
Ms M:	*Um, gracias por levantar la mano. Sí, Oswaldo* . [Um, thank you for raising your hand. Yes, Oswaldo.]
Oswaldo:	*Um cuando aventó la botella um, una amiga de él la agarró y él se enojó, porque, no me acuerdo tanto pero, luego, luego le llamó la niña y luego se enojó.* [Um when he threw the bottle um a friend of his got it and he got mad, because, I don't

remember very much but, then, then the girl called him and then he got mad.]

James: (sigh, whispers) *Quiero...* [I want to...]

Ms M: *Ok, ok, James, ¿qué querías añadir?* [Okay, okay, James, what did you want to add?]

James: *Y... y de su papá dijó um quizás el botella fue alrededor del mundo y a tu amiga.* [And... and that his father said um maybe the bottle went around the world and to your friend.]

Ms M: *Ok, entonces, la amiga..* [Okay, then the friend...]

James: *... y después todos hicieron sus propias botellas y pon – ponieron como chistes y cosas como eso y después ponieron en el agua...* [...and then everyone made their own bottles and put (verb conjugation error) put like jokes and things like this and after put in the water...]

Ms M: *Mmhmm, las pus*ieron se dice, pusieron..* [Mmhmm, put them in water, you say, put...]

James: *... *pusieron en el agua y fueron en el río y el- y no dice quién agarró.* [...put in the water and they went in the river and the – and it doesn't say who got.]

Ms M: Ok, Jonathan, um, *¿qué más te acuerdas del cuento?* [Okay, Jonathan, um, what else do you remember from the story?]

Jonathan: *Oh, que um, el niño y dos de sus amigos...* [Oh, that um, the boy and two of his friends..]

Ms M: Mhmm...

Jonathan: *O uno de sus amigos y una de sus amigas quería hacer más botellas con él, y después hicieron? más botellas y después um, echaron al agua con la papá.* [Or one of his friends (boy) and one of his friends (girl) wanted (singular) to do more bottles with him, and after they did it? more bottles and then um, they tossed them in the water with the father (incorrect article)]

Ms M: *El papá.* [The father.]

Jonathan: *El papá.* [The father.]

Ms Melanie works hard to include all five students in the conversation. She cuts off James' interruptions twice, the first time directly (i.e. 'wait, don't interrupt') and the second time more indirectly by praising his classmate Oswaldo for appropriate participation. She allows Rose and Oswaldo to contribute, and calls on Braulio, before she finally allows James to say his piece, and she gives Jonathan an opportunity before moving on to the next question.

When James holds onto the floor longer than she expects, she chooses one of his linguistic errors to correct (*'pusieron, se dice...'*). In voice tone, timing, and emphasis, this correction is far more direct and explicit than her embedded recast earlier in the lesson of Rose's gender error, *'un botella'* ('mmhmm, *una botella*, mmhmm'), in which she surrounds the correction with affirmative sounds and does not draw tremendous attention to the error. Ms Melanie's correction style with James suggests as much a reaction to James' inappropriate participation in the lesson as to his linguistic error.

After this passage, having clearly struggled to maintain relatively equitable participation among her students, Ms Melanie changes her discussion format. She turns the conversation into a round-robin in which she asks one prediction question and thereby allows each student a turn to answer. Here is her question:

Ms M: *¿Qué piensan que podría haber pasado con estas otras botellas? Si tuvieran, si tuvieran que hacer una predicción de qué iba a pasar con esas botellas...* [What do you think could have happened with these other bottles? If you had to, if you had to make a prediction about what was going to happen with these bottles...]
Braulio: Ohhh!
Ms M: *¿Qué predicción harían? Braulio?* [What prediction would you make? Braulio?]

Note that in the above exchange, Braulio, a struggling (although extremely sharp) Spanish-speaking student, interrupted Ms Melanie in much the same way that James interrupted her earlier. Yet rather than order him not to interrupt, or even send him an indirect message by choosing someone else, she chooses to call on him first. In so doing, she encourages his academic participation. Braulio offers the following prediction.

Braulio: *Que un delfín o un león lo iba a encontrar.* [That a dolphin or a lion was going to find them.]

Although pressed for time by this point, and trying to manage the participation of all five students, Ms Melanie pushes Braulio on his answer:

Ms M: *Ok, ¿Por qué por qué un delfín y un león, por qué estos animales?* [Ok, why why a dolphin and a lion, why those animals?]

Braulio answers her by changing his mind about which animals will run into the message bottles, but Ms Melanie persists:

Braulio: *Porque un delfín – digo, no un delfín, un tiburón o una ballena.* [Because a dolphin – I mean, not a dolphin, a shark or a whale.]

Ms M: *Ok, so um, ¿por qué esos animales?* [Ok, so um, why those animals?]

Braulio: *Porque están en el océano y...* [Because they are in the ocean and...]

Ms Melanie allows Braulio to change his mind about the animals, but she does not allow him to end his statement there. She requires him to explain again, why these animals? Ms Melanie's persistence in taking her student's answer seriously requires Braulio to take his own thinking seriously as well, and to provide some logic behind his response, that is, that these animals live in the ocean and so it is possible they will encounter the message bottle. Ms Melanie is working hard to give Braulio a chance to define himself as a thoughtful reader and predictor of stories.

In the following excerpt from a conflict resolution lesson, with Laura (a native Spanish speaker) and James (our native English speaker), Ms Melanie has just asked the class for suggestions on what someone can do if they are having trouble listening to a friend who is trying to tell them something:

Ms M: ... Laura?

Laura: *Puedes decir, como interrumpir pero decir 'disculpa,' y después... 'otra vez' para seguir hablando.* [You can say, like interrupt but say 'excuse me,' and then... 'again' to keep talking.]

Ms M: (tries to revoice her idea, but misses): *¿O es diferente?* [Or is it different?]

Laura: *Es diferente.* [It's different.]

Ms M: *Ok no te entendí. ¿Puedes explicarme otra vez?* [Ok I didn't understand you. Can you explain it to me again?]

Laura: *Uh huh, como si está alguien hablando y dices que otro día para seguir hablando, como si van a verse durante el recreo para seguir hablando.* [Uh huh, like if someone is talking and you say that another day to continue talking, like if you're going to see each other during recess to keep talking.]

Ms M: *¿Oh, en otro tiempo?* [Oh at another time?]

Laura: Uh huh.

Ms M: *Ok si se te hace difícil escuchar en este momento, ¿comentar que en otra ocasión tal vez sería mejor cuando puedas escuchar mejor?* [Ok if it's difficult for you to listen at that moment, to comment that at another time perhaps it would be better when you can listen better?]

Laura: (nods)

Ms M: Ok. James?

James: *Era como el idea de Laura pero un poco diferente. Tú estás* *hablando hablando y puedes decir '¿puedes hacer más tarde o tal vez lo hacer más corto?'* [It was like Laura's idea but a little different. You're talking and you can say, 'can you do it later or perhaps do it shorter?']

Ms Melanie listens carefully to Laura, attempts to revoice her idea for the class, and checks with her to be sure she's understood. In fact she hasn't, and so she asks Laura to state the idea again, and appears ready to repeat the process until she understands Laura's idea. The teacher's care in listening to her student's idea encourages English-speaking James to listen carefully to Laura's idea, and present his own idea in relation to hers. Thus Laura's classmate further validates her thinking, while at the same time they are both learning that engaging in academic discourse about important topics requires building on the words and ideas of others rather than silencing them.

Conclusion

Over and over in these data, students and teachers appear engaged in a delicate and intricate dance of identity construction, maneuvering to maximize status and build equity in every phrase they utter. It is hoped that the above samples offer the reader an idea of the challenge, and of the power, of skillful conversation management in a diverse, multilingual classroom.

Although this one-year study allows me to begin to understand the complex dynamics behind language/power transactions in this classroom, it truly is only a beginning. There is much work to be done in order to be able to translate my understandings into actual recommendations for teachers and teacher educators; my conclusions from this study are merely preliminary.

While Ms Emma struggles to keep English-speaking students from cutting off classmates and taking over the academic space of the classroom, Ms Melanie appears more aware of the implications of the micro-interactions occurring under her purview. She is skilled at re-voicing, strategically correcting or not correcting student errors, allowing (even requiring) active participation from all students as equitably as possible, and focusing students on the academic content of their oral contributions to class. In this way, it seems that she attempts to socialize students like James to participate more effectively in a multicultural and diverse society. At the same time and in the same conversations, she appears to encourage strong academic participation from Spanish-speaking students, sheltering these students when necessary by providing deliberately opened spaces for them to contribute to conversations, and by engaging with them privately when necessary. In these ways she may be attempting to communicate to her students an alternative to mainstream classroom discourses – one that takes the English-speaking students out of center stage and opens up possibilities for a wider range of students to participate meaningfully.

The ultimate question remains: Will the two-way immersion project of developing more equitable discourse patterns among linguistically and culturally diverse children have any longer term, larger influence on their futures? Through our students, are we working towards more equitable distribution of linguistic and cultural capital and the rights to claim high-status academic identities? The mutability of identity construction is at the heart of the question of whether any pedagogy can create lasting change in the larger society. Regardless, there may be advantages to offering students practice with alternative discourses, and to pushing them to take on scripts that are at first uncomfortable. But eventually the students must leave the context of the activities and participation frameworks in which they learned to define themselves in new ways. Will they carry their newly-acquired scripts with them?

Notes

1. All names are pseudonyms.
2. I chose to study Ms Melanie's classroom because I was specifically looking for an ideal setting. I had on numerous occasions watched her teach and was impressed by what I saw. She had a very strong reputation among parents, and came recommended by her principal as well as by the former bilingual resource teacher. I found Ms Melanie's teaching to be of exceptionally high caliber.
3. The asterisk (*) on two or more consecutive lines of dialogue indicates overlapping speech. The ellipse (...) indicates a pause or silence in speech. Where no name is given, this means that the child speaking could not be identified from the tape.

References

August, D. and Hakuta, K. (1997) *Improving Schooling for Language Minority-Children: A Research Agenda*. Washington, DC: National Academy Press.

Bogdan, R. and Biklen, S. (1998) *Qualitative Research for Education: An Introduction to Theory and Methods*. Boston, MA: Allyn and Bacon.

Bourdieu, P. (1991) *Language and Symbolic Power*. Cambridge, MA: Harvard University Press.

Cameron, D. (1997) Performing gender identity: Young men's talk and the construction of heterosexual identity. In S. Johnson and U.H. Meinhof (eds) *Language and Masculinity* (pp. 47–64). Oxford: Blackwell.

Cazden, C. (2001) *Classroom Discourse: The Language of Teaching and Learning* (2nd edn). Portsmouth, NH: Heinemann.

Cloud, N., Genesee, F. and Hamayan, E. (2000) *Dual Language Instruction: A Handbook for Enriched Education*. Boston: Heinle & Heinle.

Cummins, J. (2000) *Language, Power and Pedagogy: Bilingual Children in the Crossfire*. Clevedon: Multilingual Matters.
Fairclough, N. (1999) Linguistic and intertextual analysis within discourse analysis. In A.J.N. Coupland (ed.) *The Discourse Reader* (pp. 183–211). London: Routledge.
Freeman, R. (1998) *Bilingual Education and Social Change*. Clevedon: Multilingual Matters.
Garcia, E. (1991) Effective instruction for language minority students: The teacher. *Journal of Education* 173 (2), 130–141.
Garcia, E. (2001) *Hispanic Education in the United States: Raíces y Alas*. Lanham, MD: Rowman & Littlefield Publishers.
Geertz, C. (1973) *The Interpretation of Cultures*. New York: Basic Books.
Goodwin, M.H. (1990) *He Said She Said: Talk as Social Organization Among Black Children*. Bloomington: Indiana University Press.
Gumperz, J. and Hymes, D. (eds) (1972) *Directions in Sociolinguistics: The Ethnography of Communication*. New York: Holt, Rinehart and Winston.
Lindholm-Leary, K. (2001) *Dual Language Education*. Clevedon: Multilingual Matters.
Lindholm-Leary, K. (2005) *Review of Research and Best Practices on Effective Features of Dual Language Education Programs*. Washington, DC: Center for Applied Linguistics.
McCollum, P. (1999) Learning to value English: Cultural capital in a two-way bilingual program. *Bilingual Research Journal* 23 (2–3), 113–133.
Mehan, H. (1982) The structure of classroom events and their consequences for students. In P. Gilmore and A.A. Glatthorn (eds) *Children In and Out of School* (pp. 59–87). Washington, DC: Center for Applied Linguistics.
Pérez, B. (2004) *Becoming Biliterate: A Study of Two-way Bilingual Immersion Education*. Mahwah, NJ: Lawrence Erlbaum Associates
Potowski, K. (2004) Student Spanish use and investment in a dual immersion classroom: Implications for second language acquisition and heritage language maintenance. *The Modern Language Journal* 88 (i), 75–101.
Sacks, H., Schegloff, E. and Jefferson, G. (1974) A simplest systematic for the organization of turn-taking in conversation. *Language* 50, 696–735.
Schegloff, E. (1991) Talk and social structure. In A.J.N. Coupland (ed.) *The Discourse Reader* (pp. 107–120). London: Routledge.
Snow, M.A. (1987) *Immersion Teacher Handbook* (Educational Report #10). Los Angeles, CA: University of California, Center for Language Education and Research.
Thomas, W.P. and Collier, V. (2002) National study of school effectiveness for language minority students' long-term academic achievement: Final report. Available online at http://www.crede.ucsc.edu/research/llaa/1.1_final.html. Accessed 14.8.07.
Wong Fillmore, L. (1992) Learning a language from learners. In C. Kramsch and S. McConnell-Ginet (eds) *Text and Context: Cross-disciplinary Perspectives on Language Studies* (pp. 46–66). Washington, DC: Heath.

Part 2

Evolving Perspectives on Language Development in Immersion Classrooms

Chapter 6

Lexical Learning Through a Multitask Activity: The Role of Repetition

MERRILL SWAIN and SHARON LAPKIN

Introduction

It is a well-documented fact that the spoken French of French immersion students is non-target-like in a number of ways (e.g. Lyster 1999; Rehner 2004; Swain & Lapkin, 1998; see also Chapters 2, 4, 7 and 8 for additional reviews of studies on immersion student language development). Examples include their use of L1-based vocabulary including false cognates, and their overuse of *high-coverage* vocabulary items such as *les choses* [things] instead of more specific vocabulary (e.g. Harley, 1992). It is difficult to draw learners' attention – that is, to get them to notice – such features in their own oral language production. We thought that one way that might help French immersion learners to notice aspects of their spoken French would be to ask them to transcribe recordings of themselves made while working in pairs on a communicative task. Inspired by the work of Lynch (2001), we decided to try out this idea with grade 8 French immersion students.

We asked the students to imagine that an anonymous donor had given their school $2000 and to brainstorm about how this money should be spent. Students did this in pairs, and the activity gave rise to a role play about how the money should be spent. The students then transcribed the role play. Doing this, and subsequent related activities, we reasoned, would take speaking out of its rapid, real-time, meaning-making context and provide the students with opportunities to notice their own use of French.

As we analyzed our transcription for the *languaging* (see Swain, 2006) that the students did in the series of activities, we were struck by the extent to which lexical items – central to the role plays the students created – were repeated. For this reason, in this chapter, we focus on the general question of the role that repetition plays in lexical learning, and, particularly, the role it plays in the transcribing the students did of their own oral production. We will claim that repetition in transcribing draws students' attention to specific lexical items, readying them for learning the appropriate target language forms. For us, learning is the change in behavior that occurs as meaning is co-constructed with others or the self. It is often observable in learners' speaking wherein cognitive activities become visible.

Literature Review

The Lynch study

Working with adult students taking English for Academic Purposes, Lynch (2001) asked eight students in an oral communication skills class to participate in a role play activity in pairs. The students' performance was tape-recorded and students then selected an extract of 90 to 120 seconds to transcribe. Each student produced a transcript and together they agreed on a final version that they revised until they were satisfied with their product. The teacher (Lynch) reformulated that text 'changing the parts of it that were either linguistically incorrect, or expressed in a way I would not use myself' (Lynch: 2001: 127). The following day the students compared their transcript with the reformulated one, noticing differences and discussing some of these.

Among the findings were the following: the task drew the students' attention to 'language form and use in a relatively natural way' (Lynch: 2001: 128). The revising process that the students engaged in prior to the reformulation gave rise to productive noticing. The participants remained engaged in the activity throughout. The teacher had an important role to play, particularly with respect to lexical correction. Lynch's experiment encouraged us to use a similar approach in the study described below.

Repetition

Research in second language learning that has focused on repetition has demonstrated that students improve their performance with additional opportunities to repeat a task (e.g. Bygate, 2001). Bygate found a strong effect for task repetition: an encounter with a task (interview) 10 weeks prior to performing the same task a second time enhanced both fluency and complexity of task performance. As Bygate (2001: 43–44) states, '... it is possible to harness earlier work on a task to elaborate more complex and/ or more fluent performance.'

Lynch and Maclean's (2001) findings support those of Bygate. Lynch and Maclean's study involved students who were oncologists and radiothera-pists taking a course on English for Cancer Conferences that they had developed and taught. Lynch and Maclean analyzed the changing perfor-mance of these students as they discussed their poster in a mock poster carousel session with a number of different interlocuters over time. They found that over the successive cycles of talk, the speech of the hosts of the poster sessions became more accurate and more fluent. Also, all learners improved in terms of phonology and vocabulary use. Several of the learners also increased the 'semantic precision of what they were saying ... and made improvements in syntax' (Lynch & Maclean, 2001: 154).

In much of the pedagogical literature on repetition, the focus is on the teachers' use of repetition in classrooms (e.g. Verplaetse, 2000); but some research has centered on the functions of repetition in student/student interaction (e.g. Borer, 2005; DiCamilla & Anton, 1997). Duff (2000: 110) underlines the principle that repetition 'should be meaningful and relevant to the learners – a form of negotiation of messages and texts – and not merely (or entirely) a mechanical or rote parroting of structures that does not ultimately enhance students' proficiency in the target language.' Duff (2000: 134) further suggests that repetition by students may 'index prior interactions that were somehow significant (e.g. ironic, humorous) [and that function] to provide social, intellectual and discursive cohesion... .' Di Camilla and Anton (1997: 627) label the latter function as maintaining inter-subjectivity. They also point out that repetition 'distribute[s] scaffolded help throughout the activity.'

In a recent doctoral thesis, Borer (2005) studied the role of private and social speech in vocabulary learning among advanced adult ESL students. In analyzing her participants' vocabulary-related episodes, she labeled one coding category *cognitive processing*; this involved different forms of repetition: simple repetition, manipulation and generation, with manipulation and generation reflecting a greater depth of processing than unaltered repetition. Manipulation involves learners separating language items into component features, creating hypotheses about form and meaning, and comparing target words to phonologically or semantically similar words (Borer, 2005: 81). Generation involves producing, monitoring and reformulating output based on the students' sociocultural histories, world knowledge and L1/L2 linguistic conceptualizations.

In Borer's study, students read a text containing low-frequency target words (e.g. pervasive/pervade) and tried to figure out the meaning on their own or with the help of a dictionary (word study task). They also solved crossword puzzles using the words, and provided oral answers to questions eliciting the target words. This final activity required participants to generate the words, whereas the word study activity was most likely to elicit unaltered repetition, and the crossword puzzle to elicit manipulation. Manipulation and generation were shown to be more effective in vocabulary learning and retention than simple repetition.

In our study, the initial task required that students begin where Borer's students ended up – by generating lexical items needed for their role plays. These lexical items were often generated in their L1 (English) and were then repeated frequently, particularly as the students transcribed their role play. When presented with a reformulation of their own transcription of their role play, the students' heightened awareness of these lexical items brought about by transcribing led to an immediate recognition of the French equivalents in the reformulation. In this chapter, we will provide excerpts of repetition that function cognitively to support the learning of French lexical items through simple repetition, manipulation and generation processes, and function socially to provide solidarity and cohesion. In doing so, we hope to show that learning is located in the students' language use (Mondada & Pekarek Doehler, 2004).

The Study

Table 6.1 displays a chronology of six task stages and the various products associated with each. Four pairs of students were asked to imagine that their school had been given $2000 and they could have some input as to how the money should be spent. They were asked to spend some time brainstorming ideas and then to do a role play involving a meeting with the principal (our research assistant) to present their ideas (oral pretest). This was video- and audio-recorded, and product #1 is what we call the oral pretest. We will come back to the discussion of pre- and post-tests at the end of the chapter.

Next, after a short training session on how to use a transcriber, the students transcribed their role play, yielding product #2 in Table 6.1. That transcript (written pretest) was reformulated by a native speaker of French (product # 4). In Stage 3, the students compared their written pretest (which we had typed out) to the reformulation, noticing differences between the two. In Stage 4, stimulated by the video of the noticing session (we stopped the video wherever noticing had taken place), the students reflected aloud on what they were thinking as they noticed differences between the two texts. During Stage 5, the students re-did their role play orally together (the oral post-test). Each was then given the written pretest (product #2) to re-write individually, making any changes they wished. These are what we called the written post-tests (products #10 and #11 on Table 6.1).

Finally, the students were interviewed individually to give us feedback on their perceptions of the activities and their usefulness for learning French. The time taken to complete this multitask activity varied across the four pairs of students; Ruth and Zoey – who are the two students we have selected to analyze for this chapter, took two hours to complete it on five days distributed over an 11-day period (Table 6.1, second row).

Table 6.1 Data collection: Task stages and products

	Stage 1 (Day 1)	Stage 2 (Day 3)	Stage 3 (Day 5)	Stage 4 (Day 9)	Stage 5 (Day 11)	Stage 6 (Day 11)
Data collection stages	**Saynète** (role play – oral pretest)	**Transcribing** (students transcribe stage 1 tape)	**Noticing** (students compare their transcription to a reformulation)	**Stimulated recall** (students view their noticing session and comment)	**Post-test** (students re-do their role play orally and individually rewrite product #2)	**Interview** (individual)
Time spent	7.5 minutes of planning time and 2.5 minutes to perform	37 minutes; Zoey wrote and Ruth operated the transcriber	11 minutes; Zoey highlighted changes noticed on the reformulation	36 minutes	3 minutes to prepare oral role play and 3 min. to perform; 10 min. each for the written tests	9–10 minutes each
Products	#1. Transcript of preparation and performance of role play (performance = oral pretest)	#2. Transcribed role play[a] (written pretest) #3. Transcript of transcribing session #4. Reformulation	#5. Highlighted reformulation #6. Transcript of noticing session #7. Students' own annotated transcript[b] (#2)	#8. Transcribed stimulated recall	#9. Transcript of oral post-test #10. Written post-test student A #11. Written post-test student B	#12. Interview student A #13. Interview student B

Note: (a) The students' transcription of their role play was reformulated by a native speaker of French before the noticing session. This is product # 4.

(b) Ruth and Zoey did not annotate their transcript (some other pairs of students did so).

The talk resulting from all of the stages was transcribed by the researchers (products 1, 3, 6, 8, 9, 12, 13). Ruth and Zoey were both considered by their teacher to be well above average in French. As we will see, Ruth and Zoey, like most immersion students, use the L1 as a resource in vocabulary learning and still have a lot of target-language vocabulary to learn. The nature of the multitask activity they engage in is such that there are many opportunities to generate words central to their role play, and multiple occasions for repetition and manipulation that play an important role in their vocabulary learning, and create opportunities for the development of social cohesiveness.

In the next two sections of this chapter, we provide the findings. In the first section, we give examples of repetition from Ruth and Zoey's dialogue that illustrate the cognitive and social functions of learning. In the second section, we focus on a pattern that emerged in the data as we examined the learning of French nouns longitudinally, that is, across the entire sequence of the activity. Illustrative examples are provided.

Findings

Part 1: Excerpts illustrating the social and cognitive functions of repetition

Simple repetition

Excerpt 1 comes from Ruth and Zoey's transcribing session (Table 6.1, Stage 2) and illustrates simple repetition. Here Ruth is operating the tape recorder (TR), while Zoey is writing. Underlining indicates that the tape of the role play is being played back:

Excerpt 1: Simple repetition (from the transcribing session)

#241   **(TR):**   *et ... et des brosses* [and brushes]
#242   **(Ruth):**   *et des brosses*
#243   **(Zoey):**   *des peintures, des papiers et des brosses* [paints, paper and brushes]

Manipulation

Excerpt 2 comes from the stimulated recall and illustrates the process of manipulation. During the stimulated recall session the research assistant (RA) stopped the videotape of the noticing session wherever Ruth and Zoey noticed a difference between their transcribed role play (written pretest) and the reformulation. Making explicit the contrast between the English and French nouns (turns #389 and #391) constitutes one aspect of manipulation.

Excerpt 2: Manipulation (from the stimulated recall session/Stage 4)

#388 **(RA):** Okay. What were you talking about?
#389 **(Ruth):** Hmm ... about the stage. We... we said *stage* ...
#390 **(RA):** Yeah.
#391 **(Ruth):** *et ça doit être 'scène.'* [and it should be 'stage']
#392 **(Zoey):** *Scène.*
#393 **(Ruth):** *Scène, scène.*

Turns #392 and #393 constitute follow-up simple repetitions.

Generation

Excerpt 3 illustrates repetition as generation. As they prepared for the initial role play, Ruth and Zoey brainstormed a list of improvements they wanted to see in their school, often using L1 nouns to express their meaning. In #45, Zoey generates *locker* (used with English pronunciation throughout)[1] in this brainstorming part of the role play session. In #102, Zoey uses *portes* to refer to the doors of the lockers, and Ruth corrects her in #103 by using the word previously generated. In #104 Zoey elaborates, indicating that painting the lockers will make the school more attractive. Finally, in their actual performance of the role play (#157), Zoey rationalizes in a more complex sentence the need for painting the lockers.

Excerpt 3: Generation (from the role play)

#45 **(Zoey):** *Et puis on peinturer les lockers.* [and then we paint the lockers] ...
#102 **(Zoey):** *Les, peinturer les portes.* [the, paint the doors]
#103 **(Ruth):** Lockers
#104: **(Zoey):** *Oui, et les lockers de notre école pour que ça sera plus belle.* [Yes, and the lockers in our school so that it will be more beautiful.] ...
#157 **(Zoey):** *... et aussi pour nos lockers dehors pour les peinturer parce qu'ils sont très vieux et ...* [and also for our lockers outside to paint them because they are very old and...]

Social cohesion

Excerpt 4 illustrates a social function of repetition, namely to establish solidarity between the participants. As we have seen, the students generated *locker* in the initial role play, repeating it often in the transcribing session. In the noticing stage, Ruth and Zoey laugh as they notice that *locker* has been reformulated as *casier*. In the stimulated recall session, they see themselves on the videotape laughing, and pointing first to the original and then the reformulation, and again, laughing, they explain why:

Excerpt 4: Social cohesion (from the stimulated recall)

#214 **(RA):**   (shows video snippet) OK. Why were you laughing, Ruth?
#215 **(Ruth):**   Uhm...
#216 **(RA):**   What were you looking at?
#217 **(Ruth):**   Uh, I think [laughs] I noticed ... um ... again [...Ruth and
                   Zoey laugh]. Again ... hmm ... otherwise ... [the video
                   shows Zoey pointing to the original then the reformula-
                   tion] Oh, *oui*, oh, oh, yeah. We noticed that um ... lockers
                   ... that's like English ... and *casiers* is French [they laugh].
#218 **(RA):**   OK.
#219 **(Ruth):**   Yeah. That's what we were laughing at.

Turn #217 is also an excerpt of manipulation, where Ruth comments on the English and French translation equivalents.

Part 2: A pattern identified

Having reviewed excerpts illustrating cognitive and social functions of repetition, we would now like to contextualize these by focusing on specific nouns and discovering the pattern of repetition that was central to the students' learning of French nouns in this context. In fact, Ruth and Zoey learned all but one of the nouns that were the focus of language-related episodes (e.g. Swain & Lapkin, 2002) during the various task stages. These nouns and their frequency of use in oral and written products are shown in Table 6.2. The learners generated these nouns initially in English, or in one case (*brosse*) used a false cognate. The multiple repetitions of the nouns in English appear to have primed the learners to notice the French equivalents in the reformulation, permitting them to internalize/learn the target-language vocabulary items. When they were provided with the French equivalents for the meanings they wished to convey, the students immediately began to use them.

As we saw in Excerpt 1, in Ruth and Zoey's initial role play, the students were talking about the need for art supplies and used the item *brosse*. In French, *brosse* denotes a hairbrush or toothbrush, not a brush for painting.

The students use *brosse* three times as they prepare and perform the role play – see the first column of Table 6.2, item a. *Brosse* appears once in the transcribed role play (column 2). Column 3 represents our transcription of the students' talk while they transcribed their role play. During that time, Ruth and Zoey repeated *brosse* six times to help each other stay on track and keep the word salient while Zoey wrote it down.

In the reformulation (column 4), *brosse* was replaced by *pinceau*. The students noticed it in the noticing stage, highlighted *pinceau* on the printed

Table 6.2 Frequency of selected nouns by task stage/product[a]

Lexical item	#1. Oral prep. and oral pretest	#2. Student-transcribed written pretest	#3. Transcript of student transcribing session	#4. Reformulation	#5. Reform after noticing (highlighted)	#7. Transcript of Noticing session	#8. SR	#9. Researcher-transcribed oral post-test	#10. Ruth written posttest	#11. Zoey written post-test	#12. Ruth interview	#13. Zoey interview
a stage	3 (2 in prep and 1 in RP)	1	22				2	2				
a_2 *scène*				1	1	1	4	3	1	1		
b air conditioner	1	3	7				2				1	
b_2 *climatisation*		1	12	2	2	1	4	1	2	2	1	
c lockers	4						1					
c_2 *casier*		1	1	1	1	2	2	4	1	1	2	
d air freshener/ deodorant	2							2 (air freshener); 3 *déodorant* (Fr.)	1 *déodorant*	1 *déodorant*	1 deodorant (Eng.)	
d_2 *désodorisant*				1	1	1[b]	1	2[c]				
e *brosses*	2	1	6				2				1	
e_2 *pinceaux*				1	1	1	2	3	1	1	1	

Note (a) Boldface in this table indicates that item corresponds to the reformulation.
(b) Here an attempt is made at *désodorisant*; the student actually says *désodorant*.
(c) The students omit the first *s* in error and say *déodorisant*.

reformulation (column 5), evidence that they noticed the appropriate term. In the stimulated recall, Ruth explains that *brosse* is used for toothbrush (*brosse à dents*) while *pinceau* is used for paintbrush:

Ruth: Peintures et brosses, oui. Hmmm … on a comme … je pense comme … pinceau? C'est comme brosse à dents. C'est comment les faire. Et c'est comme pinceau comme les peindre. [Paints and brushes, yes. Hmmm … we have like … I think like … brush? It's like toothbrush. It's how you do {use} them. And it's like brush like paint.] [2]

Here Ruth differentiates between two semantically related nouns, realizing that only one is appropriate in the context of painting.

In sum, once Ruth and Zoey notice the reformulated term (which they are likely to have encountered in their art classes), they replace *brosse* in their developing lexicon with *pinceau*. Their post-test performances, both oral (column 9) and written (columns 10 and 11) suggest that they are now able to use together and on their own, the appropriate French term. In other words, through their talk that took place over time, learning occurred (see also Swain & Lapkin, 2002).

Finally in the interview, the students were asked to reflect on the task and its usefulness in learning French. The researcher asked what they tried to remember as they did the task. In response (#114), Ruth said: 'Actually I did because uh.. how I like to do art, right? I wrote *brosse* and it's *pinceau*. So that was quite a big mistake. And so I actually tried to remember that.'

This pattern is repeated in the other nouns shown in Table 6.2. In item a, *stage*, the English word is used because the students do not seem able to generate *scène*, the French equivalent. (They probably do not use the French false cognate, *le stage*[3] because there is no overlapping meaning between English *stage* and French *stage*.) The students appear to un-self-consciously use English *stage* every time they want to say *la scène*. In fact they do so 22 times as they transcribe their role play (column 3). After they consult the reformulation and notice the correct French word, they never use the English word again. The only times they utter *stage* in the subsequent task stages is to contrast it with *scène*:

#388　**(RA):**　OK. What were you talking about?
#389　**(Ruth):**　Hmm… about the stage. We … we said *stage* … . [4]
#390　**(RA):**　Uhm.
#391　**(Ruth):**　*et ça doit être scène* [and it should be stage]
#392　**(Zoey):**　*Scène.* [stage]
#393　**(Ruth):**　*Scène, scène* [stage, stage].

In Borer's terminology, making explicit the contrast between the English and French equivalents entails manipulation of French *scène*, as we see in #391. The subsequent repetition of *scène* by the students in #392 and #393 may serve to consolidate their knowledge of it.

A further occasion for generation and manipulation occurs in the oral post-test as the students plan their performance (product #9, Table 6.1); Ruth has difficulty retrieving *scène*, and Zoey supplies it:

Ruth: Oh! *Le ... uh ... le, le stage,* the stage.
Zoey: *Scène.*
Ruth: *Scène.*

Here Ruth is remembering components of the role play that they want to include, retrieving *stage* initially. Zoey supplies the French equivalent, which Ruth repeats, thus consolidating her knowledge of it and helping to ensure its retention. Both students use the correct French word in the oral and written post-tests.

A similar phenomenon holds for another common lexical item that is doubtless used in this school-based French context: locker or *le casier*. The students use locker(s) four times in the initial role play, once in the written pretest, and 12 times in the transcribing session. The reformulator supplies the correct French word (*le casier*); the students highlight it (column 5, Table 6.2) during the noticing session (Column 7) and comment on it in the stimulated recall (see Excerpt 4 above). Their laughter may indicate that they feel they should have known the French word. Indeed Ruth confirms in her interview excerpt that she had known the word *casier*, but had forgotten it:

#78   **(Ruth):**   So like *casier.* Like I forgot. That was *locker.* I mean *locker* was *casier.* But I forgot. So ...
#79   **(RA):**   So that was something that you've known before.
#80   **(Ruth):**   Yeah, yeah.

In two other cases, where the French nouns are less frequent, it seems that words were not forgotten but had perhaps not yet been learned. Again Ruth tells us:

#71   **(RA):**   Do you think that transcribing helped you better learn anything about your French? Did you learn anything?
#72   **(Ruth):**   Yeah. I lear ... I learned ... that I have ... I sh ... I don't know how to say *air conditioning* and *deodorant.*

In spite of not having encountered these less-frequent words before (at least in Ruth's case), both students learned one of them, *climatisation* (item

b_2 on Table 6.2). The pattern of repetition as shown in Table 6.2 was similar to the pattern for *scène, casier* and *pinceau*.[5]

This was not so evident in the case of *désodorisant* (item d_2), the French equivalent of air freshener. Notice that *air freshener* was repeated only twice in the role play; it was used once in the transcribing session (columns 2 and 3). In the noticing session, Ruth mispronounces the correct form, omitting a syllable (she says *déodorant*). In the oral post-test (column 9) the students generated the English term *air freshener* twice while preparing for the role play, and attempted *déodorant* three times (this does not mean air freshener but rather underarm deodorant). Still, when they performed the role play (column 9, Table 6.2), they managed to retrieve the term *désodorisant*, but omitted the first *s*. So the students use a partially-correct word twice in this case. Neither student used it in her written posttest, and neither referred to it in her interview.

The bolded lines in Table 6.2 indicate a clear pattern: initially Ruth and Zoey used English or a French cognate for the nouns they need. When the reformulator supplied the correct target noun, these students noticed it, discussed it in the stimulated recall and almost inevitably used it in both their oral and written posttests, as indicated by the bolded numbers in Table 6.2, columns 9–11.

Summary and Discussion

By way of summary, there are five points we wish to discuss:

(1) First and foremost, our findings show that in the context of the particular multitask activity we asked our learners to participate in, repetition – even in the first language – played important cognitive and social functions. Cognitively, students' use of repetition drew their attention to specific lexical items, readying them to notice differences between their own language use and that of others. This particular *role-play-with-self-transcription-reformulation-and-stimulated-recall* activity meant that the repetition was meaningful and relevant to the learners even though it varied from simple repetition to generation. Furthermore, over time, repetition created opportunities for the development of a sense of social cohesiveness providing support integral to the learning process.

(2) As Lynch (2001) and Lynch and Maclean (2001) reported for their participants, our learners remained engaged in the activity, which extended over five sessions and involved sustained, careful work on the part of the participants. The repetition created opportunities to learn new lexical items and consolidate their knowledge of known ones in a natural manner. Multitask activities such as these may serve

to enhance vocabulary development, which, as Met establishes in Chapter 3, becomes increasingly important as literacy and academic demands increase in upper grades.

(3) The pattern we have uncovered with Ruth and Zoey demonstrates that the use of the first language during target language use may function to make a word salient such that the learners notice it or its equivalent in a reformulation.

(4) We make a claim about learning because we have made use of pre- and post-tests. Conceptually, the pre- and post-tests do what they are supposed to do – tell us if change has occurred between them. But they differ from *traditional* pre- and post-tests because they were not developed by the researcher. The pretests were constructed by the learners, not by us. For the pretest, together, as pairs, our learners said what they were able to say, and they transcribed what they said.

The post-tests took two forms – orally what the learners could do together, and in writing, what each could do on their own. In the second case, we can therefore argue that learning has proceeded from social interactive activity to internal cognitive activity. Additionally, because we have a record of the students' talk from pre- to post-test, we can begin to understand how the students got from A to B – from pre-test to post-test.

(5) Finally, we wish to raise a pedagogical issue, of relevance perhaps only to immersion contexts such as the Canadian one we have presented (i.e., one-way foreign language immersion). The fact that Ruth and Zoey used the L1 for some quite ordinary vocabulary items leads to questions about how often immersion students have the opportunities to engage in sustained speaking activities in the target language, and what are effective ways to help them improve their speaking abilities. The type of role play we designed is a credible classroom task, and could usefully be implemented in immersion settings. It is one way of enhancing lexical development, an area that has been identified as needing attention.

Notes

1. Sometimes immersion students pronounce English words with French pronunciation as a strategy in the hope that the same word exists in French.
2. For an explanation of the use of the discourse marker *comme* by immersion students, see Rehner, K. (2004).
3. A frequent meaning of *le stage* is *training course*. When Ruth and Zoey say *stage* throughout the task, they pronounce it as the English word.
4. Italics indicate that the word *stage* is pronounced as a French word.
5. Perhaps striking about these excerpts is the lack of attempts to circumlocute as a

communication strategy when unable to access the word. This may be common with same-L1 peers.

References

Borer, L. (2005) Speaking to the self and to others: The role of private and social speech in the retention of second language vocabulary by adult academic learners. Unpublished doctoral dissertation, University of Toronto.

Bygate, M. (2001) Effects of task repetition on the structure and control of oral language. In M. Bygate, P. Skehan and M. Swain (eds) *Researching Pedagogic Tasks: Second Language Learning, Teaching and Testing* (pp. 23–48). Harlow: Longman.

DiCamilla, F. and Anton, M. (1997) Repetition in the collaborative discourse of L2 learners: A Vygotskian perspective. *The Canadian Modern Language Review* 53, 609–633.

Duff, P. (2000) Repetition in foreign language classroom interaction. In J.K. Hall and L.S. Verplaetse (eds) *Second and Foreign Language Learning Through Classroom Interaction* (pp. 109–138). Mahwah, NJ: Lawrence Erlbaum.

Harley, B. (1992) Patterns of second language development in French immersion. *Journal of French Language Studies* 2, 159–184.

Lynch, T. (2001) Seeing what they meant: Transcribing as a route to noticing. *ELT Journal* 57, 130–138.

Lynch, T. and Maclean, J. (2001) 'A case of exercising': Effects of immediate task repetition on learners' performance. In M. Bygate, P. Skehan and M. Swain (eds) *Researching Pedagogic Tasks: Second Language Learning, Teaching and Testing* (pp. 141–162). Harlow: Longman.

Lyster, R. (1999) La négociation de la forme: La suite, mais pas la fin. *The Canadian Modern Language Review* 55, 355–384.

Mondada, L. and Pekarek Doehler, S. (2004) Second language acquisition as situated practice: Task accomplishment in the French second language classroom. *Modern Language Journal* 88, 510–518.

Rehner, K. (2004) *Developing Aspects of Second Language Discourse* Competence. Munich: Lincom Europa.

Swain, M. (2006). Languaging, agency and collaboration in advanced second language learning. In H. Byrnes (ed.) *Advanced Language Learning: The Contribution of Halliday and Vygotsky* (pp. 95–108). London: Continuum.

Swain, M. and Lapkin, S. (1998) Interaction and second language learning: Two adolescent French immersion students working together. *Modern Language Journal* 82, 320–337.

Swain, M. and Lapkin, S. (2002) Talking it through: Two French immersion learners' response to reformulation. *International Journal of Educational Research* 37, 285–304.

Verplaetse, L. (2000) Mr Wonder-ful: Portrait of a dialogic teacher. In J.K. Hall and L.S. Verplaetse (eds) *Second and Foreign Language Learning Through Classroom Interaction* (pp. 221–242). Mahwah, NJ: Lawrence Erlbaum.

Chapter 7

Instructional Counterbalance in Immersion Pedagogy

ROY LYSTER and HIROHIDE MORI

Introduction

In the early days of foreign language immersion, especially in the 1970s and early 80s, the principles underlying immersion pedagogy were quite straightforward. Students' second language acquisition was expected to parallel and be similar to their first language acquisition. Second language learning was thought to be primarily incidental, without the need for any explicit attention to language. This incidental approach to language learning resulted in high levels of comprehension skills as well as fluency and confidence in second language production, but also in persistent short-comings in grammatical accuracy (e.g. Harley *et al.*, 1990; see additional reviews of studies on immersion student language development in Chapters 2, 4, 6 and 8 of this volume). This leveling-off effect has been explained by the fact that some language features, such as certain verb tenses, occur only minimally in classroom discourse, whereas other features occur frequently but lack saliency in classroom discourse (e.g. Allen *et al.*, 1990; Swain, 1988). Researchers now underscore the importance of integrating form-focused instruction into regular subject-matter instruction to allow students to notice these otherwise infrequent or nonsalient features. According to Ellis (2001: 1–2), form-focused instruction is defined as 'any planned or incidental instructional activity that is intended to induce language learners to pay attention to linguistic form.' Teachers can implement form-focused instruction that is either reactive or proactive (Doughty & Williams, 1998; Lyster, 1998c).

On the one hand, reactive form-focused instruction occurs in response to students' language production during teacher–student interaction and includes the use of feedback. Research in support of reactive form-focused instruction suggests that it may be precisely at the moment when students have something to say that focus on form can be most effectively provided, rather than postponing the focus on form until a subsequent language lesson (Lightbown, 1991, 1998; Long, 1991). On the other hand, proactive form-focused instruction involves pre-planned instruction designed to enable students to notice and use second language features that might otherwise not be used or even noticed. Proactive form-focused instruction is generally considered most effective when embedded in communicative activities and is thus different from traditional grammar lessons, which emphasize the learning and categorizing of forms out of context. See, for example, the multitask activity described in Chapter 6, which engages learners in communicative tasks to bring their attention to lexical items in context. This proactive form-focused series of tasks is used as a research tool in Chapter 6 but could also be used as a meaningful pedagogical task, as Swain and Lapkin argue in their discussion.

In this chapter, we add a new dimension to the already-complex task of orchestrating reactive and proactive form-focused instruction in immersion classrooms. Specifically, we outline a rationale for what we call *instructional counterbalance* (Lyster & Mori, 2006; see also Lyster, 2007), which we present here as a fundamental component of effective immersion pedagogy. Whether teachers draw on reactive or proactive approaches to form-focused instruction, we propose that their instructional approaches need to be counterbalanced in order to effectively target language features that have reached a developmental plateau. Our concern in this chapter, therefore, is how immersion teachers can intervene to effect change in immersion students' use of interlanguage forms. A leveling-off effect in students' language development as they progress through their immersion program has been well documented, and is a recurring theme in concerns expressed by both teachers and researchers alike. Counterbalanced instruction, as described in this chapter, does not constitute an overarching approach to immersion pedagogy, but rather one designed specifically to ensure continued growth in the immersion language by providing opportunities for students to use target forms instead of recalcitrant interlanguage forms that are more readily accessible. Implemented by selectively shifting learners' attention away from the predominant communicative orientation of the instructional setting, counterbalanced instruction has promising potential as a catalyst for interlanguage restructuring and continued second language growth.

To illustrate the effectiveness of instructional counterbalance, we draw first on a comparative study of reactive form-focused instruction observed in French and Japanese immersion classrooms (Lyster & Mori, 2006). We then draw on a comparative analysis of proactive form-focused instructional treatments implemented in French immersion classrooms (Lyster, 2004b) to further illustrate the effectiveness of instruction that serves as a counterbalance to a classroom's predominant communicative orientation.

Reactive Form-Focused Instruction

This section is based on a comparative study (Lyster & Mori, 2006) that we undertook to compare patterns of interactional feedback, uptake and learner repair in four French immersion classrooms in Canada and three Japanese immersion classrooms in the US, all at either the 4th or 5th grade level. We used two coding schemes to compare the two instructional settings. First, we used Lyster and Ranta's (1997) error treatment model to identify specific patterns of interactional feedback, uptake and repair in these two settings. Second, we used Spada and Fröhlich's (1995) Communicative Orientation to Language Teaching (COLT) coding scheme to identify similarities and differences in other instructional variables across the two settings. Part A of the COLT scheme allowed us to observe and to code pedagogical activities according to participant organization (whole class, group or individual), content (procedural, linguistic or thematic), content control (teacher, student or text), and student modality (listening, speaking, reading or writing).

The French immersion data used for analysis included transcriptions of 27 lessons totaling 1100 minutes or 18.3 hours. There were 13 French language arts lessons (7.8 hours) and 14 subject-matter lessons (10.5 hours) including lessons from science, social studies and math. The Japanese immersion data comprised transcriptions of 889 minutes or 14.8 hours of classroom interaction, including Japanese language arts lessons (10.9 hours), subject-matter lessons (2.1 hours), and other activities (1.7 hours) involving discussions before and after regular lessons pertaining to topics such as classroom procedures, daily scheduling, attendance and the weather. The French immersion data were imported into COALA (Computer Aided Linguistic Analysis, Thornton & Pienemann, 1994) and the Japanese immersion data were imported into CHILDES for Japanese (Child Language Data Exchange System for Japanese, Oshima-Takane *et al.*, 1998). These data analysis programs facilitated the quantification and identification of interactional patterns following an adapted version of Lyster and Ranta's (1997) error treatment model.

We classified teacher feedback moves as one of three types: explicit correction, recasts or prompts. Explicit correction and recasts both supply learners with target reformulations of their non-target output. In the case of explicit correction, the teacher supplies the correct form and clearly indicates that what the student said was incorrect:

Student: *Le renard gris, le loup, le coyote, le bison et la gr... groue.* (phonological error) [The gray fox, the wolf, the coyote, the bison, and the cr... cran.]

Teacher: *Et la grue. On dit 'grue'.* [And the crane. We say 'crane'.]

For recasts, the teacher implicitly reformulates all or part of the student's utterance:

Student: *Umi ya, umi ya...* (lexical error) [The sea and, the sea and...]
Teacher: *Mizuumi ya...* [The lake and...]

Prompts, on the other hand, include a variety of signals – other than alternative reformulations – that push learners to self-repair. These moves have been referred to elsewhere as negotiation of form (e.g. Lyster, 1998b; Lyster & Ranta, 1997) or form-focused negotiation (Lyster, 2002). Prompts represent a range of feedback types that include the following moves.

Elicitation

The teacher directly elicits a reformulation from the student by asking questions such as 'How do we say that in French?' or by pausing to allow the student to complete the teacher's utterance, or by asking the student to reformulate his or her utterance.

Student: *Ben y a un jet de parfum qui sent pas très bon...* (lexical error)
             [Well there's a stream of perfume that doesn't smell very nice...]
Teacher: *Alors un jet de parfum, on va appeler ça un ...?* [So a stream of
             perfume, we'll call that a...?]

Metalinguistic clues

The teacher provides comments or questions related to the accuracy of the student's utterance, such as 'We don't say that in French,' without necessarily using any metalanguage to explain the error.

Student: *Un mille six cent quatre-vingt-quinze.* (grammatical error) [One
             thousand six hundred and ninety-five, i.e. the year 1695.]
Teacher: *Non. En français ça ne se dit pas 'un mille'.* [No. In French we
             don't say 'un mille'.]

Clarification requests

The teacher uses phrases such as 'Pardon'? and 'I don't understand' following learner errors to indicate to students that their utterance is ill-formed in some way and that a reformulation is required.

Student: *Bashi ni.* (phonological error) [On the wagon.]
Teacher: *Nani?* [What?]

Repetition

The teacher repeats the student's ill-formed utterance, adjusting intonation to highlight the error.

Student: *La guimauve, la chocolat.* (gender error) [Marshmallow, chocolate. (feminine)]

Teacher: *La chocolat?* [Chocolate (feminine)?]

Although these four prompting moves – used separately or in combination – represent a wide range of feedback types, they have one crucial feature in common: They withhold correct forms as well as other signs of approval (Lyster, 1998a) and instead offer learners an opportunity to self-repair by generating their own modified response.

Feedback moves can be followed either by topic continuation moves (initiated by a student or teacher) or by learner uptake, which refers to a student's immediate response to the teacher's feedback. Uptake includes two possibilities: repair or needs repair. *Repair* can occur in the following forms: learner-generated repair (i.e. self-repair or peer-repair) and repetition or incorporation of a teacher's reformulation. Prompts can be followed by either self-repair or peer-repair, the former produced by the student who committed the error and the latter by a student other than the one who initially made the error. Repetition and incorporation follow only recasts and explicit correction because these feedback types include the target form, which can be repeated or incorporated in a longer utterance. The category of *needs repair* refers to an utterance in which the student responds to the teacher's feedback move in some way but the uptake has not resulted in repair. Following Lyster and Ranta (1997), six subcategories were identified as needs repair: acknowledgment, same error, different error, off-target, hesitation and partial repair.

Researchers concur that recasts are by far the most frequent type of feedback in a range of classroom settings: elementary immersion classrooms (Lyster & Ranta, 1997; Mori, 2002), university-level foreign language classrooms (Doughty, 1994), high school English as a foreign language (EFL) classrooms (Tsang, 2004) and adult ESL classrooms (Ellis *et al.*, 2001). There is less consensus, however, concerning the propensity of recasts for triggering learner repair. Infrequent repair following recasts has been observed in French immersion classrooms (Lyster & Ranta, 1997), adult ESL in Canada (Panova & Lyster, 2002), and EFL in Hong Kong secondary schools (Tsang, 2004), whereas more frequent repair following recasts has been observed in Japanese immersion classrooms (Mori, 2002), adult ESL classrooms in New Zealand (Ellis *et al.*, 2001) and adult EFL conversation classes in Korea (Sheen, 2004). In light of these discrepant findings, we designed our comparative study to increase our knowledge of relevant contextual variables that influence immersion students' attentional biases toward interactional feedback. The following summary of our findings is taken from Lyster and Mori (2006) and is presented here as responses to our three research questions (RQs).

- *RQ1: What is the distribution of different types of interactional feedback in French and Japanese immersion classrooms?* The teachers in French and Japanese immersion classrooms used feedback in similar ways. In both settings recasts constituted the greatest proportion of feedback (54–65%), followed by prompts (26–38%) and then explicit correction (7–9%).

- *RQ2: What is the distribution of uptake and repair following different types of interactional feedback in French and Japanese immersion classrooms?* Different patterns were observed in French and Japanese immersion classrooms. Overall, Japanese immersion students responded to feedback more frequently (i.e. uptake) and more accurately (i.e. repair) than their French immersion counterparts. Moreover, the effects of feedback type on uptake and repair were reversed in the two settings. As seen in Tables 7.1 and 7.2, in Japanese immersion settings the greatest proportion of uptake and repair followed recasts (61% and 68%, respectively), whereas in French immersion settings the greatest proportion of uptake and repair followed prompts (62% and 53%, respectively). Recasts accounted for twice as much uptake as prompts did in Japanese immersion classrooms, whereas prompts accounted for twice as much uptake as recasts did in French immersion classrooms. Thus, although no quantitative differences were detected in the teachers' choices of feedback types across instructional settings, clear differences in student behavior were apparent.

Table 7.1 Number and percentage distribution of uptake moves after each feedback type

Uptake context	*French immersion*		*Japanese immersion*	
	n	*%*	*n*	*%*
After prompts	215	62%	59	30%
After recasts	110	32%	121	61%
After explicit correction	23	7%	18	9%

Table 7.2 Number and percentage distribution of repair moves after each feedback type

Repair context	French immersion		Japanese immersion	
	n	%	*n*	%
After prompts	93	53%	28	23%
After recasts	66	38%	84	68%
After explicit correction	16	9%	12	10%

- *RQ3: What factors contribute to similarities and differences in the occurrence of feedback, uptake, and repair across these two instructional settings?* We attributed the effectiveness of recasts at eliciting student uptake and repair in Japanese immersion classrooms to at least two instructional design features with an analytic orientation, as detected by the COLT scheme – namely, the use of choral repetition and an emphasis on speaking as a skill practiced in isolation through repetition and reading aloud. We detected an emphasis in Japanese immersion classrooms on accurate oral production, apparent in various activities involving repetition of teacher models, which likely served to prime students for repeating their teachers' recasts. In contrast, in French immersion classrooms, where no such priming was observed, instances of learner uptake and repair were more likely to follow prompts than recasts. Based on these findings, we proposed that recasts and prompts, depending on a given classroom's predominant communicative orientation, may prove more or less effective at eliciting student repair, with recasts being more effective in form-oriented classrooms (see also Nicholas *et al.*, 2001) and prompts more effective in meaning-oriented classrooms.

Because recasts preserve the learners' intended meaning, Long (1996) argued that recasts free up cognitive resources that would otherwise be used for semantic processing. Thus, with meaning held constant, recasts enable learners to focus on form and to notice errors in their interlanguage production. We suggest, however, that this is especially the case in form-oriented classrooms. Learners in classroom settings with regular opportunities for focused production practice and an emphasis on accuracy are primed to notice the corrective function of recasts – that is, to notice the gap between their nontarget output and the teacher's recast and to follow up with a repair move. In these classrooms, recasts have the potential to unambiguously play their double role as both corrective and pragmatic moves, as they draw attention to form on the one hand and confirm the veracity of the learner's utterance on the other. Thus, while a teacher's recast encourages a student to stay focused on meaning, an immediate repetition of a recast is evidence that the student is also attending to form.

In more meaning-oriented classrooms, however, when students' attention is focused on meaning via recasting, they remain focused on meaning, not form, because they expect the teacher's immediate response to confirm or disconfirm the veracity of their utterances. Prompts, on the other hand, as interactional moves intended to draw learners' attention to their non-target output, enable teachers in meaning-oriented classrooms to draw their students' attention toward form and momentarily away from meaning. In meaning-oriented classrooms that do not usually provide opportunities for focused production practice with an emphasis on accuracy, learners may detect the corrective function of prompts more easily than the covert signals they need to infer from recasts and will benefit from the opportunities to produce modified output in the form of self-repair after prompts.

To further explain the potential effects of different types of feedback in accordance with instructional setting, we proposed the *counterbalance hypothesis*, which states that:

> Instructional activities and interactional feedback that act as a counterbalance to the predominant communicative orientation of a given classroom setting will be more facilitative of interlanguage restructuring than instructional activities and interactional feedback that are congruent with the predominant communicative orientation. (Lyster & Mori, 2006: 294)

The counterbalance hypothesis is predicated on the role of attention in second language learning (e.g. Robinson, 2003; Schmidt, 2001), insofar as interlanguage restructuring is hypothesized to result from the engagement of classroom learners in instructional activities or interactional feedback that require a shift in attentional focus. The effort required for learners to shift their attention to meaning in a form-oriented context and to form in a meaning-oriented context is predicted to effect changes in their use of persistent interlanguage forms, by strengthening connections between changes in long-term memory and actual language production. Following this prediction, interactional feedback that orients learners in the direction opposite to that which their target language learning environment has accustomed them to may prove effective at enabling them to restructure their current interlanguage. Skehan (1998) makes a similar argument for pushing learners who are either form-oriented or meaning-oriented in the opposite direction in order to strike a balance between the two orientations. In the next section, we further illustrate the notion of instructional counterbalance and its effectiveness in proactive form-focused instructional interventions that differ from other types of content-based activities routinely encountered in French immersion classrooms.

Proactive Form-Focused Instruction

This section is based on a comparative analysis by Lyster (2004b) of five classroom intervention studies that investigated the effects of proactive form-focused instruction on features known to be difficult for second language learners of French in Canadian immersion programs. The studies were conducted across various grade levels (2, 5, 6, 7, 8) in urban schools in or near the cities of Vancouver, Toronto and Montreal. The five studies span a period of 15 years, from 1989 to 2004, and involved almost 1200 students in 49 French immersion classrooms. The studies, which include Harley (1989), Day and Shapson (1991), Lyster (1994), Harley (1998) and Lyster (2004a), were selected because they are often grouped together as evidence for the effectiveness of form-focused instruction, even though they were not all equally effective with respect to actual learning outcomes. The purpose of the comparison was to reveal what it was about the pedagogical treatments in each study that contributed to the different outcomes.

Each study involved an intervention with a quasi-experimental design, enabling comparisons of at least two different groups of students: an experimental group exposed to a special form-focused pedagogical treatment and a comparison group exposed only to its regular immersion program. Pre-tests were given to all students in both experimental and comparison groups just prior to the pedagogical treatments and then the form-focused instruction was administered only to students in the experimental groups for roughly 10 to 12 hours distributed over an average of five to six weeks (see Lyster, 2004b: 326 for details). At the end of the instructional period, immediate post-tests were administered to all students. Then, several weeks later, delayed post-tests were administered to all students to assess the extent to which they maintained over time what they had learned.

The target features in these studies included perfect and imperfect past tenses, the conditional mood, second-person pronouns (*tu/vous*) and grammatical gender. Research into the interlanguage development of French immersion students had shown that these features were sources of difficulty and therefore required form-focused instruction, arguably because they differ from the students' first language and/or lack prominence in the discourse of subject-matter instruction.

Study 1

Harley (1989) conducted a study in immersion classrooms with 11–12 year-old students to determine the effects of form-focused instruction on the use of perfect and imperfect past tenses in French. Some of the instructional activities involved reading a legend about werewolves, working in groups to create new legends, playing language games and creating albums of childhood memories. The creation of childhood albums was the main activity, which required students to recount various childhood memories, both orally and in writing along with authentic photographs brought from home, while using the two past tenses appropriately. Students were assessed on three measures: a cloze test, a written production task, and an oral production task. Immediate post-test results revealed benefits on the cloze test and the oral task for the experimental group, but no significant differences on the written production task. Three months later, on the delayed posttest, no significant differences were found between the groups on any of the measures, in spite of the 12 hours of instructional activities.

Study 2

Day and Shapson (1991) conducted an intervention study with 12- to 13-year-old students to test the effects of form-focused instruction on the use of the conditional mood in French. The thematic context involved the planning of an imaginary space colony and thus integrated concepts from the science class. Students were asked to play the role of ecologists, and to design a space station that would recreate a natural environment where space pioneers would be able to settle. The objective was to provide students, in both speaking and writing activities, with a context for using the conditional to express possible yet uncertain outcomes in the future. A cooperative-learning approach was adopted to maximize student interaction and to ensure the use of the conditional in communicative situations. In addition, every lesson began with a language game or exercise that served as a reminder to students of the forms and functions of the conditional. On immediate posttest measures, the experimental group demonstrated significant gains on a cloze test and a written composition, but not in oral production. Students maintained the significant gains on the composition and cloze test at the time of delayed post-testing 11 weeks later, confirming that no gains were made in oral production, even after 17 hours of instructional activities.

Study 3

Lyster (1994) examined the effect of form-focused instruction on the sociolinguistic competence of 13–14 year-old immersion students, focusing specifically on their use of second-person pronouns in formal and informal contexts. The instructional unit included the following types of activities:

(1) explicit comparisons of various speech acts in formal and informal contexts;
(2) role plays with peer feedback in contexts contrived to be either formal or informal;
(3) structural exercises highlighting verb inflections;
(4) analysis of second-person pronouns in dialogues extracted from a novel;
(5) comparison of formal and informal letters and invitations;
(6) creation of formal and informal letters and invitations.

Test results showed significant improvement, both in the short- and long-term, in students' ability to accurately use second-person pronouns in formal contexts in both written and oral production tasks. Their overall awareness of sociolinguistic appropriateness, as demonstrated by their performance on multiple-choice tests, also improved significantly over time.

Study 4

Harley (1998) conducted a study with young 7–8 year-olds, using form-focused activities designed to draw children's attention to noun endings that predict grammatical gender. Each student created two illustrated dictionaries (one for masculine words and the other for feminine words) and labels were prominently displayed around the classrooms to identify the names of objects along with their gender-specific determiners. In addition, the treatment incorporated a series of language games, including I Spy, Simon Says, Concentration, Bingo and My Aunt's Suitcase, all of which were designed to provide opportunities for practice in associating grammatical gender with noun endings. The study revealed significant long-term progress for students exposed to form-focused instruction, as demonstrated by three of the four measures (two listening tasks and an oral picture description task). The only measure that did not reveal significant improvement was an oral task requiring students to identify the gender of low-frequency unfamiliar nouns.

Study 5

Building on Harley's (1998) study, Lyster (2004a) conducted a classroom study at a higher grade level with 10–11-year-old students, focusing on grammatical gender. The instructional unit was designed around the children's regular curriculum, and contained simplified versions of texts found in their commercially produced materials. Typographical enhancement was used to highlight, in bold, the endings of target nouns embedded in these texts. Students were asked to fill in the missing gender-specific article before each noun by checking its gender in the original text. Students were then asked to classify target nouns according to their endings and their gender, and to induce the rules governing gender attribution. Some of these tasks revolved around the students' history program, while others pertained to their science program.

This study was designed to examine not only the overall effects of instruction, but also the effects of different types of feedback. In addition to the comparison group, then, there was not just one but rather three experimental groups, each receiving the same instructional unit, but each exposed to a different oral feedback option: either recasts, prompts or no feedback. Results revealed that all three treatment groups demonstrated significant long-term improvement on all but one measure at the time of delayed post-testing, but had shown short-term improvement on this measure at the time of immediate post-testing. Prompts proved to be the most effective type of feedback, with the prompt group distinguishing itself as the only group to significantly outperform the comparison group on all immediate and delayed post-test measures.

Comparison

To summarize, the instructional treatment targeting two forms of the past tense in Harley's (1989) study yielded short-term improvement on two of the three measures, but no long-term significant improvement on any measures. Form-focused instruction on the conditional mood in Day and Shapson's (1991) study yielded short- and long-term significant improvement in written production, but none in oral production. In contrast, the other three studies on second-person pronouns and grammatical gender generally yielded more positive results.

The selected target features are from such different linguistic domains that these linguistic differences might have caused the differences in learner outcomes. For example, the functional distinctions expressed by the perfect and imperfect past tenses, as well as the hypothetical meanings expressed by the conditional mood, are arguably more complex than the ostensibly binary distinctions apparent in grammatical gender and second-person pronouns. To level the playing field for the sake of comparing these studies, however, we suggest instead that grammatical gender also constitutes a relatively complex subsystem, which is not simply binary in nature when one factors into the equation several hundred noun endings (e.g. Lyster, 2006) as well as the multiple effects that grammatical gender has on morphosyntax within and across sentences. Even the learning of second-person pronouns in French does not entail simple binary choices when we consider: first, the complexity of social variables that need to be taken into account; second, the use of the singular pronoun to mark indefinite and even plural reference in classroom discourse (Lyster & Rebuffot, 2002); and third, the effects of pronoun choice on morphosyntax, again within and across sentences.

Harley (1989: 335) stated that one of the main objectives of the form-focused instruction targeting the functional distinctions between two past tenses was to provide 'more opportunities for students to express these functions in the realization of interesting, motivating tasks.' The main communicative activity, which involved the creation of childhood albums, was indeed interesting and motivating, so much so that Harley reported that teachers and students alike seemed to overlook the linguistic focus. It was found in the end that, not only did students have difficulty distinguishing the functional distinctions of these two tenses, they had not mastered their formal characteristics either. In cases like these, more meaningful content-based interaction may not be what immersion students need to be pushed in their interlanguage development.

Similarly, Day and Shapson (1991) described the principles that guided the design of their instructional treatment as follows: (1) integration of language and content teaching, (2) interaction characterized by negotiation of meaning and (3) curriculum-based activities that are intrinsically motivating. In both the Harley and Day and Shapson studies, the emphasis on negotiation of meaning along with intrinsically motivating content-based activities, arguably did not push students to notice and to use the target verb forms more accurately. That is, the main thematic activities in their studies may not have created contexts that were sufficiently different from other immersion activities. By focusing students on meaningful interaction and motivating content, the instructional units may not have drawn learners' attention to linguistic accuracy any more than is typically the case, and, furthermore, may not have pushed students to actually use the target forms in oral production. For example, Day and Shapson reported having observed a tendency during the oral tasks for students to use the present tense as they interacted together in groups, avoiding the conditional and thereby decreasing opportunities to use conditionals in a meaningful context.

The production activities included in the instructional units in the Harley (1989) and Day and Shapson (1991) studies – the creation of childhood albums and the design of futuristic space colonies, respectively – emphasized meaning-focused practice much more than form-focused practice. In contrast, interventions in the other three studies, all of which demonstrated more robust changes to students' interlanguage, included production activities involving more form-focused practice. For example, in Lyster (1994), form-focused practice activities with peer feedback engaged students in various role plays in which they alternately addressed either a friend or an adult stranger. In Harley (1998), form-focused practice activities required students to recall and associate nouns with similar endings in games such as Concentration and to associate gender-specific articles with target nouns in various games such as Bingo and My Aunt's suitcase. In Lyster (2004a), form-focused practice activities required students to accurately assign gender-specific articles to target nouns whose endings had been typographically enhanced and that had been contrived to recur frequently in the students' curriculum-related materials and in various language games.

Production practice that was more form-focused than meaning-focused was likely more effective across these five studies because of the selected areas of difficulty, all of which are well-known sources of persistent error. In other words, continued opportunities for the same type of meaning-based interaction so characteristic of immersion classroom discourse is unlikely to change the students' use of easily accessible and recalcitrant interlanguage forms (Ranta & Lyster, 2007). Specifically, we suggest that the activities about childhood memories and futuristic space colonies were less effective because they were similar to other types of content-based activities routinely encountered in immersion, involving meaningful interaction and motivating content, and so did not require a shift in students' attention toward linguistic accuracy any more than is typically the case in immersion. In contrast, the activities with role plays, linguistic games and typographically enhanced texts were more effective because they were intrinsically *different* from the other instructional activities going on at the same time in other parts of the immersion curriculum, and thus required a shift in attention, from meaning to form, that proved beneficial in effecting change in students' interlanguage. We thus return to the counterbalance hypothesis to explain the different outcomes, and reiterate that, with respect to language features that have reached a developmental plateau, the effectiveness of proactive instructional interventions is commensurate with the extent to which they differ from the classroom's overall communicative orientation.

Conclusion

Drawing on studies of both reactive and proactive approaches to form-focused instruction, we have suggested that instructional counterbalance contributes to the effectiveness of classroom interventions that are intended to ensure continued immersion language growth, especially in the case of language features that have reached a developmental plateau. Instructional counterbalance involves pedagogical interventions that trigger interlanguage restructuring by shifting learners' attention away from the predominant communicative orientation of their instructional setting. For example, learners in meaning-oriented classrooms can benefit from form-focused intervention, such as feedback in the form of prompts and focused production practice, designed to increase their awareness of form and to push them beyond the use of interlanguage forms. Learners in form-oriented classrooms, to avoid an overemphasis on form, may benefit from meaning-oriented interventions, such as implicit feedback in the form of recasts and communicative production practice that involves open-ended tasks with fewer constraints to ensure accuracy.

The notion of instructional counterbalance facilitates our understanding of how to integrate analytic and experiential teaching strategies at the curriculum level, as recommended by Stern (1990, 1992), who argued that 'analytic' and 'experiential' (i.e. form-focused and meaning-focused) instructional options are best seen, not as dichotomous, but as complementary pairs along a continuum (see also Allen *et al.*, 1988; Allen *et al.*, 1990). Stern (1992: 106) recommended that 'where languages are taught as a subject ... there should be more emphasis on experiential strategies; for immersion-type programs, more attention should be paid to analytic strategies.' Even within a single immersion classroom, there is a need to counterbalance instructional options. In our comparison of the widely researched setting of French immersion in Canada with the much less researched setting of Japanese immersion in the US (Lyster & Mori, 2006), subtle yet distinctive characteristics emerged to confirm that immersion classrooms are multi-faceted and multidimensional. We found that both French and Japanese immersion alike are predominantly experiential in that teachers minimize explicit language instruction and instead use theme-based approaches to integrate language skills across content areas. However, Japanese immersion teachers, but not French immersion teachers, incorporated into this predominantly experiential backdrop two instructional options with an analytic focus: choral repetition and oral production practice in isolation. As a result of these form-focused episodes, Japanese immersion students appeared to benefit more than French immersion students from their teachers' extensive use of recasts.

Counterbalanced instruction also has relevance in other immersion settings that are defined by different entry points (early, middle or late). Dicks (1992) observed that language arts lessons tended to be more experiential for early French immersion students and more analytic for middle and late French immersion students. Harley and Hart (1997), in their comparison of early and late French immersion students who had all reached grade 11, indeed found that second language outcomes were predicted by memory ability in the case of early immersion students and by analytical language ability in the case of late immersion students. In line with the counterbalance hypothesis, we suggest that:

- older students in late immersion will benefit from the inclusion of more meaning-focused activities that encourage spontaneous production and quick access to unanalyzed language chunks stored as such in long-term memory (Skehan, 1998);
- younger students in early immersion will benefit from the inclusion of more form-focused age-appropriate activities (e.g. Harley, 1998), because developing their analytic language ability will prime them for the kind of implicit analysis of naturalistic input they need to engage in to drive forward their interlanguage development (see Ranta, 2002; Skehan, 1998).

Genesee (1987: 59) suggested that 'continuous growth in the second language will occur only if there are increased demands made on the learners' language system.' Counterbalanced instruction increases such demands by pushing learners to shift their attentional focus in a way that then balances their awareness of both form and meaning alike. For a teacher to effectively do so during the instructional day and throughout the school year requires considerable flexibility and orchestration (Tedick & de Gortari, 1998). Our hope is that this chapter will help teachers to reflect on their daily classroom activities and to make use of instructional counterbalance as a tool for guiding interventions that ensure continued growth in their students' target language proficiency.

References

Allen, P., Swain, M. and Harley, B. (1988) Analytic and experiential aspects of core French and immersion classrooms. *Bulletin of the Canadian Association of Applied Linguistics* 10, 59–68.

Allen, P., Swain, M., Harley, B. and Cummins J. (1990) Aspects of classroom treatment: Toward a more comprehensive view of second language education. In B. Harley, P. Allen, J. Cummins and M. Swain (eds) *The Development of Second Language Proficiency* (pp. 57–81). New York: Cambridge University Press.

Day, E. and Shapson, S. (1991) Integrating formal and functional approaches to language teaching in French immersion: An experimental study. *Language Learning* 41, 25–58.

Dicks, J. (1992) Analytic and experiential features of three French immersion programs: Early, middle, and late. *The Canadian Modern Language Review* 49, 37–59.

Doughty, C. (1994) Finetuning of feedback by competent speakers to language learners. In J. Alatis (ed.) *GURT 1993: Strategic Interaction* (pp. 96–108). Washington, DC: Georgetown University Press.

Doughty, C. and Williams, J. (1998) Pedagogical choices in focus on form. In C. Doughty and J. Williams (eds) *Focus on Form in Classroom Second Language Acquisition* (pp. 197–262). Cambridge: Cambridge University Press.

Ellis, R. (2001) Investigating form-focused instruction. *Language Learning* 51 (Supplement 1), 1–46.

Ellis, R., Basturkmen, H. and Loewen, S. (2001) Learner uptake in communicative ESL lessons. *Language Learning* 51, 281–318.

Genesee, F. (1987) *Learning Through Two Languages: Studies of Immersion and Bilingual Children*. Cambridge, MA: Newbury House.

Harley, B. (1989) Functional grammar in French immersion: A classroom experiment. *Applied Linguistics* 10, 331–359.

Harley, B. (1998) The role of form-focused tasks in promoting child L2 acquisition. In C. Doughty and J. Williams (eds) *Focus on Form in Classroom Second Language Acquisition* (pp. 156–174). Cambridge: Cambridge University Press.

Harley, B., Cummins, J., Swain, M. and Allen, P. (1990) The nature of language proficiency. In B. Harley, P. Allen, J. Cummins and M. Swain (eds) *The Development of Second Language Proficiency* (pp. 7–25). Cambridge: Cambridge University Press.

Harley, B. and Hart, D. (1997) Language aptitude and second language proficiency in classroom learners of different starting ages. *Studies in Second Language Acquisition* 19, 379–400.

Lightbown, P. (1991) What have we here? Some observations on the influence of instruction on L2 learning. In R. Phillipson, E. Kellerman, L. Selinker, M. Sharwood Smith and M. Swain (eds) *Foreign/Second Language Pedagogy Research* (pp. 197–212). Clevedon: Multilingual Matters.

Lightbown, P. (1998) The importance of timing in focus on form. In C. Doughty and J. Williams (eds) *Focus on Form in Classroom Second Language Acquisition* (pp. 177–196). New York: Cambridge University Press.

Long, M. (1991) Focus on form: A design feature in language teaching methodology. In K. de Bot, R. Ginsberg and C. Kramsch (eds) *Foreign Language Research in Cross-Cultural Perspective* (pp. 39–52). Amsterdam: John Benjamins.

Long, M. (1996) The role of the linguistic environment in second language acquisition. In W.C. Ritchie and T.K. Bhatia (eds) *Handbook of Second Language Acquisition* (pp. 413–468). San Diego, CA: Academic Press.

Lyster, R. (1994) The effect of functional-analytic teaching on aspects of French immersion students' sociolinguistic competence. *Applied Linguistics* 15, 263–287.

Lyster, R. (1998a) Recasts, repetition and ambiguity in L2 classroom discourse. *Studies in Second Language Acquisition* 20, 55–85.

Lyster, R. (1998b) Negotiation of form, recasts, and explicit correction in relation to error types and learner repair in immersion classrooms. *Language Learning* 48, 183–218.

Lyster, R. (1998c) Immersion pedagogy and implications for language teaching. In J. Cenoz and F. Genesee (eds) *Beyond Bilingualism: Multilingualism and Multilingual Education* (pp. 64–95). Clevedon: Multilingual Matters.

Lyster, R. (2002) Negotiation in immersion teacher–student interaction. *International Journal of Educational Research* 37, 237–253.

Lyster, R. (2004a) Differential effects of prompts and recasts in form-focused instruction. *Studies in Second Language Acquisition* 26, 399–432.

Lyster, R. (2004b) Research on form-focused instruction in immersion classrooms: Implications for theory and practice. *Journal of French Language Studies* 14, 321–341.

Lyster, R. (2006) Predictability in French gender attribution: A corpus analysis. *Journal of French Language Studies* 16, 69–92.

Lyster, R. (2007) *Learning and Teaching Languages Through Content: A Counterbalanced Approach.* Amsterdam: John Benjamins.

Lyster, R. and Mori, H. (2006) Interactional feedback and instructional counterbalance. *Studies in Second Language Acquisition* 28, 269–300.

Lyster, R. and Ranta, L. (1997) Corrective feedback and learner uptake: Negotiation of form in communicative classrooms. *Studies in Second Language Acquisition* 19, 37–66.

Lyster, R. and Rebuffot, J. (2002) Acquisition des pronoms d'allocution en classe de français immersif. *Acquisition et Interaction en Langue Étrangère* 17, 51–71.

Mori, H. (2002) Error treatment sequences in Japanese immersion classroom interactions at different grade levels. Unpublished doctoral dissertation, University of California, Los Angeles.

Nicholas, H., Lightbown, P. and Spada, N. (2001) Recasts as feedback to language learners. *Language Learning* 51, 719–758.

Oshima-Takane, Y., MacWhinney, B., Sirai, H., Miyata, S. and Naka, N. (eds) (1998) *CHILDES for Japanese* (2nd edn). Nagoya: Chukyo University.

Panova, I. and Lyster, R. (2002) Patterns of corrective feedback and uptake in an adult ESL classroom. *TESOL Quarterly* 36, 573–595.

Ranta, L. (2002) The role of learners' language analytic ability in the communicative classroom. In P. Robinson (ed.) *Individual Differences and Instructed Language Learning* (pp. 159–180). Amsterdam: John Benjamins.

Ranta, L. and Lyster, R. (2007) A cognitive approach to improving immersion students' oral language abilities: The awareness-practice-feedback sequence. In R. DeKeyser (ed.) *Practice in a Second Language: Perspectives from Applied Linguistics and Cognitive Psychology* (pp. 141–160). Cambridge: Cambridge University Press.

Robinson, P. (2003) Attention and memory in SLA. In C. Doughty and M. Long (eds) *The Handbook of Second Language Acquisition* (pp. 631–678). Oxford: Blackwell.

Schmidt, R. (2001) Attention. In P. Robinson (ed.) *Cognition and Second Language Instruction* (pp. 3–32). New York: Cambridge University Press.

Sheen, Y. (2004) Corrective feedback and learner uptake in communicative classrooms across instructional settings. *Language Teaching Research* 8, 263–300.

Skehan, P. (1998) *A Cognitive Approach to Language Learning.* Oxford: Oxford University Press.

Spada, N. and Fröhlich, M. (1995) *COLT, Communicative Orientation of Language Teaching Observation Scheme: Coding Conventions and Applications.* Sydney: National Centre for English Language Teaching and Research.

Stern, H.H. (1990) Analysis and experience as variables in second language pedagogy. In B. Harley, P. Allen, J. Cummins and M. Swain (eds) *The Development of Second Language Proficiency* (pp. 93–109). New York: Cambridge University Press.

Stern, H.H. (1992) *Issues and Options in Language Teaching.* Oxford: Oxford University Press.

Swain, M. (1988) Manipulating and complementing content teaching to maximize second language learning. *TESL Canada Journal* 6, 68–83.

Tedick, D. J. and de Gortari, B. (1998) Research on error correction and implications for classroom teaching. In *The Bridge: From Research to Practice. American Council for Immersion Education Newsletter* 1 (3), 1–4 (insert).

Thornton, I. and Pienemann, M. (1994). *COALA: Computer-Aided Linguistic Analysis.* Sydney: Language Acquisition Research Centre.

Tsang, W. (2004) Feedback and uptake in teacher–student interaction: An analysis of 18 English lessons in Hong Kong secondary classrooms. *Regional Language Centre Journal* 35, 187–209.

Chapter 8

Teacher Strategies for Second Language Production in Immersion Kindergarten in Finland

MARGARETA SÖDERGÅRD

Introduction

Immersion teachers are expected to create a stimulating and challenging environment for second language (L2) learning. Although comprehension of the L2 is especially important in the early years of immersion, L2 production should be promoted from the start as well. An important issue is how kindergarten immersion teachers can invite children to use the L2 even though their proficiency in the language is minimal.

When Swedish immersion for Finnish-speaking children was introduced in Finland, one of the aims was to give the learners confidence in speaking Swedish (Laurén, 1998). Hence, developing working methods that support students' productive language skills and their motivation to use the L2 is considered important. Research has shown that although immersion students' L2 proficiency develops to a high level, their productive skills are not on a par with their receptive skills (e.g. Swain, 1996). See Chapters 2, 4, 6 and 7 in this volume for further discussion and review of research on immersion student language development.

Although it is important not to overestimate children's ability to produce the L2 early on, it is equally important to encourage the children to use the L2 whenever possible. Thus, the immersion kindergarten teacher is expected to create situations where the children can use the L2 in meaningful communication (Mård, 1997). In the early years of immersion the children's cognitive ability and their linguistic means to express this ability develop hand in hand, and natural communication in the L2 is easy to achieve (Björklund *et al.*, 2005). Nevertheless, research by Mård (1997) has shown that immersion kindergarten teachers are uncertain of how much output they can expect and how actively they can promote the children's use of the L2.

Södergård (2002) observed an immersion kindergarten classroom during the children's first two months in the program and reported that the children's ability to understand the L2 developed quickly. The communication between the teacher and students gradually became very smooth, since the teacher used the immersion language and the children used their L1. However, there may be some risk in allowing this pattern to become too established. That is, when the teacher understands the children's L1, the children may not experience any authentic need for communicating in the L2. Döpke (1992) emphasizes the importance of a natural need for communication as a stimulus for language acquisition, but argues that the children's need to understand the L2 does not automatically result in their need to use it. Scholars (e.g. Cummins & Swain, 1986; Genesee, 1991; Swain, 1985) have also long argued for a balance between input and output for language acquisition to occur.

To contribute further to our understanding of how teachers in the early stages of immersion promote children's L2 use, a study was conducted in a Swedish immersion kindergarten classroom in Finland. To gain insight into how language learning can be promoted in immersion contexts, researchers need to go into actual classrooms and study how authentic interaction between teachers and children works. The focus of the study reported in this chapter is on teacher strategies that relate to the children's L2 production in natural classroom interaction.

Background to the Study

Several studies (e.g. Long, 1983) have paid attention to the role of interaction between learners and their interlocutors in providing effective conditions for L2 learning. Chaudron (1988) reports that teachers make adjustments in their speech when talking to language learners, and these adjustments serve to maintain the communication, to clarify information and to elicit learners' responses. Tardif's (1994) research focuses on teacher talk in early total immersion in Canada, and one of the objectives was to describe how teacher speech is modified to aid learner comprehension and output in the L2. Her study was based on video recordings primarily made in immersion kindergarten, accentuating the fact that the quality of teacher speech is especially important when the teacher is the main source of oral input in the L2.

Tardif identified five major modification strategies used by the teachers in her study: self-repetition, modelling, information, expansion and teacher questions. Linguistic modelling, that is, the teacher providing a word or a complete statement as a model for the students to imitate, was a common interactional feature in immersion classes. A typical feedback strategy was expansion, which Tardif divided into three subcategories:

grammar, concept, and paraphrase, depending on what the feedback targeted. The majority of the questions asked at the kindergarten level were context dependent and at a low level of complexity. Tardif also identified other strategies such as the teacher's use of the L1 and what she called *prompting*, where the teacher invited student response by tone of voice, but noted that these strategies were infrequent.

Teacher–student communication in kindergarten has also been studied by Arnau (1994) in Catalan immersion for Spanish-speaking children. His study focused on two teachers in classrooms with four-year-old children and in addition to teacher strategies, it also focused on student language use. One of the objectives was to study what interactional adjustments teachers made to facilitate and sustain student language. Arnau divided interactional adjustments into strategies and tactics, making a subtle distinction between the two. Strategies were defined as conversational procedures that teachers used when demanding a verbal message or an action. They are 'prior to the temporal space that is left so that the pupils respond, act or give an indication that they know how to do' (Arnau, 1994: 54). In contrast, tactics were defined as 'conversational procedures used by the teachers after the presence or absence of a message requested of a pupil' (Arnau, 1994: 54). Arnau identified tactics of corrective feedback, tactics of non-corrective feedback and tactics of meaning.

Arnau's observations in the classrooms showed that the teachers frequently asked questions that offered information to imitate, showing individual preferences for certain strategies, such as questions with alternatives. He also noticed that the proportion of clues given was related to the linguistic and academic competence of the students.

Regarding the teachers' use of tactics, Arnau's study showed some general features. When the students' expressions were understood in terms of their meaning but were not linguistically correct, the teachers offered an alternative model for expressing the same meaning. The teachers rarely informed the students that they had expressed themselves incorrectly or that they should express themselves in the L2. Use of the L2 was generally requested in an implicit way and only when the teachers knew that the students actually were able to produce it. Positive responses had a salient role in the classroom discourse, and Arnau suggested that positive response is a subtle way of stimulating use of the new language.

Studies of teacher and student interaction in authentic immersion school settings have been carried out as well by Lyster and Ranta (1997), who conducted their research in four grade 4 French immersion classes in Canada. Their study focuses on corrective feedback and learner uptake, that is, learner responses to feedback given. Lyster and Ranta identified six different types of feedback: explicit correction, recasts, clarification requests, metalinguistic feedback, elicitation and repetition. See Chapter 7 in this volume for a discussion of ongoing research in this area.

The most frequently used feedback type among teacher participants was the recast, or teacher's reformulation of all or part of the student's utterance, minus the error. However, recasts were the least likely to lead to uptake and only a small percentage led to repair. Lyster and Ranta drew the conclusion that recasts are less successful since young learners often do not take notice of them. Their observations showed that many teachers also repeated well-formed utterances to reinforce what students had said, and this habit of repeating created ambiguity. Clarification requests, metalinguistic feedback, elicitation and repetition were all considered to be more successful in the study because they allowed for *negotiation of form*, that is, they promoted the students' participation in finding the correct answer.

The study presented in this chapter continues this vein of inquiry by expanding on previous work done in actual immersion classrooms. It focuses on teacher strategies used in an immersion kindergarten classroom to elicit children's L2 production and to offer feedback after children's L2 production.

Context of the Study: Immersion in Finland

Finland is a bilingual nation that has had two official languages, Finnish and Swedish, since it became an independent country in 1917. Finnish is the native language of the majority (about 92.3% of the population) while Swedish is the native language of the minority (about 5.7%). The rest of the population represent other first languages (L1), such as Russian, Estonian, English and Somali. There are also about 6500 indigenous Saami in Finland, but only about half speak a Saami language as their L1 (Latomaa & Nuolijärvi, 2002).

The national school system is divided into Finnish-speaking and Swedish-speaking sections, and children from both groups have equal rights to education in their L1. The curricular content is similar for both Finnish-speaking and Swedish-speaking schools, with the only difference being the language of instruction. Proficiency in several languages is considered important in Finland, and all children have the right and obligation to study at least two languages in addition to their L1 within their basic education (7 to 16 years of age). One of the compulsory languages studied is always the second national language; the other is most often English. In general, students in Finland also choose to study one or two optional languages (most often German or French). Until the latter part of the 1980s, languages were exclusively taught as subjects in school, with instruction occurring in separate lessons focused on language learning (Björklund, 1997).

Traditionally, second and foreign language teaching in Finland was based on grammar instruction with very little importance given to the students' ability to use the languages learned, but in the last few decades there has been a growing demand for communicative-pragmatic L2 teaching (Björklund, 1997). As a result, language immersion was introduced in Finland in 1987, starting in the bilingual city of Vaasa, where Finnish-speaking children were offered the opportunity to learn Swedish through immersion.

The one-way Swedish immersion program in Vaasa is based on the Canadian early total immersion model. See Chapter 2 by Genesee for detailed discussion of the Canadian immersion model and its variations. One criterion for the program is that all the children have the same linguistic background (cf. Baker, 1996; Laurén, 1999; Mård, 1997). In Finland, children begin school at the age of seven, and pre-school education is optional. However, most children spend at least one year in half-day kindergarten or nursery school before starting primary school. In Vaasa, children from families who choose this optional school program begin immersion kindergarten at the age of five and spend two years there before continuing in a grade 1–9 immersion school (basic education). In kindergarten the immersion language, Swedish, is the only language of instruction. In the primary grades in the immersion schools most of the instruction is given in Swedish, with literacy skills being taught entirely in the L2. However, the students' L1, Finnish, is already introduced in the first grade, with an emphasis on communication and cultural activities, like songs, rhymes and literature. There is a gradual increase in the amount of instructional time in Finnish and in grades 3 and 4 Finnish is used for instruction in handicrafts, physical education and language arts. From grade 5 on, about 50% of the instruction is given in Finnish. In order to enable the students to acquire functional multilingualism (cf. Baker, 1996), a third language, English, is introduced as early as grade 1 and a fourth optional language, German or French, in grade 5. The students can study four languages all through basic education. The immersion program ends in grade 9, when the students are 16 years of age.

Since the start of the Swedish immersion program the intention has been to teach all the languages of the program in accordance with immersion principles (Björklund & Suni, 2000), and gradually the L3 and L4 have also become more integrated parts of the program. Although the lessons are defined as language lessons in the curriculum and are restricted to one to two hours per week, the teachers of English and German have introduced content-based instruction and use the language as the medium of instruction (Björklund, 2005).

Since its inception in Vaasa, Swedish immersion has been introduced in about ten other cities in Finland, with slightly varying characteristics such as the children's age when starting immersion (see Björklund, 1997). The first cities to follow Vaasa's example were Kokkola, north of Vaasa, and Turku in the southwest. In the mid 1990s the number of schools offering Swedish immersion increased rapidly with a concentration in the capital of Helsinki and surrounding regions, i.e. Espoo, Vantaa, Kirkkonummi, Kauniainen, Sipoo and Porvoo (Buss & Mård 2001). Figures gathered in 2006 indicate that Swedish immersion is offered in more than 30 schools and 30 kindergartens.

One city, the predominantly Swedish-speaking city of Jakobstad to the north of Vaasa, serves as an exception in that it offers immersion education to both language groups. Because immersion in Swedish became very popular, the Swedish-speaking parents in Jakobstad wanted immersion in Finnish for their children. According to Østern's (2000) studies, Finnish immersion has had no negative influence on the children's development of their L1, Swedish.

A nationwide survey conducted by Buss and Mård (2001) shows that the schools offering immersion are satisfied with the design of their immersion programs and with student achievement. However, Buss and Mård express concerns about variation in the implementation of Swedish immersion programs. They emphasize the need for a detailed national immersion curriculum for all grade levels where the immersion program is seen as a holistic program from kindergarten to grade 9. They argue that a national model for immersion programs would guarantee that new immersion programs would be based on previous research and best practices.

Scholars at the University of Vaasa have engaged in continuous research on Vaasa's immersion program. From the beginning there has been intense interaction and cooperation between immersion teachers at the school and researchers at the university. Initially, the primary focus of the research was evaluating the success of the program. The research focus has gradually shifted from an emphasis on product to an emphasis on the process of second language acquisition in immersion. Consequently, there has been a demand for classroom-based studies, and the present study (based on Södergård 2002) serves as a response to this demand.

Nunan (1992: 102) states that in the wide field of immersion and second language learning research there have been few studies where the data are collected in genuine classrooms, that is 'classrooms which were specifically constituted for the purpose of teaching and learning, not to provide a venue for research.' The study presented in this chapter is based on genuine class-room interaction, and its findings increase our knowledge of what is happening in an immersion kindergarten classroom.

The Study

Setting and study participants

In Finland, the kindergarten curriculum is regulated by a national curriculum but, because attending kindergarten is optional, the children are not taught to read and write (though early literacy activities are common), and they are not required to learn academic subject matter. The curriculum is not divided up into specific lessons but is rather based on larger themes, such as *Me and My Family, Winter* and *Water*. When working with a theme the children sing songs, study picture books, play games and do a range of activities related to the theme. Each kindergarten teacher can decide on the themes for his/her class, and this freedom of choice enables all teachers to take the children's needs and interests into account (Mård, 1995; Södergård, 2002). It also allows the immersion kindergarten teachers to concentrate on their role as language teacher (Snow, 1987) and create a learning environment favorable for second language acquisition.

Although the teaching in immersion kindergarten differs somewhat from the teaching in the immersion school, how language is learned in this context remains the same. The children acquire the L2 through partici-pating in classroom activities where the major focus is on the content and a minor, more implicit, focus is on the language to be learned.

This study on teacher–student interaction is an ethnographic case study based on classroom observations with one kindergarten teacher and her group of children in Vaasa. Classroom observations began in August, when a new group of 26 five-year-old children entered the program, and continued for two school years, ending in May when the children left immersion kindergarten. The children were all Finnish-speaking monolinguals, and none of them had any command of Swedish when they were enrolled. They attended the immersion class five days a week for four hours a day.

A kindergarten teacher and two assistants, all native speakers of Swedish with high levels of proficiency in Finnish, served as the classroom instructors. The children were allowed to use Finnish but following the principle of one person-one language, the staff spoke only Swedish with the children from the very first day (Laurén, 1999). The kindergarten teacher was an experienced immersion teacher; she had a degree in early childhood pedagogy, and she had participated in in-service professional development in multilingualism and immersion education. This teacher was also known to achieve good results, which led me to conclude that her classroom would provide a rich context for a study on teacher strategies.

Data collection and analysis

Data collection included classroom observations as well as an interview with the teacher about her personal view of second language acquisition in immersion (Södergård, 2002). I visited the class regularly, beginning on the children's first day in immersion and continuing throughout both of their years in immersion kindergarten, taking field notes on classroom procedures and routines, and the general nature of classroom communication. I also videotaped between the teachers and the children during selected classroom situations.

For this study I concentrated on one classroom situation, which is called 'small group work'. When working in small groups, the larger class of 26 children is divided into three small groups all of which are instructed by an adult, either the teacher or one of the assistants. One of the advantages of small group work is that all the children get more individual attention and assistance. Small group composition did not vary once groups were formed, so I observed the kindergarten teacher instructing the same group of nine children over time.

Small group activities can be described as typical of kindergarten and they are in general connected to whatever theme is of focus in the whole class instruction. Some activities are more practical and hands-on, like modeling with clay or planting a flower; others are planned to provide more systematic linguistic instruction. For example, the students might make up a story and dictate it to the teacher, who writes it down, and then the children provide an illustration. Usually the children engage in small group work about twice a week for about 45 minutes each time.

I chose to observe the small group work because it is a recurrent and easily defined teaching situation in this particular classroom context. Though recurrent, it is not a daily routine like morning circle and thus the language is not particularly ritualized. In addition, because the teacher is directing only nine children, she can use all the devices she deems effective to promote the children's understanding and use of the L2.

Although I observed and videotaped a total of 14 small group sessions, the data for this study are based on five such sessions, starting when the children had spent six months in immersion and one could expect some production in the L2 (see Vesterbacka, 1991). The recorded activities lasted between 45 and 60 minutes each, and they can be classified as activities that were planned to offer the children systematic linguistic practice. All small group activities included three predictable stages:

(1) a short discussion initiated and structured by the teacher related to a theme;
(2) a drawing task;
(3) an oral task (a language development task) with reference to the picture(s) drawn.

In the first stage, the discussion was supposed to be on-task, although occasional off-task behaviors did occur. In the second stage, the children had time and many opportunities to initiate conversation with the teacher and to interact on an individual basis. In the third stage the children were asked to perform an oral task and were implicitly expected to do so in the L2. For example, one time the children dramatized a story from a picture book and, because the characters in the book spoke Swedish, it was natural for the children to do the same.

I started data analysis by excerpting all utterances that the children made in the L2. I defined these as *utterances that contain at least one identifiable word in the L2*. The L2 utterances varied in number between 130 and 150 per recorded session, showing a clear, though not continuous, increase in utterances from the first recording to the last one. During the first few observations, the children's production of L2 generally consisted of one-word answers, mostly *yes* or *no*, but the complexity of their utterances grew noticeably from one observation to the next, as did their tendency to initiate discourse in the L2.

After excerpting the children's utterances in the L2, I focused on the teacher's linguistic behaviors, identifying utterances that preceded and followed children's L2 production. The process of data analysis was inductive, as I began with specific utterances and then tried to detect patterns and regularities that ultimately form the categories of strategies that I present in this study. The teacher's utterances were analyzed merely from a grammatical viewpoint, characterized, for example, as questions. However, I also discuss what influence the different types of utterances and moves may have on the children's willingness to use the L2. Hence, I also approach the data from a more pedagogical stance, thereby attempting to expand the research perspective *vis-à-vis* more linguistically-oriented research.

Findings

Two general types of strategies were identified in this study: strategies the teacher used to elicit the L2, which preceded children's L2 production, and feedback strategies, which followed students' L2 production.

Strategies to elicit L2 use

The strategies the teacher used to elicit the L2 fell into four main categories:

(1) questions (which were directly followed by L2 production);
(2) offering an answer;
(3) signals for a language switch (from L1 to L2);
(4) teacher utterances leading to spontaneous L2 production.

Questions

As might be expected, the children's L2 utterances were in many cases responses to questions asked by the teacher (Lindberg & Håkansson, 1988; Tardif, 1994). Examples of both close-ended (those offering fixed alternatives) and open-ended questions were observed in this study. The questions were divided on the basis of their linguistic form into three main subcategories: yes/no questions, wh-questions, and either/or questions.

Yes/no questions

Yes/no questions were those that could be answered by a simple yes or no, and this type of question often preceded the children's use of the L2. In the example below, the student has been telling the others in Finnish about the houses he has lived in so far. The teacher then brings the Swedish language into the conversation and asks three yes/no questions of which the final is asked in the negative form.

Teacher: *Har du bott i många hus där?* [Have you lived in many houses there?]
Student: *Jå-å.* [Ye–es.(With intonation as if to say 'yes, really.')]
Teacher: *Är det så?* [Is that right?]
Student: Mm-m.
Teacher: *Bodde du inte alltid i det där vita? Apotekshuset?* [Didn't you always live in the white one? The drug store house?]
Student: *Nä-ä.* [No-o.]

These questions are clearly important in the beginning of the immersion experience, since they require comprehension on the part of the learner and permit the children to take a somewhat active (albeit minimal) part in an L2 conversation (Lindberg & Håkansson, 1988). However, yes/no questions do not challenge the learners like the more demanding questions identified below, and a discourse based on yes/no questions can hardly extend the linguistic repertoire of the learner (see Lindberg & Håkansson, 1988; Swain 1985). As the children's linguistic competence grew, the yes/no questions in many cases could have been replaced by more demanding question types that would have been more on a par with the children's cognitive and linguistic abilities, by requiring more decision-making and output on the part of the children.

Wh-questions

The next type of questions that emerged in the data was wh-questions, which were open-ended and required more production from students. What- and who-questions emerged even in the earlier recordings as they could be followed by a one word answer in Swedish, usually a noun or a verb. In the next example the student tells the teacher what pictures he has drawn on his memory cards.[1]

Teacher: *Så det här var halsduk. Och vad är det här?* [So this was scarf. And what is this?]
Student: *Halsduk.* [Scarf.]
Teacher: *Mm. Och vad har vi här?* [Mm. And what do we have here?]
Student: Vantar. [Gloves.]

Why- and how-questions required more complex answers, preferably clauses or other types of phrases, and thus were followed by children's responses in the L2 only in the later observations. In the next example the student is telling the teacher in Swedish about the best place in Vaasa, and the teacher is writing down her explanations.

Teacher: *Maria tycker att Wasalandia... är bäst. För...* [Maria likes Wasalandia... the best. Because...] *Varför tycker du att Wasalandia är bäst? För...* [Why do you like Wasalandia the best? Because...]
Student: *Där är den där båten.* [There is that boat.]
Teacher: (writing) *För där... är... den där... båten.* [Because there... is... that... boat.] *Vad gör båten då?* [What does the boat do?]
Student: *Gungar.* [Swings.]
Teacher: *Där är den där båten som gungar.* [There is the boat that swings.]

Either/or questions

Either/or questions offer choices to learners and are helpful in the sense that they offer a model that the learner can imitate. In this study, either/or questions were the most likely to elicit answers in the L2, a finding that is consistent with results that have been reported by others (see Long, 1983; Arnau, 1994). These questions did not change in quantity over time, but they grew increasingly more difficult, from two or three symmetric alternatives *Vill du ha ett gult kort eller ett vitt kort?* [Would you like a yellow card or a white card?] to more complex alternatives like *Vill du rita pärmen på boken eller sista sidan?* [Would you like to draw the cover of the book or the last page?].

Related to questions, another strategy that was observed is parallel to what Lyster and Ranta (1997) call *filling in the blank,* and Tardif (1994) calls *prompting.* The teacher started uttering a compound or a sentence, and then paused after having signalled by tone of voice that she expected the child to continue and complete the utterance. In general, this strategy elicited use of the L2.

Offering an answer

The second category of strategies used to elicit L2 use was called *offering an answer* and was divided into two subcategories based on whether the answer offered was incorrect or correct. The strategy of offering an incorrect answer implied that the teacher tried to guide the child's thoughts towards the correct answer, by mentioning, for example, an antonym (see Met, 1994) or by making silly suggestions like *Vad var det för ett torn vi var till i går? Var det ett mjölktorn?* [What tower did we visit yesterday? Was it a milk tower?] This was successful since the child was familiar with the needed word, *water tower,* and water and milk were opposites that the children were confronted with every day at the kindergarten lunch table.

Offering the correct answer came into use when several other strategies had failed. Mostly the teacher asked a question and let the child answer *yes* or *no.* These questions were deliberately asked to ultimately elicit L2 use, to give the child the opportunity to take the final move in the dialogue. Hence, I interpreted them to be more strategically used than the yes/no questions described in the first category, even though in form they were essentially the same. Another example of offering the correct answer was when the teacher modelled the needed utterance by whispering it into the child's ear and letting the child say it out loud.

Signals for a language switch

Often the children used Finnish (the L1) although they knew the words and were familiar with the sentence structure needed in Swedish (the L2). In later observations the teacher was not as willing to accept children's use of the L1. However, the teacher, being reluctant to emphasize that the children actually were involved in an L2 learning program (an attitude she revealed in the interview), never explicitly asked the children to use the L2. Instead she used different signals to show that an answer in the L2 was expected. Most signals were questions such as *What? What is that? What did you say?* Gradually, the children learned that these questions did not mean that the teacher did not hear or understand but rather functioned as requests to switch languages. These signals are similar to what Lyster and

Ranta (1997) called clarification requests, although they appeared in this study after students' utterances in the L1, whereas Lyster and Ranta observed them after students produced an incorrect utterance in the L2. In the next example the student switches to the L2 in line 9.[2]

1	**Student:**	*Mä piirrän täss' siniseks'.* [I will draw this blue.]
2	**Teacher:**	*Vad sa' du?* [What did you say?]
3	**Student:**	*Mä piirrän tässä näin.* [I will draw this like this.]
4	**Teacher:**	*Va?* [What?]
5	**Student:**	*Ja laitan kokonaan sen värilliseks'.* [And I will color all of it.]
6	**Teacher:**	*Vad sa' du?* [What did you say?]
7	**Student:**	*Mä laitan tään kokonaan siniseks'.* [I will make all of this blue.]
8	**Teacher:**	*Vad sa' du?* [What did you say?]
9	**Student:**	*Jag gör hela den här blått.* [I will make all of this blue.]
10	**Teacher:**	*Och du gör/du trycker hårt.* [And you do/you press hard.]
11	**Student:**	*Jå.* [Yes.]
12	**Teacher:**	*Så det blir fint.* [To make it nice.]

Another signal involved repetition of the same question again and again until the child answered in Swedish. The children gradually learned to interpret these signals correctly and understood that there was nothing wrong with the content, only with the code. In the next example, Student 2 switches into Swedish in line 9 with '*ei vaan röd.*' In the following turns both Student 1 and Student 2 switch to Swedish.

1	**Teacher:**	*Och vilken färg har Mars-planeten?* [And what color is the planet Mars?]
2	**Student 1:**	*Punaista.* [Red.]
3	**Teacher:**	*Va? Vilken färg var det?* [What? What color was it?]
4	**Student 2:**	*Punaista oli.* [It was red.]
5	**Student 3:**	*Punaista ja oranssia.* [Red and orange.]
6	**Teacher:**	*Vilken färg var det?* [What color was it?]
7	**Student 3:**	*Punaista ja oranssia.* [Red and orange.]
8	**Teacher:**	*Vilken färg var det?* [What color was it?]
9	**Student 2:**	*Punaista ja/ei vaan röd.* [Red and/no but red.]
10	**Student 1:**	*Röd.* [Red.]
11	**Teacher:**	*Lite röd och...* [A little red and...]
12	**Student 2:**	*Orange.* [Orange.]
13	**Teacher:**	*Orange, jå.* [Orange, yes.]

Although the signals usually were interpreted correctly, at times they appeared to confuse the children, and in these cases one could presume that it would have been preferable to ask the children explicitly: 'How do we say it in Swedish?' instead of simply repeating the question, especially since the teacher knew that the students had no problems with expressing the phrase in their L2.

The data also revealed that the children's production of the L2 in many cases was a result of systematic pushing by the teacher. The teacher tried one strategy, and if it failed she tried another until she found a way of interacting that brought the child to expressing his or her thoughts in the L2.

Teacher utterances leading to spontaneous L2 production

The fourth category of strategies used to elicit the L2 is called *teacher utterances leading to spontaneous L2 production*. To this category I have assigned the use of L2 that was produced spontaneously by the children following the teacher's utterance, but that was not deliberately provoked by the teacher. For example, the students might spontaneously imitate the teacher's utterance or some part of it. The children also showed proof of linguistic reflection, i.e. they either commented on some features of the second language, as in the next example, or focused on some element of an utterance and tested it (see Vesterbacka, 1991).

Student: *Miks' tuossa on tommosta?* [Why is there such one?]
Teacher: *Därför att det står och här.* [Because I have written and her.]
Student: *Och.* [And.]
Teacher: *Ibland måst' man ha såna småord också.* [Sometimes you need these short words too.]

One important observation related to this strategy was that some of the children very alertly reflected on the input they were offered and also noticed errors, for example, if the teacher pronounced something wrong. In the next excerpt the student notices the teacher's mispronunciation of the word *bläckfisk* [octopus], interrupts the conversation and struggles to imitate the incorrect pronunciation. The student knows how to pronounce the word, since the children are familiar with the picture book character *Mamma Bläckfisk*. The teacher chooses to interpret his move as difficulties with the pronunciation and models the word for him.

Teacher: *Jå precis. Hon väntar tills bläck/Mamma Bläsk/Bläckfisk simmar iväg.* [Yes exactly. She waits until octo/Mamma Bläsk/ Bläckfisk swims away.]
Student: *Mamma Bläck... fisk, Mamma Bläskfisk.*
Teacher: *Är det svårt att säga?* [Is it difficult to say?] *Mamma Bläckfisk, Mamma Bläckfisk, Mamma Bläckfisk.*

These interactions occurred only occasionally, but they show how observantly some students listen to the teacher's speech, and they underline the importance of the teacher's role as a model for the children's own language use.

Feedback strategies

In addition to strategies used to elicit students' L2 production, feedback strategies were also observed in this study. The teacher's feedback strategies fell into five main categories: (1) non-corrective repetition, (2) positive feedback, (3) corrective feedback and recasts, (4) either/or questions and (5) turn-taking in the dialogue.

Non-corrective repetition

Initially, when the children entered immersion and had no other means of expressing their thoughts than by using their L1, the teacher mostly repeated their utterances in the L2 in order to communicate how the message could be conveyed in the L2. The teacher's repetition could also be classified as a form of modeling through translation, only with the reservation that she did not expect the children to repeat after her. However, once the children started using the L2, the teacher continued this pattern of repeating their utterances in the L2, either in identical or in a somewhat expanded form. The observations showed that in all the recordings the most frequent feedback strategy used was non-corrective repetition, echoing Lyster and Ranta's (1997) finding of a large number of teacher repetitions of well-formed utterances in their data. In the next excerpt the student tells the teacher what pictures she has drawn on her memory cards. The word *snöhund* is mentioned twice, since the idea of memory games is that there are duplicates of all pictures.

Teacher: *Vad är det här?* [What is this?]
Student: *Snöhund.* [Snowdog.]
Teacher: *Snöhund. Och det här?* [Snowdog. And this?]
Student: *Snöhund.* [Snowdog.]
Teacher: *Och sen?* [And then?]
Student: *Vantar.* [Gloves.]
Teacher: *Vantar. Och det här?* [Gloves. And this?]

In the next example, the teacher is asking questions about a character in a picture book. The student's answer is accurate in both meaning and form.

Teacher: *Och vad gör Lilla Anna då?* [And what is Little Anna doing then?]
Student: *Simmar.* [Swimming.]

Teacher: *Hon simmar, jå.* [She's swimming, yes.]

In many cases the repetition may have been intended as confirmation that the utterance was correct in both meaning and form, as Lyster (1998a) has noted; in other cases the intention was to further expand and develop the utterance. Repetition certainly can be useful in the classroom, but this teacher's (somewhat routine-like) habit of repeating can also be criticized from the point of view that teachers, even without repeating students' utterances, already dominate the conversation in the classroom (Chaudron, 1988; Tardif, 1994).

Positive feedback

Another feedback strategy that was observed was positive feedback, which primarily consisted of minimal feedback like *okay, yes, mm* and so forth. The teacher very infrequently used praise markers like *Good!* or *Well done!* As revealed in the interview, this may have been due to her interpretation of the recommendation that language and linguistic achievements should not have too much focus in immersion contexts (Södergård, 2002). This teacher's cautious behavior with respect to providing positive feedback can be contrasted with the fact that many researchers consider positive feedback an effective strategy for promoting language acquisition (Arnau, 1994).

Corrective feedback and recasts

As the children's proficiency in the L2 increased, they started to produce longer utterances and simultaneously to produce them with less dependence on models offered by the teacher (see Vesterbacka, 1991). Consequently, their utterances contained more phonological, lexical, and syntactic errors. Because the teacher consistently repeated what the children said, there were multiple opportunities to observe her treatment of these errors.

Sometimes the teacher corrected the children immediately after they had made an error. For example, if the utterance consisted of only one word that was mispronounced, she gave the correct form: *tövlar* for *stövlar* [boots]. If a child said the wrong word, she provided the correct one: *testar* [to test] for *provar* [to try on], or if a child incorrectly conjugated a verb, she gave the correct form: *skrikte* [screamed, incorrectly conjugated] for *skrek*. This strategy of immediately providing the correct form can be compared to what Lyster (1998a) calls *explicit correction*, but it differs in the sense that she never indicated overtly that something was wrong with markers like '*no*' or '*we say....*'

The most frequently applied corrective feedback strategy was recasts (see Lyster, 1998a) or what Chaudron (1988) called *repetition with change*.

This corrective feedback strategy involved the teacher reformulating the utterance slightly to eliminate the error. Recasts were observed to follow lexical or syntactic errors. Mostly the recasts focused on one word, for example, the adding of a preposition. Whereas the teacher made explicit corrections immediately after the child produced an incorrect utterance (as explained above), she offered a recast after the child completed an entire utterance and repeated the whole phrase with the error corrected. At least in the short term, recasts seemed to encourage some of the children to notice their errors and use the right form the next time, as in the next excerpt where the student notices the need for the indefinite article *en*.

Teacher: *Vad har du börja' med att rita?* [What have you started to draw?]
Student: *Laivan. Båt.* [Ship. Boat.]
Teacher: *En båt. Är det en segelbåt eller en motorbåt eller...?* [A boat. Is it a sailing boat or a motor boat or...?]
Student: *En segelbåt.* [A sailing boat.]
Teacher: *En segelbåt.* [A sailing boat.]

That being said, learner uptake was not a focus of this study and therefore a firm statement that recasts appeared to lead to learner uptake (contrary to Lyster's findings) is not possible.

Either/or questions as feedback strategies

Just as in strategies used to elicit the L2, the teacher also used either/or questions as a feedback strategy. However, this feedback strategy was only observed in the final lesson in which students were individually creating stories. While interacting with the children, the teacher would bring the plot forward by asking '*What happens then ... ? And then...?*' To provide feedback to students as they were creating these stories, the teacher offered either/or questions to implicitly point out errors and attempt to elicit more accurate language. For example, when a child used an incorrect preposition, the teacher offered the correct preposition and the incorrect one as alternatives: *Gömde du dig i skogen eller på skogen?* [Did you hide in the woods or on the woods?] Lyster and Ranta (1997) term this corrective feedback strategy a metalinguistic clue.

Occasionally these either/or questions appeared to be focused on meaning although they were really focused on form. For example the question *Hoppade du från båten eller på båten?* [Did you jump from the boat or on the boat?] was asked when the student's drawing clearly showed him jumping from a boat although he had used the prepositon *på* [on]. This type of feedback mostly led students to choose the right alternative. Some of the children managed to tell their story very independently, but in several cases the linguistic form of the story was a result of intense negotiation with the teacher. This storytelling activity is a good example of *pushing output* at the kindergarten level (see Allen *et al.*, 1990), and the teacher's way of pushing the correct form can be compared to what Lyster (1998a) calls *negotiation of form*.

The either/or questions were both stimulating and challenging, but there were other types of feedback given during the storytelling activity that were not as easy for the children to interpret correctly. Sometimes the teacher paused or changed her intonation in an effort to prompt the child to repeat his or her previous utterance in L2 or part of it. In general, the child drew the conclusion that something needed to be changed in the utterance and attempted to reformulate parts of it (see. Lyster, 1998a). Sometimes these signals for repetition were actually signals that correction was needed. However, the teacher at times gave the same signals although the utterance was correct. This ambiguity caused obvious confusion, because the children could not be sure how to interpret the signals. This observation in my study corresponds to observations made by Allen *et al.* (1990) and Lyster (1998b), who have argued that the feedback given by immersion teachers is often confusing, unsystematic and fraught with ambiguity.

Turn-taking in the dialogue

Sometimes as a response to the children's L2 production, the teacher just took her turn in the dialogue, either by continuing the same topic or changing to another topic, without explicitly noticing the child's utterance in the L2.

Teacher: *Vad har du laga'?* [What have you made?]
Student: *Jag har laga' raketen.* [I have made the space-ship.]
Teacher: *Sen skall du komma ihåg att färglägga också.* [Then you must remember to color, too.]

In these turns the teacher did not apply any strategy typical of discussions between teachers and learners but simply took her turn in the dialogue. By acting like this the teacher refrained from giving the child explicit feedback on the use of the L2. However, turn-taking can be seen as implicit feedback, that is, confirmation that both content and form are correct and that the utterance does not need further attention. As might be expected, instances in which the teacher engaged in turn-taking seemed to increase towards the end of the observation period, as the children's L2 proficiency increased.

Discussion

This study took place in an actual classroom context, suggesting that the observed activities would have been carried out without researcher presence. The discourse between the teacher and children was authentic, and classroom discourse focused on topics typical of kindergarten classrooms. The teacher was observed to consistently use the immersion language (Swedish), but in general the children most often used their L1 (Finnish) especially during the early observations that comprised this study.

The teacher tried to create an inspiring and encouraging learning environment, and the atmosphere in the immersion group was nurturing and accepting. Since the teacher wanted the children's language learning to happen unnoticed, she avoided mentioning explicitly that the children were participating in immersion to learn a new language. Nevertheless, she made continuous efforts to establish a good basis for the children's L2 learning. One manifestation of this was that she tried to create situations where the children were encouraged and slightly pushed to use the L2.

Many of the strategies the teacher applied to elicit L2 use have been identified in other studies of teacher–student interaction in communicative classrooms (e.g. Arnau, 1994) and this is true also for feedback strategies such as recasts and negotiation of form (Lyster & Ranta, 1997). However, my observations also showed that the teacher avoided strategies found in other studies (Tardif, 1994), such as linguistic modeling and explicitly requesting the students to repeat after her. It is obvious that, by using different strategies to elicit production, immersion teachers can focus on certain aspects of grammar also present in natural communication.

The teacher in this study used a set of devices she found effective to promote L2 use, and she also clearly adapted her expectations and insistence to the children's proficiency (cf. Arnau, 1994). The system of signals that she had developed in order to show the children that she wanted an answer in the L2 instead of the L1 seemed to work. However, an explicit request for an expression in the L2 instead of implicitly requesting (that is, repeating the same question until the child actually replied in the L2) would have made the discourse situation clearer, more authentic and easier to understand in many cases.

Furthermore, because the teacher was in the habit of repeating the children's utterances, she sometimes repeated incorrectly formed utterances without reformulating them. This way of responding to the children's L2 production must be criticized for at least two reasons. First, the speaker might interpret the teacher's repetition of an erroneous utterance as confirmation that the utterance was correct and, second, the teacher's repetition served as input for the children who were listening. In immersion contexts, the teacher's language use must be of high quality, because the children must be able to rely on it as a model for their own production. Especially when the children are testing linguistic hypotheses (e.g. Swain, 1996) related to such things as word order, it is important that the teacher, by following the norms of the L2, consistently offer accurate input.

The teacher constantly responded to the children's production of the L2, either by repeating, by giving positive feedback or correcting by modifying and slightly reformulating their utterances. Nevertheless, as Lyster and Ranta (1997) also point out, giving feedback is a complicated process, and this was also apparent in my study. This meant that the feedback was not systematic and the children could not always be sure how to interpret it. The teacher also used different signals as feedback, but the signal system was at times confusing and caused ambiguity. Sometimes an implicit signal for repetition of an utterance was a wish for correction, and sometimes it was not.

Several studies have shown that corrective feedback is an aspect of experiental language teaching that needs further research and discussion. With respect to correcting mistakes it is obvious that the teachers must be aware of the importance of different types of errors. Leaving an isolated lexical mistake uncorrected causes little harm to the child's total L2 development. However, there are some aspects of the L2, such as word order in Swedish, where the teacher must consistently offer correct models to consolidate correct language use. The teacher also needs to be able to identify and focus on aspects of the L2 that cause the children specific problems. Furthermore, it is important that the teacher be sensitive to the children's hypothesis-testing about correct language use and consistently offer them supporting feedback.

This study was carried out in close cooperation with the immersion kindergarten teacher, and the results of my study have also been presented to other immersion teachers through in-service workshops. An interesting topic for further research is how the results of a study based on classroom observation affects teachers' attitudes and makes them reflect upon their work in the immersion classrooms, for example, their use of corrective feedback. Another interesting research topic is how teachers view their role as language models both in immersion classrooms and in other classrooms with young children, who need stimuli of high quality for their ongoing language development.

Notes

1. Memory cards are created by the children for a common game used in kindergarten (known as Concentration in the US), where children create cards

having identical pairs and then play a game where they turn all the cards face down and need to find the identical pairs.
2. In all data excerpts presented, Finnish utterances are underlined.

References

Allen, P., Swain, M., Harley, B. and Cummins, J. (1990) Aspects of classroom treatment: Toward a more comprehensive view of second language education. In B. Harley, P. Allen, J. Cummins and M. Swain (eds) *The Development of Second Language Proficiency* (pp. 57–81). Cambridge: Cambridge University Press.

Arnau, J. (1994) Teacher–pupil communication when commencing Catalan immersion programs. In C. Laurén (ed.) *Evaluating European Immersion Programs, From Catalonia to Finland* (pp. 47–76). *Vaasan yliopiston julkaisuja. Tutkimuksia No 185. Linguistics 27.* Vaasa: Vaasa University Press.

Baker, C. (1996) *Foundations of Bilingual Education and Bilingualism* (2nd edn). Clevedon: Multilingual Matters.

Björklund, S. (1997) Immersion in Finland in the 1990s. A state of development and expansion. In R.K. Johnson and M. Swain (eds) *Immersion Education: International Perspectives* (pp. 85–101). Cambridge: Cambridge University Press.

Björklund, S. (2005) Toward trilingual education in Vaasa/Vasa, Finland. *International Journal of the Sociology of Language* 171, 23–40.

Björklund, S. and Suni, I. (2000) The role of English as L3 in a Swedish immersion program in Finland: Impacts on language teaching and language relations. In U. Jessner and J. Cenoz (eds) *English in Europe: The Acquisition of a Third Language* (pp. 198–221). Clevedon: Multilingual Matters.

Björklund, S., Kaskela-Nortamo, B., Kvist, M., Lindfors, H. and Tallgård, M. (2005) *Att uppmuntra till språk i språkbadsgrupper. Kompendium 4.* Levon-institutet. Vasa: Vasa universitet.

Buss, M. and Mård, K. (2001) Swedish immersion in Finland: Facts and figures. In S. Björklund (ed.) *Language as a Tool: Immersion Research and Practices* (pp. 157–175). *Proceedings of the University of Vaasa. Reports 83.* Vaasa: University of Vaasa.

Chaudron, C. (1988) *Second Language Classrooms: Research on Teaching and Learning.* Cambridge: Cambridge University Press.

Cummins, J. and Swain, M. (1986) *Bilingualism in Education: Aspects of Theory, Research and Practice.* London: Longman.

Döpke, S. (1992) *One Parent One Language: An Interactional Approach.* Amsterdam: John Benjamins Publishing.

Genesee, F. (1991) Second language learning in school settings: Lessons from immersion. In A.G. Reynolds (ed.) *Bilingualism, Multiculturalism and Second Language Learning* (pp. 183–201). Hillsdale, NJ: Lawrence Erlbaum.

Krashen, S. (1987) *Principles and Practice in Second Language Acquisition.* New York: Prentice-Hall International.

Laurén, C. (1998) The more, the easier: Immersion for multilingulism. In J. Arnau and J.M. Artigal (eds) *Els Programes d'Immersió: Una Perspectiva Europea* [*Immersion Programmes: A European Perspective*] (pp. 33–42). Barcelona: University of Barcelona

Laurén, C. (1999) Språkbad: Forskning och praktik. *Proceedings of the University of Vaasa. Research Papers 226. Språkvetenskap 36.* Vaasa: University of Vaasa.

Latomaa, S. and Nuolijärvi, P. (2002) The language situation in Finland. *Current Issues in Language Planning* 3 (2), 95–202.

Lindberg, I. and Håkansson, G. (1988) Vad är det frågan om? In K. Hyltenstam and I. Lindberg (eds) *Första symposiet om svenska som andraspråk. Volym I: Föredrag om språk, språkinlärning och interaktion* (pp. 42–54). Stockholm: Stockholms universitet.

Long, M. (1983) Native speaker/non-native speaker conversation and the negotiation of comprehensible input. *Applied Linguistics* 4, 126–141.

Lyster, R. (1998a) Immersion pedagogy and implications for language teaching. In J. Cenoz and F. Genesee (eds) *Beyond Bilingualism. Multilingualism and Multilingual Education,* (pp. 64–95). Clevedon: Multilingual Matters.

Lyster, R. (1998b) Form in immersion classroom discourse: In or out of focus? *Canadian Journal of Applied Linguistics* 20 (1), 53–82.

Lyster, R. and Ranta, L. (1997) Corrective feedback and learner uptake: Negotiation of form in communicative classrooms. *Studies in Second Language Acquisition* 19 (1), 37–66.

Mård, K. (1995) Immersion pre-school as an environment for early second language acquisition. In M. Buss and C. Laurén (eds) *Language Immersion: Teaching and Second Language Acquisition, From Canada to Europe* (pp. 141–151). *Vaasan yliopiston julkaisuja. Tutkimuksia No 192. Linguistics 30.* Vaasa: Vaasan Yliopisto.

Mård, K. (1997) *Fyra språkbadsbarns tidiga kommunikation på andraspråket. Vaasan yliopiston julkaisuja. Tutkimuksia 215. Språkvetenskap 28.* Vaasa: Vaasan yliopisto.

Met, M. (1994) Teaching content through a second language. In F. Genesee (ed.) *Educating Second Language Children* (pp. 159–182). Cambridge: Cambridge University Press.

Nunan, D. (1992) *Research Methods in Language Learning.* Cambridge: Cambridge University Press.

Østern, A. (2000) Research into future possibilities: Genre proficiency in Swedish as a mother tongue in Finnish immersion. In K. Sjöholm and A. Østern (eds) *Perspectives on Language and Communication in Multilingual Education* (pp. 145–165). Vaasa: Åbo Akademi University.

Snow, M.A. (1987) *Immersion Teacher Handbook.* Los Angeles, CA: University of California, Center for Language Education and Research.

Södergård, M. (2002) *Interaktion i språkbadsdaghem. Lärarstrategier och burnens andraspråksproduktion. Acta Wasaensia Nr 98. Linguistics 20.* Vaasa: University of Vaasa.

Swain, M. (1985) Communicative competence: Some roles of comprehensible input and comprehensible output in its development. In S.M. Gass and C.G. Madden (eds) *Input in Second Language Acquisition* (pp. 235–253). Rowley, MA: Newbury House Publishers.

Swain, M. (1996) Discovering successful second language teaching strategies and practices: From programme evaluation to classroom experimentation. *Journal of Multilingual and Multicultural Development* 17 (2–4), 89–104.

Tardif, C. (1994) Classroom teacher talk in early immersion. *Canadian Modern Language Review* 50 (3), 466–481.

Vesterbacka, S. (1991) *Elever i språkbadsskola: social bakgrund och tidig språkutveckling. Vaasan yliopiston julkaisuja. Tutkimuksia No 155.* Vaasa: Vaasan yliopisto.

Part 3

Evolving Perspectives on Social Context and its Impact on Immersion Programs

Chapter 9

Language Development and Academic Achievement in Two-Way Immersion Programs

KATHRYN LINDHOLM-LEARY and ELIZABETH R. HOWARD

Introduction

Two-way immersion (TWI) programs in the US integrate English Language Learners (ELLs) from a common native language background and native English-speaking (NES) students for academic instruction through both languages, with the goals of academic achievement, bilingualism and biliteracy development and cross-cultural competence for all students. TWI programs have surged in popularity over the past 20 years. From only 37 programs in 1987, there are currently at least 325 TWI programs in public schools in 29 states and Washington DC, with new programs added every year.[1] While most of the programs are Spanish/English, other languages include Chinese (Mandarin and Cantonese), Korean, French, Portuguese, Navajo and Russian. These programs serve a culturally, linguistically and socioeconomically diverse population in an integrated environment.

The body of literature on TWI programs has also increased in the past decade. While there is an increasing variety of articles written on two-way immersion, most papers include program descriptions, educator experiences or recommendations in two-way programs, or they provide an overview of two-way programs in a local area, a particular state or the nation (e.g. Christian *et al.*, 1997; Gomez *et al.*, 2005; Howard, 2002, 2004; Howard & Christian, 2002), or they present a review of literature on two-way programs (Bikle *et al.*, 2004; Howard *et al.*, 2003; Lindholm-Leary, 2001). Most of the research has focused on academic achievement, followed by studies of language and literacy development, cross-cultural attitudes and behaviors, the perceptions of students and teachers, parental involvement and other issues germane to the field. Very few of these studies have been quasi-experimental (e.g. Bae & Bachman, 1998). Further, studies of TWI programs that use languages other than Spanish are rare.

We will now turn to a presentation of research findings about students' academic achievement and language development in TWI programs. First, we will provide a brief description of two-way immersion programs.

Description of Two-Way Programs in the United States

The definition of two-way immersion programs encompasses four critical features:

(1) the program involves instruction through two languages, where the non-English language is used for a significant portion (from 50% to 90%) of the students' instructional day;
(2) the program involves periods of instruction during which only one language is used (i.e. there is no translation or language mixing);
(3) approximately equal numbers of ELLs and NESs are enrolled;
(4) the students are integrated for most or all instruction.

Two major variants of the TWI model exist – usually referred to as the *90/10* and the *50/50* models. The principle factors distinguishing these two elementary-level program variations are the distribution of languages for instruction and the language in which reading is taught. The amount of time spent in each language varies across the grade levels in the 90/10 design, but not in the 50/50 design.

In the *90/10 model*, at the kindergarten and first grades, 90% of the instructional day is devoted to content instruction in the partner language (the language other than English that is used for instruction, for example, Spanish or Korean), with the remaining 10% of instruction provided in English. All content instruction occurs in the partner language, and English time is used to develop oral language proficiency and some pre-literacy skills. Reading instruction begins in the partner language for both the native speakers of that language and for the native English speakers. At the second and third grade levels, students receive 80% of their instruction through the partner language, and 20% through English, and all students continue to receive reading instruction through the partner language. Students begin formal English reading in third grade, but they may be *exposed* to English print and English literature as early as kindergarten or first grade. By third grade, they might be studying mathematics, social studies and science in the partner language, and language arts in both languages. Physical education, music, art and other subjects would be taught in either language, depending on teacher availability and site-specific needs. By fourth, fifth and sixth grades, the students' instructional time is balanced between English and the partner language, and students continue to receive formal language arts instruction through both languages. Content instruction is equally divided between the two languages as well. This can be accomplished either by alternating the language of instruction for different units within each content area, or by designating a consistent language of instruction for each content area (e.g. math in Spanish and social studies in English).

In the *50/50 model*, students receive half of their instruction in English and the other half in the partner language throughout all of the elementary years. Literacy instruction varies slightly in this model. At some school sites, students learn to read first in their primary language (e.g. English speakers learn to read in English and Spanish speakers learn to read in Spanish) and then add second language literacy at grade 2 or 3. At other school sites, students learn to read in both languages simultaneously.

Academic Achievement

The academic achievement of students in TWI programs has been a central concern of US educators, parents and policymakers and, as a result, much of the research on two-way immersion has focused on the academic outcomes of students. The majority of TWI studies that deal with student outcomes rely on standardized measures of oral language, literacy and academic performance in the content areas, as standardized test scores are usually needed to demonstrate program effectiveness from a policy perspective.

There have been three longitudinal, large-scale, comparative studies (Lindholm-Leary, 2001; Thomas & Collier, 1997, 2002). Thomas and Collier (1997) analyzed 700,000 student records to track the long-term educational outcomes of ELLs in five school districts who were educated during the elementary grades through various program types: English as a second language (ESL) pullout (traditional), ESL content (including content curriculum as well as English language arts), transitional bilingual education, developmental bilingual education, and two-way immersion education[2] (see Genesee, Chapter 2 of this volume, for further discussion). Choosing programs that were well implemented, Thomas and Collier aimed to describe a best-case scenario regarding the effectiveness of each program type. They found a significant program effect that was apparent by late high school. Only those groups that received strong, grade-level cognitive and academic support in both their first and second languages for many years (often up until grades 7 or 8) were successful by the end of high school. Formal schooling in the first language in elementary school was the largest single predictor of long-term success. Length of time in the program was also found to be crucial: four to seven years were required for ELLs to close the gap between their test scores and those of their NES peers. In addition, specific program models that attend to language/academic content integration and offer sociocultural support for ELLs were identified as contributing factors. TWI was found to be the program type with the highest long-term success, with students achieving well above grade level. Developmental bilingual education also showed above-grade-level success. ELLs in other types of programs were unable to close the gap with NES peers by the end of high school. These findings are consistent with a synthesis of research on the effectiveness of various language education programs for ELLs (Lindholm-Leary & Borsato, 2006).

In a later report, Thomas and Collier (2002) presented findings from their 1985–2001 longitudinal study. The authors found that only developmental bilingual programs and two-way immersion programs enabled ELLs to reach or surpass the 50th percentile on standardized tests on all subjects in both languages. They also found that the fewest dropouts came from these programs. After four to seven years of program participation, bilingually-schooled students in 90/10 and 50/50 program varieties were found to outperform their peers who were educated monolingually in English in all subjects.

In another large-scale study (Lindholm-Leary, 2001) of 21 schools and 9000 TWI students, results indicated that native Spanish speakers (NSS) and NES in Spanish/English TWI programs performed at or above grade level in the content areas in their first language, achieving standardized mathematics and reading test scores on par with their state-wide peers by about grade 7. In addition, both groups of students demonstrated high levels of academic achievement through their respective second languages. As Figure 9.1 illustrates, on norm-referenced standardized tests of reading and math achievement in English, NES students outscored their English-only peers in English-only classrooms, and NSS students scored not only significantly higher than NSS students in the state, but they also performed on par with NES students in English-only classrooms (Lindholm-Leary, 2005b; Lindholm-Leary & Borsato, 2005, 2006). These results extend to studies of Chinese and Korean TWI students as well (Garcia, 2003; Lindholm-Leary, 2001, 2003).

Similar results were reported by Christian *et al.* (2004) with TWI students in two different states. In this study, state-mandated standardized achievement test data were collected from two schools in different states. Both schools were K–8 Spanish/English 90/10 programs, one in the Southwest (School A) and one in the Midwest (School B). While School A is very diverse in its racial/ethnic composition and socioeconomic status, School B

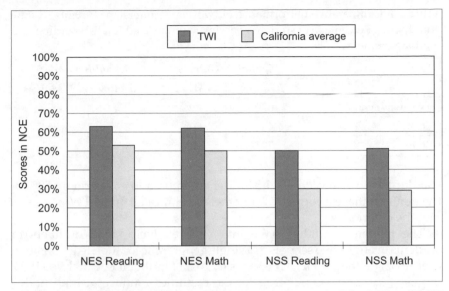

Figure 9.1 English reading and math achievement in grade 7 for NES and NSS students, TWI and California state averages

Note: NCE 50th percentile is equivalent to grade level performance

includes a majority of students of Latino origin, but of varying native language and socioeconomic backgrounds. With the exception of state performance on the math assessment, a higher percentage of School A third-grade students met or exceeded district and state performance on reading and math (see Table 9.1). This is particularly interesting given that School A had higher percentages of ELLs, ethnic minority students and low-income students than the state, and a higher percentage of ELLs and a comparable percentage of ethnic minority students as the district. At School B, comparison findings from the state achievement test administered when the students were in 5th grade were also very favorable. In School B a higher percentage of students met or exceeded state expectations for math, reading and for all tests taken than was the case for either the district or the state.

Gomez *et al.* (2005) reported on the achievement of TWI students in a 50/50 program in Texas. In the analysis of three schools with a high concentration of Latino (99%) and economically disadvantaged (91%) students, 88% of the NSSs and 91% of the NESs met the third-grade level reading standard on the Texas-developed, criterion-referenced test (the Texas Assessment of Knowledge and Skills). Unfortunately, the criterion for meeting the

Table 9.1 Comparative performance of two-way immersion students to state and district: Percentage of students passing standardized English reading and math assessments

	School A: Grade 3		*School B: Grade 5*	
	Reading	*Math*	*Reading*	*Math*
Two-way school	87%	89%	97%	97%
District	44%	80%	91%	96%
State	72%	92%	87%	92%

standard was set very low, with students required to answer only 53% of the items on the test correctly. Nonetheless, almost all of the TWI students met the criterion.

The remaining studies have involved relatively small numbers of students in one or two schools in a single geographic location (e.g. Cazabon *et al.* 1998; de Jong, 2002; Kirk Senesac, 2002; Lindholm & Fairchild, 1990; Stipek *et al.*, 2001). On aggregate, these studies found that both native Spanish speakers and native English speakers in TWI programs perform as well as or better than their peers educated in other types of programs, both on English-medium standardized achievement tests and Spanish-medium standardized achievement tests. Within TWI programs, native speakers tend to outperform second-language learners, such that NES tend to score higher on English achievement tests and NSS tend to score higher on Spanish achievement tests.

Reading and Writing Development

Reading

As part of a large-scale study of language and literacy development in TWI programs, Howard *et al.* (2004) looked at the English and Spanish reading performance of 344 students in 11 TWI programs across the United States. Cloze measures of English reading comprehension were collected at the beginning of grade 3 and the end of grade 5, while a cloze measure of Spanish reading comprehension was collected only at the beginning of grade 3. In English, the native Spanish speakers made slightly more mean progress than the native English speakers, but this was likely due in part to the fact that their mean score in third grade was lower than that of the native English speakers. At both time points, the mean scores of the native Spanish speakers were lower than those of the native English speakers, although the gap narrowed over time and was very slight by fifth grade. In

Spanish, there was also a native language effect, where the average scores of native Spanish speakers in third grade were significantly higher than those of native English speakers. Comparing across languages at the beginning of third grade, the native English speakers had a slightly higher mean score on the English reading assessment than on the Spanish reading assessment, and the opposite was true for the native Spanish speakers. In other words, both groups had slightly higher mean scores in their native language than in their second language.

In a longitudinal study of one 50/50 school site, Lindholm-Leary (2005c) examined the vocabulary scores of NES and NSS students in their *first language*. Assessments included the Woodcock Johnson and Woodcock Muñoz Language Battery (standardized tests measuring cognitive and language abilities) in kindergarten and grade 3, and then the Spanish and English norm-referenced achievement tests at grade 6. Results showed that NES students began kindergarten with an above-grade-level mastery of vocabulary in English (75th percentile) and maintained it through grade 3. Their English vocabulary scores in grade 3, but not in kindergarten, were highly correlated with their reading achievement scores at the sixth and seventh grade levels in English ($r = 0.91$), but not with their 6th grade vocabulary and total reading achievement scores in Spanish ($r = 0.25$ and $r = 0.14$, respectively). In contrast, NSS students began kindergarten with low vocabulary scores in Spanish (33rd percentile), but they made substantial gains by grade 3 to above average (61st percentile). For NSS students, Spanish vocabulary scores in grade 3 were equivalent to the slightly above grade-level Spanish achievement vocabulary percentiles in grade 6. In addition, their Spanish vocabulary scores in grade 3, but not kindergarten, were highly correlated with their reading achievement on norm-referenced achievement tests in both Spanish ($r = 0.49$) and English ($r = 0.51$). These findings suggest that strengthening L1 vocabulary development in the early primary grades supports later achievement in L1 reading for NES and NSS students, and for NSS students, L2 reading achievement also benefits.

Writing

Howard *et al.* (2004) investigated the English and Spanish writing development of 344 native English speakers and native Spanish speakers in 11 Spanish/English TWI programs across the United States. Nine waves of writing data in each language were collected over a three-year period, from the beginning of grade 3 to the end of grade 5. An analytic rubric was used to score these writing samples according to composition, grammar and mechanics. On average, the NSS and NES students had remarkably similar trends. At all time points, the mean scores of the native speakers were higher than the mean scores of second language speakers (such that NES students had higher mean scores in English and NSS students had higher mean scores in Spanish), but the shapes of the trajectories of mean performance in each language were comparable for the two groups. Moreover, there was a tremendous amount of overlap in scores across the two groups. While the mean scores of native speakers were consistently higher than the mean scores of second language speakers, there were many second language speakers who scored higher than their native language peers, and vice versa. In other words, many native Spanish speakers scored higher than native English speakers in English, and many native English speakers scored higher than native Spanish speakers in Spanish. As a final point, the mean English writing ability of NES students was always clearly higher than their mean Spanish writing ability. For NSS students, however, the situation was very different. Their mean scores in English and Spanish were virtually identical at all time points.

In a more detailed analysis of the same dataset, Howard (2003) used an individual growth modeling framework to estimate average growth trajectories in each language, as well as to assess the predictive power of native language background and home language use on average final status (end of fifth grade performance) and average rate of change. Controlling for other variables in the model, among students who were not eligible for free/reduced lunch there was a consistent effect of home language use over time, with students who spoke more Spanish at home having higher estimated performance at all time points than students who spoke less Spanish at home. Among students who were eligible for free/reduced lunch, however, the situation was different. While students who spoke more Spanish at home always had higher estimated Spanish writing scores than students who spoke less Spanish at home, the gaps among the home language groups narrowed over time. The reason for this difference across free/reduced lunch eligibility groups is not clear, but may be due at least in part to the fact that the native English speakers who were eligible for free/reduced lunch tended to include a larger percentage of minority students, particularly Latinos who may have had some exposure to Spanish outside of school.

Serrano and Howard (2003) investigated English influence on the Spanish writing development of 55 native Spanish speakers in three 90/10 TWI programs. They found that many samples demonstrated evidence of English influence, but, most students exhibited just a small amount of English influence in their Spanish writing. English influence was found to be most common in the domain of vocabulary, followed by grammar and then mechanics.

Howard and Christian (1997) analyzed the English and Spanish writing samples of eight focal students in the upper elementary grades of a 50/50 TWI program. Four students (two NES and two NSS) were followed from grade 3 to grade 4, and four additional students (two NES and two NSS) were followed from grade 5 to grade 6. Their writing samples were analyzed according to organization, topic development, mechanics and language use. The authors found that in general, writing in both languages showed reasonable sophistication in all four domains, particularly with regard to organization. The Spanish essays were usually comparable to the English essays with regard to organization and topic development, but they showed more mechanical errors and more linguistic/grammatical errors, usually regarding word order, word choice and agreement. There was no code switching in the English essays and only a few instances in the Spanish ones, though all were flagged with quotation marks. The English writing samples of NESs and NSSs were generally comparable, especially in the grade 5–6 cohort. The Spanish samples of NSS students tended to be more sophisticated in terms of vocabulary and grammar than those of their NES peers. However, NSS students did make some grammatical mistakes in Spanish, generally at a higher frequency than evidenced in their English writing.

Oral Language Development

As part of the large-scale study discussed earlier, Howard *et al.* (2004) investigated the Spanish and English oral language development of 131 NSS and 110 NES students in 11 TWI programs across the United States. Using a modified version of the SOPA (Student Oral Proficiency Assessment), English and Spanish oral proficiency assessments were conducted with these students at the end of grade 3 and the end of grade 5. The average oral English proficiency of both groups of students was quite high in both grade 3 and grade 5, with average scores in the mid to high 4 range on a scale of 0 to 5, indicating advanced skills on the part of both NES and NSS students. In addition, standard deviations for both groups dropped to extremely low and equivalent levels, indicating that the very high mean scores of both groups in fifth grade were reflective of most individual scores as well.

In Spanish, both groups of students showed progress from grade 3 to grade 5. NES students showed more growth than their NSS peers, which was possible because their initial score at the end of grade 3 was much lower than that of the NSS students. By the end of grade 5, the mean scores of both groups were in the advanced range, with a mean score of 4.8 for NSS and 4.14 for NES students. Additionally, the standard deviations of both groups decreased over time, but the standard deviations of the native English speakers were always much higher than those of the native Spanish speakers, which indicates much more variability in Spanish language proficiency among native English speakers than among native Spanish speakers. In addition, as a group, the NSS students experienced a subtle shift from slight dominance in Spanish in grade 3 to comparable scores in English and Spanish by the end of grade 5, while the NES students were always clearly dominant in English.

Based on classroom observations and testing in a 50/50 TWI program in Virginia, Howard and Christian (1997) studied the oral development of elementary students in English and Spanish. In English, all NES students entered as fluent English speakers and remained that way, so there was no evidence of the TWI program causing delay or interference. The NSS students also developed strong English oral skills: all NSS third graders were rated as fluent according to the LAS-O (Language Assessment Scales, Oral), and no significant differences were found in oral English proficiency between NES and NSS students. In Spanish, development was strong but not quite as strong as in English. Some 88% of native Spanish speakers students tested as fluent in Spanish in first grade as compared to 100% of the native English speakers testing fluent in English in first grade, which may be attributed to the fact that most NSSs had lived all or most of their life in the US, and therefore had experienced some level of English exposure to English. In grades two and above, 100% of the NSS students tested fluent in Spanish. About 20% of NES students rated fluent in Spanish in grades 1–2, and about 50% rated fluent in grades 4–5. Overall, native Spanish speakers tended to be more balanced bilinguals than native English speakers were.

Similar results were reported by Lindholm-Leary (2001) using the Student Oral Language Observation Matrix (SOLOM). The oral language proficiency results indicate that TWI students scored at or near the top of the SOLOM in their first language in grades 1–2, and almost all students were rated as proficient in their two languages, particularly by the upper elementary grade levels. In general, students made excellent progress in both languages across the grade levels. In both 90/10 and 50/50 programs, NSS students developed proficiency in English and by grade 4, most were rated as proficient in English. NES students also became proficient in Spanish by grade 6, though more 90/10 students were proficient in Spanish compared to 50/50 students. These results were consistent whether they were examined from a cross-sectional or a longitudinal perspective, and regardless of the language measures (e.g. Language Assessment Scale, Bilingual Syntax Measure, SOLOM) utilized.

Students' ratings of their Spanish proficiency

Lindholm-Leary and Ferrante (2005) examined 199 TWI middle school students' ratings of their proficiency in Spanish listening comprehension, fluency, vocabulary and grammar. These students had participated for six to eight years in a two-way program, and all NSS and most NES had been rated as proficient in Spanish by their teacher, and had scored at or above grade level in Spanish reading achievement. Students were given rubrics to self-rate their Spanish listening comprehension, fluency, vocabulary and grammar on a scale from 1 to 5. Like most rubrics, there were descriptions of each numerical score for each language component. Results showed that there were no statistically significant differences between the means of the Latino NSS, Latino NES, and Euro[3] NES students. Overall, findings indicated that:

(1) *Spanish listening comprehension:* almost 75% of Latino NSS and Latino NES students and 50% of Euro NES students rated themselves at a level 4 or 5 on the five-point scale for listening comprehension (from 1= understand simple questions/statements, to 5 = understand everything at normal speed);

(2) *Spanish fluency:* 50% of Latino NSS, and more than 33% of Latino NES and Euro NES students rated their fluency as a 4 or 5 (from 1 = participate in simple conversations on familiar topics at slower-than-normal speed, to 5 = native-like fluency);

(3) *Spanish vocabulary:* nearly 50% of Latino NSS students, 33% of Latino NES students, and 25% of Euro NES students gave themselves a 4 or 5 (from 1 = enough vocabulary to make simple statements/ask simple questions, to 5 = extensive native-like vocabulary);.

(4) *Spanish grammar:* received the lowest ratings overall, with 11–45% of students perceiving that they had at least a good command of grammar (levels 4–5) (from 1 = produce very basic sentence patterns with frequent errors, to 5 = native-like command of complex grammatical patterns).

Relationships between oral proficiency and academic achievement: Within and across languages

Research in TWI programs joins the literature in bilingual education in the US that indicates that bilingual proficiency and biliteracy are positively related to academic achievement in both languages (Genesee *et al.*, 2005, 2006; Lindholm & Aclan, 1991; Lindholm-Leary & Borsato, 2006). As syntheses of the research (e.g. Genesee *et al.*, 2006) show, bilingual Latino students tend to have higher achievement scores, grade point averages and educational expectations than their monolingual English-speaking Latino peers. While this finding is not as strong for Latino native English speakers in English reading, it is certainly true for Latino native English speakers in Spanish reading and for native Spanish speakers in English and Spanish reading. Thus, higher levels of bilingual proficiency are associated with higher levels of reading achievement, in particular L2 (second language) reading achievement. Further support for this interpretation is that across the grade levels, as students become more proficient in both languages, the correlation between reading achievement in English and Spanish increases (Howard, 2006; Lindholm-Leary, 2001; Lindholm & Aclan, 1991). In addition, the Lindholm-Leary and Borsato (2005) study noted earlier found that the best NSS and NES readers in English (advanced level on California's criterion-referenced test) had the highest reading scores in Spanish. Interestingly, among those who scored in the lowest categories of reading achievement in English, NSS students scored low in English, but tended to score average in Spanish whereas NES students who scored low in English tended to also achieve at low levels in Spanish.

Thus, students, in bilingual and TWI programs, rated as balanced bilinguals with high levels of proficiency in both languages tend to outperform other students, perhaps lending support to Cummins' threshold hypothesis (Cummins, 1991), which states that high levels of bilingualism are required before cognitive benefits can be attained. Finally, there is some indication of transfer of content knowledge, as students were sometimes instructed in one language and assessed in the other, and still demonstrated grade-appropriate mastery of the content. For all these studies, there are concerns related to non-random assignment of participants in the TWI and other programs. In other words, any differences found or not found across groups of students within TWI and across program models may have to do with differences in student backgrounds, general quality of school environment independent of program model, etc. As a result, these findings should be interpreted cautiously. At the same time, the consistency of findings across studies suggests that the conclusions discussed here have credibility.

Program Model Differences

Several studies have included comparisons of the performance of students in 90/10 and 50/50 TWI programs, as the question of whether there are program differences in student outcomes is of great interest to educators, parents and policy makers. The research presented here with a variety of different schools shows that both TWI models, 90/10 and 50/50, promote proficiency and achievement in two languages, although not necessarily at the same time or to the same levels. Taken together, the findings are consistent in indicating that:

(1) In *English language development*, there is no long-term program effect; both NES and NSS in both 50/50 and 90/10 programs demonstrated high levels of oral English proficiency (Christian *et al.*, 2004; Lindholm-Leary, 2001).

(2) While the paths towards *English literacy and reading and math achievement* do vary by program model and there are short-term advantages for 50/50 programs, these differences disappear by the upper elementary grades and performance remains comparable through the secondary grades (Christian *et al.*, 2004; Lindholm-Leary, 2005b).

(3) In Spanish, by the end of elementary school and into middle school, there is clearly an advantage for the 90/10 programs, with greater Spanish oral language and literacy attainment by both NES and NSS students in these programs (Christian *et al.*, 2004; Lindholm-Leary, 2001).

(4) With respect to bilingual proficiency, students in 90/10 programs develop higher levels of bilingual proficiency than students in the 50/50 program (Lindholm-Leary, 2001).

These results show that more instructional time spent in Spanish positively impacts achievement in Spanish, and has no negative effect on achievement measured in English. That is, receiving less English in their curriculum does not negatively affect these students' English language proficiency relative to students who receive half their instruction in English, regardless of linguistic background. The results for NSS students are consistent with findings reported in the bilingual education literature. Additional instruction in Spanish is typically associated with higher levels of proficiency in Spanish and with no loss to English proficiency; ELL students in developmental bilingual programs (like the 90/10 program) also acquire higher levels of proficiency in English than students in transitional bilingual education programs (August & Hakuta, 1997; Genesee *et al*, 2006; Lindholm-Leary & Borsato, 2006). Further, these findings for first language (L1) and second language (L2) proficiency are similar to results obtained from foreign language (one-way) immersion research, in which English speakers develop high levels of proficiency in their *L1*, regardless of whether they participate in a partial (50/50 type) or full (90–100% in L2) immersion program. Native English-speaking immersion students also develop high levels of *L2* proficiency in both partial and full immersion programs (e.g. Genesee, 1987), though their proficiency has been found to be higher in full immersion programs.

Student Background Differences

There is evidence to suggest that participation in TWI programs meets the language and achievement needs of most student participants regardless of certain student characteristics. Results from a number of different schools in a variety of states using both program models (90/10 and 50/50) consistently demonstrate that students of different ethnicities, language backgrounds, socioeconomic levels and even those in special education develop proficiencies and reading and content area (e.g. mathematics) skills in the two languages of the TWI program. That is, by the upper grade levels, these students are able to score at least as well as their non-TWI same background peers. There is no evidence to support the belief among some educators that a few specific student characteristics ought to limit participation in TWI programs.

In several different studies of TWI students from three ethnic groups (Christian *et al.*, 2004; Howard, 2003; Lindholm-Leary, 2001, 2005c), results showed that students from Euro-American, Hispanic, and African-American (and Asian-American, though there were few such students) backgrounds all benefited from the TWI program. This was true regardless of the students' social class backgrounds, though middle-class students typically outperformed lower-class students.

Howard (2003) and Lindholm-Leary (2001, 2005c) found that native language background, socioeconomic status, gender and special education participation all had significant effects on the outcomes of TWI students in the upper elementary grades. Controlling for native language, gender, and participation in special education, higher socioeconomic status was associated with higher average outcomes in English literacy and achievement. Similarly, controlling for other variables in the model, girls outperformed boys on average.

Howard (2003) found that the achievement gap for special education students diminished over time, meaning that while their predicted performance still lagged behind that of their peers who did not receive special education services, the difference in predicted performance between the two groups was not as large at the end of fifth grade as it was at the end of third grade. Similarly, Lindholm-Leary (2005c) reported that students identified as special education scored very low in reading achievement in English. However, there was no difference in English reading scores between NSS and NES special education students, and there was no difference between TWI special education students and the California average for students with disabilities in grades 4–8, despite the greater exposure to English instruction in the California state sample. In reading achievement in Spanish, students identified as special education scored only slightly below average, and there was little difference in Spanish reading scores between NSS and NES special education students.

An important implication of these results is that TWI programs may better serve TWI special needs students because, although the students may be low in their literacy in English, they are at least biliterate, and some of them are scoring average in Spanish reading achievement. Their English monolingual special needs peers are low in the only language in which they are *literate*. Thus, the fact that the TWI special needs students are bilingual and at least semi-biliterate seems to provide an important benefit over the English-only students who are monolingual and semi-literate in their only language. Because of this, the decision to keep them in the TWI program may be well advised and is consistent with practices in one-way immersion education (Genesee, 1987), in which students with special education needs or learning disabilities are typically accepted in the program.

Taken together, data from these various studies indicate that TWI programs are capable of promoting academic performance for students of different backgrounds, including those subpopulations identified as *at risk* for academic difficulty. Based on the current research knowledge base, there is no reason *per se* not to include such children in TWI programs, though much more research is needed in this area, as argued by Genesee in Chapter 2 of this volume.

Instructional Implications

A substantial body of literature has been created about school or program effectiveness in English-medium programs and in bilingual and TWI programs. There is tremendous consistency between certain factors that define exemplary two-way immersion programs and practices that are found in effective mainstream education programs, although different labels may be used. The importance of these factors is evident from the frequency and consistency with which they are found in programs that produce more successful student outcomes in numerous studies with various populations, especially culturally and linguistically diverse students. These factors are elaborated in a recent document entitled *Guiding Principles for Dual Language Education*, which provides a comprehensive literature review (Lindholm-Leary, 2005a) and a set of key indicators of program quality in TWI programs (Howard *et al.*, 2005).[4] These Guiding Principles consider the significant influence of several factors on culturally and linguistically diverse students' educational outcomes, including:

(1) school environment;
(2) curriculum and instruction;
(3) program planning;
(4) assessment and accountability;
(5) staff quality;
(6) professional development;
(7) family involvement.

The guiding principles will be briefly characterized here; for a more thorough discussion and review of the research, see Lindholm-Leary (2005a).

School environment

Studies of effective schools consistently and conclusively demonstrate that student educational outcomes are enhanced when schools have a cohesive school-wide shared vision and a set of goals that define their expectations for achievement, as well as an instructional focus and commitment to achievement and high expectations that are shared by administrators, teachers, students and parents. Establishing a vision of bilingualism and multicultural competence requires a clear understanding of and equitable treatment directed toward the needs of culturally and linguistically diverse students, as well as consistently integrating multicultural themes into instruction.

Successful schools have effective leadership, who assure that there is a high degree of faculty cohesion, collaboration and collegiality; in schools with a TWI strand and one or more other strands, all teachers and other staff are engaged in promoting achievement for all students.

Curriculum and instruction

Studies show that more successful schools and programs provide a curriculum that establishes a clear alignment to standards and assessment, is meaningful, academically challenging and incorporates higher order thinking and is enriched, rather than remedial in nature. Because of the vision and goals associated with bilingualism and biliteracy, language instruction is integrated within the curriculum, and language and literature are developed across the curriculum to ensure that students learn the content as well as the academic language associated with the content. See further discussion in Chapter 3 by Met which emphasizes the mutual interdependence of language, literacy and academic achievement and Chapter 4 by Fortune, Tedick and Walker, which focuses on teachers' perspectives on language and content integration. Promoting highly proficient oral language skills necessitates providing both structured and unstructured opportunities for oral production. It also necessitates establishing and enforcing a strong language policy in the classroom that encourages students to use the instructional language and discourages students from speaking the non-instructional language. Grouping strategies, such as cooperative learning, are utilized to optimize student interactions and shared work. Further, since the vision and goals also include multicultural competence and equity, the curriculum needs to reflect and value the students' culture(s). Palmer's discussion in Chapter 5 illustrates how TWI teachers must systematically and skillfully manage classroom talk to foster more equitable discourse patterns in the classroom.

Program planning

Strong planning processes are in place that focus on meeting the goals of the program (in two-way immersion, this means promoting the students' bilingualism, biliteracy and multicultural competence) as well as improving *all* students' achievement. Program articulation should be both vertical (across grade levels) and horizontal (within grade levels) and should include proper scope, sequence, and alignment with developmentally appropriate practices and language proficiency levels in both languages.

Assessment and accountability

Effective schools use assessment measures that are aligned with the school's vision and goals, appropriate curriculum and related standards. TWI education programs require the use of multiple measures in both languages to assess students' progress toward meeting bilingual and biliteracy goals along with the curricular and content-related, and bilingual proficiency goals.

Staff quality

Teachers in language education programs, just as in mainstream programs, should be high-quality teachers with high levels of knowledge relating to the subject matter, curriculum development and technology, instructional strategies, classroom management skills and assessment. In addition, teachers need to understand the importance of and demonstrate the ability to reflect on their own teaching. Effective TWI programs require additional teaching and staff characteristics: native or native-like ability in either or both of the language(s) in which they are instructing – in speaking, listening, reading and writing skills and knowledge of the language education model and appropriate curriculum design and instructional strategies.

Professional development

To effectively administer and teach in a TWI program, administrators and teachers also need professional development related to the theories and philosophies underlying dual language education and to L2 and biliteracy development, cooperative learning, assessment and educational equity.

Family involvement

Effective programs make the school environment a welcoming and warm one for parents of all language and cultural groups, where multilingualism is valued and there is a sense of belonging for students and their families. In Chapter 10 Dagenais describes the inclusion of language awareness activities in a one-way French immersion program in Canada that has a linguistically diverse student population. Such classroom-based activities place value on multilingualism and multiculturalism and contribute to inclusion of families in subtle yet important ways.

In TWI programs that place a high priority on family involvement, culturally and linguistically diverse parents are treated equitably, and English-speaking parents do not dominate the advisory committees to the exclusion of the non-English-proficient parents. In addition, when parents come to the school, they must see a reflection of the vision and goals associated with bilingualism and biliteracy, for example, signs are in both languages and front office staff members are bilingual.

Conclusions and Suggestions for Further Research

As we have shown here, research has examined the language and literacy development and math achievement of students in two-way immersion programs at late elementary or secondary levels to determine the progress of students in such programs. These studies are consistent in showing that overall: (1) both NSS and NES students make significant progress in both languages, (2) both groups typically score at or above grade level in both languages by middle school, and (3) they perform at comparable or superior levels compared to same-language comparison peers. Findings are consistent across studies that included both TWI models (90/10 and 50/50), students from different demographic backgrounds, and a variety of districts and states. In addition, the results are similar across longitudinal and cross-sectional data, with small-scale and large-scale studies and with research studies in various TWI program environments.

Several important findings can be drawn from this research. First, there seems to be a native language effect, such that native speakers generally perform higher than second language speakers in terms of both oral and written language proficiency (Howard, 2003; Howard *et al.*, 2004; Lindholm-Leary, 2001). Second, not surprisingly, there seem to be slightly different patterns for NES and NSS students, with NESs always showing a clear dominance in and preference for English, and NSS students demonstrating more balanced bilingualism (Howard, 2003; Howard *et al.*, 2004; Lindholm-Leary, 2001). Sometimes the NSS students tend to perform slightly higher in their native language, and other times slightly higher in English, but in general, their performance on language and literacy measures across the two languages is much more similar than that of their NES peers. Third, there is some evidence for transfer of skills across languages, with some studies reporting similar writing processes and products across the two languages (Gort, 2002; Howard, 2003). This was not the case, however, in a writing study conducted in a Korean/English program (Ha, 2001), and may point to differences in the amount of potential cross-linguistic transfer and/or interference that may occur depending on the similarities or differences in orthographies in the two languages of instruction. Finally, several studies point to inter-relationships between language and literacy skills as well as mathematics within and across languages (Bae & Bachman, 1998; Lindholm-Leary, 2001; Lindholm-Leary & Borsato, 2005, 2006).

Much current research suffers from a short-term perspective; only a few studies have examined the long-term results of various program alternatives. Retrospective studies and those that rely wholly on school records, while valuable, provide incomplete information, and certainly cannot address the complex teacher and instructional factors that can affect student outcomes. Considerably more research is necessary that focuses on the specific teacher and instructional factors that are associated with successful content learning in TWI programs. In addition, observational and ethnographic studies on academic achievement and language and literacy development in TWI programs are clearly lacking. This research focus would add considerable depth to understanding children's language development within various contexts, their use of language with each other and how they learn language from each other, the types of conversations in which children engage with each other, how they use reading in context, and a whole variety of other topics. Research on the influence of peer interactions in promoting content and language learning would provide information on the kinds of interactional contexts that help both groups of students develop language and content skills, a point that was raised by Genesee *et al.* (2006).

While research has examined the characteristics of effective content instruction (Lindholm-Leary, 2005a), most of these findings emanate from studies in which the primary focus was not on the instructional characteristics. There is little research into how to make instruction more accessible and meaningful to students, particularly in areas considered challenging by all students – that is, science and math. Extant research provides some starting points, but a research program that includes ELLs with different language backgrounds, ages and previous educational experiences prior to immigrating should be considered in future research. Another significant factor to consider in examining learners is the cognitive challenge they may experience when learning academic content area through a second language.

Considerably more information is also needed about model variations. From the research reviewed above, it would appear that 90/10 and 50/50 are both viable models. However, some schools alternate languages by day, week or instructional units. More information is needed about whether alternating instruction by weeks or longer-term by instructional units is an effective way to deliver instruction through two languages and, if so, whether it is appropriate at all grade levels or only at later grade levels.

Developing reading and writing proficiencies in two languages is another important topic for further research. While TWI programs incorporate biliteracy, there is some confusion about how to best promote biliteracy, and how to help students who are struggling with reading in their second language. While many schools say they are using a standards-based curriculum, lesson plans often do not integrate language and content standards, and the publishers do not provide materials that adequately address language and content standards for dual language programs (be they two-way, one-way, indigenous immersion or developmental bilingual).

Assessment is also an important need. There are many challenges in assessing the content area knowledge of students learning through two languages. Test norms may be inappropriate because of differences between TWI students and students in the norming samples; and language proficiency and other background factors may influence test performance. Results from the few studies that have investigated testing accommodations suggest that the language of assessment should match the language of instruction and that modifying test questions to reduce language complexity may help narrow the performance gap between native English speakers and ELLs. Given the high-stakes nature of standardized testing, it is imperative to develop assessment procedures that allow *all* students to demonstrate what they know. Another potential problem with respect to assessment in TWI programs is that the development of state criterion-referenced tests has yielded results that are not comparable across different states. Some states have much higher criteria for reaching grade level norms than others, which can lead to differential interpretations of assessment data and different expectations for success or failure.

In conclusion, the research presented here provides solid evidence that on average, TWI students, both English language learners and native English-speaking students, succeed at becoming bilingual and biliterate in addition to achieving at or above grade level in content areas. However, much more is left to be learned regarding specific contextual factors that influence these patterns of achievement, and how particular program factors (e.g. program model, path of initial literacy instruction and allocation of languages) interact with student factors (e.g. native language, level of bilingualism at time of entry, socioeconomic status, special learning needs).

Notes

1. The national directory can be found at www.cal.org/twi/directory. The state directories for California and Texas are at www.cde.ca.gov/sp/el/ip and at http:/texastwoway.org. Other states may have directories of their programs, but that information is not available to the authors of this chapter.
2. In *one-way* developmental bilingual education, most or all of the students are ELLs; *two-way* bilingual education is the same as two-way immersion, in that students from two language backgrounds are integrated for instruction and both 90/10 and 50/50 variants exist.
3. Euro refers to American students of European backgrounds, often also referred to as Anglo students.
4. This document was funded by the US Department of Education's Office of English Language Acquisition, through a contract with the National Clearinghouse for English Language Acquisition.

References

August, D. and Hakuta, K. (eds) (1997) *Improving Schooling for Language Minority Children: A Research Agenda*. Washington, DC: National Academy Press.

Bae, J. and Bachman, L.F. (1998) A latent variable approach to listening and reading: Testing factorial invariance across two groups of children in the Korean/English two-way immersion program. *Language Testing* 15 (3), 380–414.

Bikle, K., Hakuta, K. and Billings, E.S. (2004) Trends in two-way immersion research. In J.A. Banks and C.A. McGee Banks (eds) *Handbook of Research on Multicultural Education* (2nd edn; pp. 589–606). New York: Macmillan.

Cazabon, M., Nicoladis, E. and Lambert, W.E. (1998) Becoming bilingual in the Amigos two-way immersion program (Research Report 3). Available online at http://www.cal.org/crede/pubs/research/rr3.htm. Accessed 14.8.07.

Christian, D., Genesee, F., Lindholm-Leary, K. and Howard, E. (2004) Final progress report: CAL/CREDE study of two-way immersion education. Available online at http://www.cal.org/twi/CREDEfinal.doc. Accessed 14.8.07.

Christian, D., Montone, C., Lindholm, K. and Carranza, I. (1997) *Profiles in Two-Way Immersion Education*. Washington, DC: Delta Systems and ERIC Clearinghouse on Languages and Linguistics.

Cummins, J. (1991) Conversational and academic language proficiency in bilingual contexts. *AILA Review: Reading in Two Languages* 8, 75–89.

De Jong, E.J. (2002) Effective bilingual education: From theory to academic achievement in a two-way bilingual program. *Bilingual Research Journal* 26 (1), 65–84.

Garcia, Y. (2003) Korean/English two-way immersion at Cahuenga Elementary School. *NABE News* 26, 8–11, 25.

Genesee, F. (1987) *Learning Through Two Languages.* Cambridge: Newbury House Publishers.

Genesee, F., Lindholm-Leary, K., Saunders, W. and Christian, D. (2005) English language learners in US schools: An overview of research findings. *Journal of Education for Students Placed at Risk* 10 (4), 363–385.

Genesee, F., Lindholm-Leary, K.J., Saunders, W. and Christian, D. (2006) *Educating English Language Learners: A Synthesis of Empirical Evidence.* New York: Cambridge University Press.

Gomez, L., Freeman, D. and Freeman, Y. (2005) Dual language education: A promising 50–50 model. *Bilingual Research Journal* 29, 145–164.

Gort, M. (2002) On the threshold of biliteracy: Bilingual writing processes of English-dominant and Spanish-dominant first graders in a two-way bilingual education program. Unpublished doctoral dissertation, Boston University.

Ha, J.H. (2001) Elementary students' written language development in a Korean/English two-way immersion program. Unpublished masters thesis, California State University – Long Beach.

Howard, E.R. (2002) Two-way immersion: A key to global awareness. *Educational Leadership* 60 (2), 62–64.

Howard, E.R. (2003) Biliteracy development in two-way immersion education programs: A multilevel analysis of the effects of native language and home language use on the development of narrative writing ability in English and Spanish. Unpublished doctoral dissertation, Harvard University.

Howard, E.R. (2004) Two-way immersion education: An integrated approach to bilingual education in the United States. In X.P. Rodriguez-Yanez, A.M. Lorenzo-Suarez and F. Ramallo (eds) *Bilingualism and Education: From the Family to the School* (pp. 229–236). Munich: Lincom Europa.

Howard, E.R. (2006) Additive bilingualism through dual language education. Presentation at the annual conference of the National Association for Bilingual Education: Phoenix, AZ.

Howard, E.R. and Christian, D. (1997) The development of bilingualism and biliteracy in two-way immersion students. Paper presented at the Annual Meeting of the American Educational Research Association, Chicago, IL. (ERIC Document Reproduction Service No. ED 405741).

Howard, E.R. and Christian, D. (2002) *Two-Way Immersion 101: Designing and Implementing a Two-Way Immersion Education Program at the Elementary Level* (Educational Practice Report 9). Santa Cruz, CA: Center for Research on Education, Diversity & Excellence.

Howard, E.R., Christian, D. and Genesee, F. (2004) *The Development of Bilingualism and Biliteracy from Grades 3 to 5: A Summary of Findings From the CAL/CREDE Study of Two-Way Immersion Education.* Santa Cruz, CA: Center for Research on Education, Diversity & Excellence and Center for Applied Linguistics.

Howard, E.R., Sugarman, J. and Christian, D. (2003) *Trends in Two-Way Immersion: A Review of the Research* (Report 63). Baltimore, MD: Center for Research on the Education of Students Placed at Risk.

Howard, E.R., Sugarman, J., Christian, D., Lindholm-Leary, K.J. and Rogers, D. (2005) *Guiding Principles for Dual Language Education*. Washington, DC: US Department of Education and National Clearinghouse for English Language Acquisition. Available online at www.cal.org/twi/guidingprinciples.htm. Accessed 14.8.07.

Kirk Senesac, B.V. (2002) Two-way immersion education: A portrait of quality schooling. *Bilingual Research Journal* 26 (1), 85–101.

Lindholm-Leary, K. (2001) *Dual Language Education*. Clevedon: Multilingual Matters.

Lindholm-Leary, K. (2003) Language and education issues affecting Asian Pacific American students. Keynote speech at California Association for Asian and Pacific American Education and National Association for the Education and Advancement of Cambodian, Laotian, and Vietnamese Americans Conference on Quality Public Schools for Every Child: Opportunities and Challenges for Asian and Pacific American Children and Educators, Woodland Hills, California.

Lindholm-Leary, K.J. (2005a) Review of research and best practices on effective features of dual language education programs. Available online at http://www.lindholm-leary.com/resources/review_research.pdf . Accessed 14.8.07.

Lindholm-Leary, K.J. (2005b) The rich promise of two-way immersion. *Educational Leadership* 62, 56–59.

Lindholm-Leary, K.J. (2005c) Understanding outcomes of diverse students in two-way bilingual immersion. Paper presented at the 13th Annual National Two-Way Bilingual Immersion Summer Conference, Monterey, California.

Lindholm, K.J. and Aclan, Z. (1991) Bilingual proficiency as a bridge to academic achievement: Results from bilingual/immersion programs. *Journal of Education* 173, 99–113.

Lindholm-Leary, K.J. and Borsato, G. (2005) Hispanic high schoolers and mathematics: Follow-up of students who had participated in two-way bilingual elementary programs. *Bilingual Research Journal* 29, 641–652.

Lindholm-Leary, K.J. and Borsato, G. (2006) Academic achievement. In F. Genesee, K. Lindholm-Leary, W. Saunders and D. Christian (eds) *Educating English Language Learners* (pp. 176–222). New York: Cambridge University Press.

Lindholm, K.J. and Fairchild, H.H. (1990) First year evaluation of an elementary school bilingual immersion program. In A.M. Padilla, H.H. Fairchild and C. Valadez (eds) *Bilingual Education: Issues and Strategies* (pp. 126–136). Beverly Hills, CA: Sage Publications.

Lindholm-Leary, K.J. and Ferrante, A. (2005) Follow-up study of middle school two-way students: Language proficiency, achievement and attitudes. In R. Hoosain and F. Salili (eds) *Language in Multicultural Education* (pp. 157–179). Greenwich, CT: Information Age Publishing

Serrano, R. and Howard, E.R. (2003) Maintaining Spanish proficiency in the United States: The influence of English on the Spanish writing of native Spanish speakers in two-way immersion programs. In L. Sayahi (ed.) *Selected Proceedings of the First Workshop on Spanish Sociolinguistics* (pp. 77–88). Somerville, MA: Cascadilla Proceedings Project.

Stipek, D., Ryan, R. and Alarcón, R. (2001) Bridging research and practice to develop a two-way bilingual program. *Early Childhood Research Quarterly* 16 (1), 133–149.

Thomas, W.P. and Collier, V. (1997) School effectiveness for language minority students. Available online at http://www.ncela.gwu.edu/pubs/resource/effectiveness/. Accessed 14.8.07.

Thomas, W.P. and Collier, V. (2002) A national study of school effectiveness for language minority students' long-term academic achievement. Available online at http://www.crede.ucsc.edu/research/llaa/1.1_final.html. Accessed 14.8.07.

Chapter 10

Developing a Critical Awareness of Language Diversity in Immersion

DIANE DAGENAIS

Introduction

With increases in population movements over the last decades, researchers and educators in many parts of the world have begun to attend to the presence of children of diverse backgrounds in immersion programs as is evident in a growing body of literature on the topic (Cenoz, 1998; Dagenais & Berron, 2001; Dagenais & Day, 1998, 1999; de Courcy, 2002; Hurd, 1993; Lamarre, 1997; Rolstad, 1999; Swain & Lapkin, 1991, 2005; Taylor, 1992). While relatively little is known about the progress of these students compared to their counterparts from majority language backgrounds, there is a consensus among researchers working in this area that they may experience considerable success in such programs when their home languages are valued and maintained.

At the same time, as researchers (Cenoz & Genesee, 1998; Genesee, Chapter 2 this volume, Hornberger, 2003) have noted, studies of bilingualism and immersion education have led to an increased interest in issues related to multilingualism. Cenoz and Genesee observed how the emerging literature on multilingualism has made evident links between forces of globalization, population shifts, language diversity, community affiliations and program options in education. Elsewhere (Dagenais, 2003), I signalled how these connections were made as well by immigrant parents in Vancouver who chose to enrol their children in one-way French immersion programs as a means of promoting multilingual development. I argued that immigrant parents considered multilingualism to be valuable linguistic capital that could be converted eventually into economic capital on national and international markets. Moreover, I suggested that they adopted a transnational perspective by associating multilingualism with increased social capital that could ensure access to desirable bilingual and multilingual communities across national boundaries. This research highlighted how immersion programs offer opportunities for various language groups that were unforeseen when the first French immersion program was implemented in Canada four decades ago.

Immersion programs now serve a wide variety of purposes for diverse communities. For example, Richards and Burnaby (Chapter 11 this volume) propose that immersion programs for Aboriginal students might foster language revitalization as it has in other indigenous communities around the world (e.g. for the Maori of New Zealand and the Hawaiian people of Hawaii) and Rolstad (1999) suggests that two-way immersion provides an enriching approach for supporting language maintenance, identity formation and community affiliations among Korean speakers. In Chapter 9 Lindholm-Leary and Howard present similar evidence for speakers of other languages (predominantly Spanish) in two-way programs.

Recently, Swain and Lapkin (2005) reviewed the core features of immersion education identified in Swain and Johnson (1997) to determine whether they are still applicable today in light of changing demographics. Reminding us that immersion programs in Canada originally aimed at serving Anglophone students, they observed that population shifts now beg for a need to change immersion pedagogy and overtly support home languages other than English. Swain and Lapkin (2005: 182) suggested that we consider applying the principles of multilingual education to immersion programs in contexts characterized by diversity, arguing that: 'It is important to allow for the use of multiple L1s in the classroom and celebrate the diverse cultures represented. In this way additive bilingualism/multilingualism is made possible.'

In this chapter, I begin by reviewing findings from my ethnographic research on the home and school language experiences of multilingual immersion students that point to differences in opportunities for multilingual development afforded in both contexts. I describe how this work led me to pursue teacher-researcher projects aimed at transforming pedagogical practices that marginalize students of diverse language origins. Then, I briefly outline the theoretical perspective associated with critical language awareness and critical pedagogies to situate the lens I adopt in examining a few excerpts of data from language awareness activities implemented in a Canadian French immersion classroom. Finally, I conclude by considering the potential and limitations such activities present for multilingual children to take up desirable identities at school and for transforming stereotypes of languages and speakers of diverse languages.

Multilingual Children's Language Practices at Home and School

Between 1994 and 2001 my research teams conducted four studies with multilingual immersion students. The teams included one or two video ethnographers and from one to four research assistants who worked alongside me at various stages of the research. This work was situated in an ethnographic methodology and epistemological stance (Green & Wallat, 1981; Lecompte & Preissle, 1993). The first study extended over six months to document the school literacy practices of three children of diverse language origins (Spanish, Vietnamese, Polish) who were enrolled in different school districts of Metropolitan Vancouver. A second project was conducted over a year to examine these same children's literacy practices at home. This work was then expanded over four years in a third study of the home literacy practices of 12 other children of diverse language backgrounds (English, Spanish, French, Mandarin, Cantonese, Korean, Punjabi, Gujarati, Urdu and Hindi) who were enrolled in one school district in a Vancouver suburb. The scope of fieldwork was expanded in a fourth, three-year study of their literacy practices at school.

My research teams audiotaped children's conversations at home; we observed children's literacy practices at home; parents kept written records of their children's literacy activities over the period of a week; we video-taped and audiotaped the children's classroom interactions; and we conducted open-ended interviews with the children, their parents and teachers. More detailed discussions of this research are provided elsewhere (Dagenais, 2005; Dagenais & Berron, 2001; Dagenais & Day, 1998, 1999; Dagenais & Jacquet, 2001).

In keeping with ethnographic approaches, fieldwork and analysis phases of research were undertaken recursively so that the initial analysis and validation procedures were ongoing throughout the fieldwork and informed subsequent data collection. Data were organized, reduced, coded and categorized using qualitative data analysis packages. Analysis procedures included triangulating the data collected from all sources as well as reviewing memos and interpretive summaries of the data. Interviews, fieldnotes and videotapes were indexed to identify language interactions and participants' interpretations of them. Recurring patterns, relationships and analytic categories were identified in repeated readings of the data corpus.

Our analysis revealed that the multilingual children regularly alternated between languages at home. For example, in a family of South Asian origin, the grandparents spoke only Punjabi with all members of the family; the parents alternated between Hindi (the mother's heritage language) and English in their conversations together; and the mother spoke a combination of Hindi and English with the children, whereas the father spoke a combination of Punjabi and English with them. The children spoke to each other mainly in English but eventually used some French with each other on occasion as the youngest child progressed through school.

The children also engaged in a range of multilingual literacy practices at home. For instance, one girl wrote letters in Spanish to relatives, did her homework in French and English, read recipes in Spanish when she helped her mother cook and read Spanish language magazines that were available at home. As well, she read novels for pleasure in English and in French for homework, watched television in English and occasionally in French, watched videos in Spanish and English. She listened to the local radio station in English and sometimes listened to cassettes or CDs in Spanish. Thus, at home, this child and her multilingual peers drew on each language in their repertoire for particular literacy tasks according to their needs and their communication partners.

At home, these children learned to juggle the communicative demands of a complex multilingual context. Their parents did not view the introduction of new languages as a threat to family languages, rather, they highly valued multilingualism and actively sought out opportunities for their children to learn new languages. They enrolled their children in immersion education to learn French and English while adopting a range of strategies to maintain the family language at home, such as insisting on using the family language at the dinner table, registering their children in community-based language classes on evenings or weekends, providing individual tutoring, participating in religious activities in the family language or making regular trips to the parents' country of origin.

Contrary to the multilingual practices we documented at home, observations in the children's French immersion classrooms revealed that a monolingual norm prevailed as most teachers focused on the language of instruction, either French or English, to the exclusion of other languages. Other researchers have made similar observations more recently about the absence of support for the home languages of students from a variety of origins, noting 'in most immersion programs diverse students' first languages are invisible and inaudible in the classroom' (Cummins, personal communication cited in Swain & Lapkin, 2005: 171).

Nevertheless, we did document a few exciting exceptions when teachers recognized children's knowledge of more than two languages, as illustrated in a French literacy activity in grade 3. In that classroom, the French teacher asked students to write a text titled *Pourquoi je suis fier de parler deux langues* [Why I am proud to speak two languages]. One girl we were observing asked: 'Well, can I write about the other languages I speak?' In response, the teacher proposed as an alternative *Pourquoi je suis fier de parler trois langues* [Why I am proud to speak three languages]. When the children were later asked to read their texts out loud, the girl volunteered to do so and in response, her classmates asked her to say something in Spanish, which she did. Then, she shared her observation of similarities in the Spanish word for cat, *gato,* and the French word for cake, *gateau.* She made her classmates laugh by warning them of the risks of confusing one word for the other: 'If you say *gato* [cat] in Spanish. ... And in French its like *gateau* [cake]. ... If you say *Yo quiero comer un gato.* ... They will think you want to eat a cat.' (Classroom audiotape transcription, April 7, 2000).

Thus, given the opportunity to write and talk about her home language, this multilingual child was able to demonstrate her expertise in translation and knowledge of similarities and differences between languages. As analysis of such ethnographic data progressed, I became increasingly concerned about practices that marginalized students of diverse language origins and intrigued by the transformative potential of instances when immersion teachers invited children to share what they knew of languages beyond the target languages of instruction. Consequently, in collaboration with colleagues in Montreal and Vancouver, I have turned to teacher-researcher projects aimed at examining the relevance of language awareness activities that attend to a broad diversity of languages and foster multilingualism.

Language Awareness

Language awareness activities were first proposed by Eric Hawkins (1984, 1992) and his team in Britain. In these activities, students attend systematically to language diversity by examining the role of language in society and comparing the patterns of their own languages and other languages. One objective of these activities was to develop an appreciation for language diversity and speakers of different languages.

In the 1990s, language awareness activities were redeveloped in France and became known as *Eveil au langage* and later *Eveil aux langues* (Moore, 1995). These activities focused on the use of minority, migrant and immigrant children's knowledge of diverse regional, national and international languages as a teaching resource. One aim was to lead students to view diverse languages that once seemed distant as more familiar and accessible. Extensive research and curricular innovations conducted in a number of countries such as France, Switzerland, Spain, Italy, Germany and Austria have shown that language awareness operates as a powerful means of acquiring knowledge of language patterns, learning about the unequal statuses of languages in school and society, developing positive attitudes towards speakers of other languages, and increasing metalinguistic capacities such as auditory discrimination of non-familiar languages (Billiez, 1998, 2000; Candelier, 2003a; Castellotti & Moore, 2002; Dabène, 1994; de Pietro, 1998; Perregaux *et al.*, 2003; Sabatier, 2004). Such results have drawn the attention of education policy makers in the European Union to language awareness as a promising approach to language teaching in multilingual contexts (Candelier, 2003b; Castellotti & Moore, 2002).

Recently, language awareness activities developed by Francophone teams in Europe were adapted by Armand and her research group in Montreal for use in Francophone classrooms (Maraillet, 2005). Armand and I then expanded this work to include a comparative examination of language awareness activities implemented in Montreal and Vancouver. In Vancouver, we readapted these activities for an early French immersion program (Dagenais, 2005; Walsh, 2005), where we gathered the data I discuss later in this chapter. Currently, my colleagues Armand, Moore and Sabatier and I are extending this research further in a longitudinal study in both cities. In this latest project, we are exploring how language awareness activities might rely more on contextual data about the local linguistic landscape (Cenoz & Gorter, 2006; Cenoz *et al.*, 2004; Landry & Bourhis, 1997) to develop children's knowledge of multilingual practices in their own communities. Our work is inspired in part by critical perspectives, reviewed below, that have been applied to language awareness specifically and to language education more generally.

Language awareness and critical perspectives

Fairclough (1992) proposed critical language awareness as an extension of language awareness activities developed by Hawkins (1984). Based on critical perspectives in education, critical language awareness aims to:

(1) raise students' awareness of the values attributed to different languages and language speakers;
(2) address and change stereotypic representations of languages, language speakers and language learning;
(3) empower students to take greater control of their learning;
(4) question inequalities and work toward greater equity.

English language variations of critical language awareness activities have been taken up in some Canadian classrooms and developed in particular with Aboriginal communities (Bélanger, 1996; Bilash & Tulasiewicz, 1995; Labercane *et al.*, 1997; Rowney, 1994).

Thus far, in French work on language awareness there have been relatively few explicit references to critical language awareness or to critical theoretical perspectives. Nevertheless, a close look at francophone literature on language awareness indicates that authors do presuppose that social relations are based on an unequal distribution of power and that engagement in these pedagogical approaches implies a commitment to educational projects aimed at justice and social equity.

In keeping with the critical perspectives outlined below, but without referencing them directly, a number of francophone sociolinguists engaged in language awareness research and classroom innovations in Europe clearly assume that power issues are central to human interactions (for example, see contributors to Moore, 2001). To analyze the transformation of stereotypes in students' discourse during language awareness activities, they attend to discursive positioning and highlight the role that power and unequal status play in dialogic processes.

Critical perspectives in education

In English language publications, critical perspectives have emerged as a powerful theoretical lens over the last few decades to analyze the links between social inequities and educational processes. This work is situated in a long tradition of scholarship that traces its roots to the writings of Apple (1979), Bourdieu (1977), Bourdieu and Passeron (1977), Freire (1970), Giroux (1983) and others whose discussions of power differences in social relationships were pivotal in shaping contemporary critical theory in education. Bourdieu's work on the links between economies, education and language is widely cited in English language scholarship, though it has been critiqued as well for its inability to surpass a pessimistic and deterministic logic in his descriptions of the reproduction of inequality. Freire and Giroux focused instead on possibilities for change by examining how social actors such as students and teachers can counter the constraints of the system and shape their own destiny. Today, educational approaches based on critical perspectives that aim at providing students and teachers with opportunities and tools for redressing social inequities are generally known as critical pedagogies.

As Norton and Toohey (2004) suggested, language educators who engage in critical pedagogies focus on language as a vehicle for pursuing equity. To emphasize the broad diversity of approaches that interrogate the relationship between power and second language education, they referred to critical pedagogies in the plural in their recent edited volume that examined how language researchers and teachers from different parts of the world engage in such practices.

Earlier, Pennycook proposed that within a critical stance:

> the view of language or of language learning cannot be an autonomous one that backs away from connecting language to broader political concerns ... and the focus on politics must be accountable to broader political and ethical visions that put inequality, oppression and compassion to the fore. (Pennycook, 1999: 334)

Pennycook further argued that critical approaches should not be seen as:

> a static body of knowledge and practices, but rather as always being in flux, always questioning, restively problematizing the given, being aware of the limits of their own knowing ... (Pennycook, 1999: 329)

In a similar vein, Goldstein (2003) and Heller (2003) developed approaches for language teaching in Toronto that drew attention to issues of equity and gave students greater control over the curriculum. Goldstein's critical ethnography explicitly aimed at challenging linguistic inequities in an English language secondary school serving a multilingual student population where there was a tendency to focus exclusively on English in teaching. Drawing on ethnographic data she had gathered, Goldstein wrote a play about language controversies at the school, had students engage in performing it and then making connections between the play and their own lives.

Likewise, Heller (2003) worked in collaboration with teachers in Francophone schools to combine aspects of the ethnography of communication with cooperative learning strategies and develop a series of classroom activities. These activities drew on ethnographic data she had gathered on students' language practices that revealed they had limited capacities to express themselves in French. They aimed at expanding students' verbal repertoires and changing their attitudes towards French by having them document and examine their own language practices outside of school. Moreover, Heller adopted a critical reflexive stance to consider the possibilities and limits of such teaching innovations for changing language education.

This body of literature points to a desire to move beyond ethnographic descriptions of inequities in language education to pedagogical action that enables students to question the status quo. Classroom activities based on critical perspectives encourage students to develop a greater awareness of their social context and consider how diverse language choices and practices are embedded in value systems and are related to power.

In the following section, I describe the context of language awareness activities we implemented in French immersion. Next, I adopt a critical lens to analyse the transformative potential of student–teacher discussions on language diversity. I conclude with a reflection on teaching materials, research approaches and researchers' stances that might better support children in developing a critical awareness of language diversity.

Language awareness in French immersion

During the 2003–2004 school year, our research team readapted and expanded on language awareness activities[1] so they could be implemented in an early total immersion grade 5–6 class in metropolitan Vancouver. While the school was situated in a middle class enclave and was attended by students who were predominantly of English language heritage, it was also part of a large suburban school district that served a highly diverse population with over 92 languages represented in the student body (Surrey School District, 2004, January, as cited in Walsh, 2005).

The class included 11 boys and 16 girls, between the ages of 10 and 12. Most students came from monolingual English-speaking families and had been in the French immersion program since kindergarten. Five students spoke a language other than English at home. One girl, Lorraine, who was born in Quebec, spoke French with her family. Another girl, Louisa, was born in Taiwan and spoke only Mandarin with her mother. Maria, whose father was Swedish and mother British, spoke both English and Swedish at home. One boy, Vacya, spoke Russian and English at home and another boy, Chun, spoke a combination of Korean and English with his family.

The classroom teacher incorporated the language awareness activities in French language arts lessons on a weekly or bi-weekly basis. She designed her lessons in response to the interests, needs and abilities of her immersion students and she took into account the expected learning outcomes of the official curriculum for the province of British Columbia. The teacher had learned about language awareness activities a year earlier when she began a graduate program at the local university and volunteered to participate in a teacher-researcher group that explored how issues of identity and inclusion could be addressed in teaching.[2] Aiming to draw students' attention to language diversity in their immediate community and larger environment, she organized activities in which they observed patterns across a range of languages. Students explored topics such as greetings in 17 languages, families of languages, borrowings between languages, the origins of local and national name places, the evolution of writing across the ages, diverse scripts, fairy tales and proverbs across cultures, the construction of negation in various languages and sign languages.

Our research team documented the implementation process and student perceptions through classroom observations, videotaping, a student questionnaire, and two series of open-ended group interviews with focal children in the Fall and Spring terms. Of the 22 lessons in which language awareness activities were implemented, 10 were videotaped. A member of the Vancouver research team recorded observations in fieldnotes during 8 lessons, a researcher from the Montreal team recorded observations during 2 other lessons and the classroom teacher kept retrospective fieldnotes that she recorded after each lesson. All relevant lesson plans, curriculum documents and student work were gathered as well.

The questionnaire was an adaptation of an instrument designed by Harter (1998, as cited in Maraillet, 2005) and aimed at obtaining information on their representations of diverse languages, language speakers and language learning. It was administered in French to all students who were asked to indicate their responses to opposing statements such as: 'Children think that they could become friends with someone who does not speak the same language as them' and 'children think that they could not become friends with someone who does not speak the same language as them.'

The semi-structured group interviews were audiotaped and conducted in English. Eight students were selected to participate in the first round of interviews. One interview group was composed of all four students who spoke another language than English or French at home. Another group was composed of students who spoke only English at home and they were selected randomly from among the remaining students in the class. The interview questions aimed at having students talk about different languages, language speakers, bilingualism and multilingualism. These same eight students participated in a second round of interviews in the spring in which students were asked to talk further about these same issues and expand on responses given in the earlier interviews and the questionnaire.

Fieldnotes, audiotapes and videotapes were transcribed throughout the fieldwork phase of the project. As they were gathered, the data were discussed by the research team and these discussions oriented further data collection and implementation activities in the project. Once transcription of all data was completed, the transcripts and all relevant classroom documents were read over by the research team as part of an analysis process LeCompte and Preissle (1993) refer to as scanning. A software package (N6, 2002)[3] was then used to categorize qualitative data and identify emerging themes.

Findings and Discussion

Multilingual students as informants about language diversity

When we adopted a critical lens to closely analyze the data we gathered over the school year, we were able to confirm our initial interpretations that language awareness activities had potential to transform inequities insofar as they allowed some multilingual students to take up identities as language experts. For example, in a series of lessons that focused on the evolution of the alphabet, students read accounts of the historical development of writing. Typically, the teacher opened by engaging the whole class in a discussion through open-ended and closed questions about their observations of similarities and differences in the script of various languages. A detailed discussion of interactions in these language awareness activities is provided in Walsh (2005). In the following excerpt of a videotape transcript, the spontaneous participation of two students, the boy of Russian origin and the girl whose mother is Swedish, aptly illustrates how class discussions in language awareness activities provided a forum for multilingual children to share what they knew about their family languages:

Excerpt 1

Vacya: There are many languages, many different languages in the world whose alphabet is not always a, b, c, d... because in Russian, it's a, b, d, g... .

Teacher: So it changes. Are the letters the same? Are they the same as ours?

Vacya: Euh, no.

Teacher: Not all, eh? We will be looking at that next week. We will look at the Russian alphabet. I have a copy of the Russian alphabet. We'll be able to show our friends how it is different. Yes?...

Maria: The Swedish alphabet is like the same, but it has five other letters added. (Videotape transcript, lesson on the invention of the alphabet, February 23, 2004)

This transcript reveals that when the focus of instruction expanded beyond French and English, the target languages of this immersion program, multilingual children became key informants in the class discussions. They volunteered information about their family languages that was new to their peers and demonstrated that they had insight into language diversity. Their knowledge about their family languages was no longer marginalized and instead became central to informing their peers and their teacher about similarities and differences in languages. As their language repertoires were valued and recognized by the teacher, multilingual students began to reposition themselves and were repositioned by others as being knowledgeable and rich in language resources. (See Palmer, Chapter 5, for discussion of additional strategies immersion teachers can use to reposition language and status inequities in the classroom.)

The topics of teacher-led discussions in language awareness activities focused on subjects that enabled multilingual students to draw on their personal knowledge and adopt an expert role in the joint construction of knowledge, thereby gaining access to a desirable identity position. These discussions allowed the teacher to introduce subjects that legitimized what some students knew while challenging all to think in new ways about who had expertise in the classroom community.

Nevertheless, in this type of exchange, all students might not necessarily act on the opportunity to express a desired identity as expert, as did the two students in the transcript above. A discussion with the whole class in which the teacher directs turn taking and topic changes might constrain some students who would prefer not to speak their mind in a public forum. Elsewhere (Dagenais *et al.*, 2006), we reported on how a multilingual immersion student was identified by some of her teachers as at-risk because she was reluctant to engage in such large group structures and yet took up a different identity in small groups and pair activities where she readily shared her knowledge of her family language and practices.

The need for a critical perspective

As our research team pursued a critical analysis of the data from language awareness activities, we turned our gaze from the videotapes of classroom interactions back to earlier transcripts of interviews with the students conducted during the fall term. During the open-ended group interviews, students openly expressed stereotypes about speakers of diverse languages. The teacher's role in the interviews was to elicit students' responses to a few questions and allow them to express themselves freely, so she limited her own interventions to encourage them to talk more. As indicated in the next two interview excerpts, some powerful stereotypes emerged in the students' discourse.

Excerpt 2

Student 1: Yeah, I went around houses and I sold cookie dough for my gymnastics, and there's a whole bunch of different, like, euh, different people that were like different, euh, like from

different religions and stuff. But they're mostly all white,
like, but there were some Chinese and some East Indians.

Student 2: Yellow people.

Teacher: Sorry?

Student 2: Yellow people. That's what they call the Chinese...

Student 1: Bananas!

Student 2: Yellow.

Teacher: Really? (Group interview transcript, October 23, 2003)

In this excerpt, the first student struggled to describe racial, ethnic and religious diversity in his community. The second student interjected with a physical characterization that is associated with racial slurs and the first student responded to this with another derogatory name used to refer to people of Asian ancestry living in Vancouver.

In the next excerpt, the teacher asked students whether there were languages they would not like to learn.

Excerpt 3

Teacher: Have you got any idea about languages that you would not like to learn? ...

Student 1: How about, I don't know what it's called but the one that Saddam Hussein knows. I don't like that one.

Teacher: Why don't you like it?

Student 1: I don't know. Just like, I don't know! I just don't like it!

Teacher: Ok.

Student 1: It's, it's like pretty, euh, I think it's hard to learn. Just like.

Teacher: Where have you heard that language?

Student 1: On the news.

Teacher: Do you know what it's called?

Student 1: No. Urakanese?!

Teacher: Ok. So you've heard it on the news. Have you seen it written anywhere?

Student 1: Nn, no.

Teacher: So just from hearing it on the news, you think that it's hard to learn. So this is the reason why you wouldn't want to learn it?

Student 2: Some languages are very hard to learn. (Group Interview Transcript, October 23, 2003)

As the interview date indicates, this excerpt was recorded after the war in Iraq had begun. In response to the teacher's question, a first student expressed a negative view of Arabic and associated the language with

Saddam Hussein, adding that he thought it would be a hard language to learn. With some probing by the teacher, it was revealed that his representation of this language was based on viewing media reports about the war. Focused discussions related to these specific stereotypes did not resurface during the school year, but in her research, Walsh (2005) examined changes in these students' representations of other languages, language speakers and language learning. Her analysis of interviews conducted in the fall and spring terms of the school year revealed that some students had learned to provide more nuanced descriptions and use specific, non-discriminatory terms to talk about language speakers, the status of languages, bilingualism, language competence and Asian scripts.

It was only during the final phase of analysis that the Vancouver team became aware that in our focus on adapting language awareness materials that already existed elsewhere, we had not considered using these - transcripts of early interviews with the children as contemporary, contextualized pedagogical resources. In retrospect, we began to see the transformative potential of having students analyse these transcripts themselves to stimulate a critical reflection on stereotypes that circulate among them, in the local community and in the media at large. However, we were not able to follow up by having students engage in such an analysis because we had not obtained prior ethical consent to use the interview transcripts as teaching materials in the immersion classroom, though we did receive consent to use them as teaching resources at the university.

In activities situated explicitly in critical perspectives, students and teachers typically question and challenge social inequities, including the unequal distribution of power between students and teacher, and the inequitable exchanges in linguistically diverse classrooms, as in the study described by Palmer in Chapter 5. Moreover, students tend to engage in Freirean-inspired problem-posing and student-led projects aimed at fostering equity. In language awareness activities based on an implicit critical stance, students of diverse language origins may be repositioned as knowledgeable partners and discussions may allow for the emergence of stereotypes of languages, language speakers and language learning. Yet, as Fairclough (1992) has suggested, the transformative potential of such language awareness activities is limited unless they adopt an explicit critical stance and make issues of equity central to classroom initiatives.

According to Pennycook (1999: 340), critical pedagogies view 'such issues as gender, race, class, sexuality and postcolonialism as so fundamental to identity and language that they need to form the basis of curriculum organization and pedagogy.' This assumes that by critically examining their own discourses, those of others and the media, students may begin to recognize how they are situated in contexts of power and domination. Yet, change in students' stereotypes is not necessarily guaranteed by such activities. After having a group of Swiss students engage in language awareness that focused on examining their own stereotypes about the German language and learning German, Muller and De Pietro (2001) found that some negative representations were reinforced through group discussion rather than eliminated. They concluded that changing stereotypes is a long-term process that may not be achievable in short-term pedagogical interventions.

Avenues for further work

This first attempt at implementing language awareness activities in an immersion class has provided some useful insights for further study that my colleagues and I are considering in our ongoing longitudinal work in Vancouver and Montreal. First, a critical analysis of stereotypes might be included usefully in language awareness activities by having students examine how racism is reproduced through the use of names that hurt in their own conversations and in the media's negative portrayals of speakers of certain languages such as Arabic. To engage in such an analysis, teachers could tactfully use, with prior permission, excerpts from audiotaped classroom discussions and from the local media as contemporary, highly contextualized resources. In order to pursue this avenue, it would be essential first to establish a trusting dialogic relationship between teacher and students and create a safe environment in which all students are able to express themselves without feeling targeted.

Second, a critical stance may be developed among students by having them attend to the status of diverse languages in the local linguistic landscape to consider which languages are given importance and which ones are marginalized or absent. For example, in a context such as metropolitan Vancouver where a number of Aboriginal communities live, students might consider what place Aboriginal languages are accorded in public space. In fact, students may not only examine data about the linguistic landscape gathered by researchers, but could be encouraged to undertake their own mini-ethnographies as they circulate in the metropolis in order to document the role diverse languages occupy in their communities and examine the relationship between language and power in their own lives and the lives of people they live near.

Finally, language awareness activities might include more open-ended multi-modal literacy projects with objectives and methods defined by the students themselves as they identify equity issues that need to be addressed in their communities. As Norton and Toohey (2004: 12) suggest, providing students with increased curricular control 'is seen not only as a way to respectfully recognize students' backgrounds, but also as a way to ensure that critical language instruction has relevance to the issues and problems students face in their daily lives.' However, as they also observe, such initiatives sometimes have ambiguous results, which might make some teachers uneasy about moving beyond the usual paper and pencil tasks or teacher-led discussions.

Activities such as those described above may hold much promise because they have the potential to significantly move immersion pedagogy beyond developing competence in two languages to fostering 'critical bilingualism,' which Walsh (1991 as cited in Pennycook, 2001: 15) defined 'as the ability to not just speak two languages but to be conscious of the sociocultural, political, and ideological contexts in which the languages (and therefore the speakers) are positioned and function, and the multiple meanings that are fostered in each.'

Yet, there remain unresolved challenges in attempting to respond to calls for a more critical approach to language awareness activities specifically and language lessons generally. In teacher-researcher projects such as ours, there is a need to be sensitive to the scope and pace of change desired by teachers and to resist the temptation to impose researcher agendas in the classroom. As well, by having students critically examine their own texts in audiotape transcripts, teachers and researchers run the risk of appropriating child discourse and using it for their own ends. In his research on the use of rap and hip-hop among Francophone youth, Ibrahim (1999) signalled the danger of co-opting students' language for pedagogical purposes. Finally, as Pennycook (1999: 335) so aptly put it, 'how to reconcile degrees of freedom with degrees of constraint is one of the toughest conundrums in critical work.'

Acknowledgements

I am indebted to Linda Hof and Randy Rotheisler who videotaped the classroom interactions described in this chapter, and to my research assistants Marie-Josée Beaulieu, Elaine Day, Marianne Jacquet, Rumiana Ilieva, Linda Laplace, Shaheen Sharif, Noëlle Mathis and Nathalie Walsh who worked alongside me at different stages of this research program. This chapter expands on presentations given at several conferences, including, more recently, the 14th World Congress of *l'Association internationale de linguistique appliquée*, Madison, Wisconsin in July, 2005, the Canadian Association of Applied Linguistics Annual Conference, London, Ontario in May 2005 and the 2nd International Conference on Immersion Education held by CARLA (Center for Advanced Research on Language Acquisition) at the University of Minnesota, Minneapolis, Minnesota in October, 2004. As well, I am grateful to the immersion students, their parents and teachers who warmly welcomed us into their homes and classrooms. This program of research was funded by the Social Sciences and Humanities Research Council of Canada through a standard grant (Dagenais: 1999–2002), a Metropolis grant from the Vancouver Centre of Excellence for Research on Immigration and Integration in the Metropolis (Dagenais: 2003–2005) and a grant from the Program on Questions of Multiculturalism in Canada (Armand, Dagenais: Jan–Dec 2004).

Notes

1. Numerous language awareness activities have been developed in French and other languages for classrooms in projects that group together researchers and teachers. They include the Evlang (*Éveil aux langues à l'école primaire*) project initiated in France under the direction of Candelier (2003a) and expanded to several other countries (website: http://www.jaling.ecml.at); the EOLE (*Éveil au langage et ouverture aux langues à l'école*) implemented in Switzerland under the leadership of Perregaux, de Goumoëns, Jeannot and de Pietro (2002) and the ELODiL (*Éveil aux langues et à la diversité linguistique)* project in which Françoise Armand and her team adapted activities from the above projects and created new ones for Montreal schools. The website for this latter project (http://www.elodil.com) provides examples of activities implemented in Montreal and Vancouver classrooms, a comprehensive bibliography and links to the above projects.

2. This teacher-researcher study, *Pedagogical Models for Inclusion & Equity in Diverse School Communities*, was funded by Social Sciences and Humanities Research Council of Canada through the Metropolis Project and the Vancouver Centre of Excellence for the Study of Immigration and Integration (Beynon, Bai, Cassidy, Dagenais, Toohey: April 2001–2004)

3 This software package for qualitative data analysis is a tool that enables researchers to manage, code and categorize text data in a flexible manner, allowing them to rapidly retrieve and view emerging patterns as they construct grounded theoretical interpretations. While this tool facilitated analysis for our team in many respects, it was also onerous as we had to find ways to move between PC and Macintosh computers, as well as French and English texts. Since N6 was not available for Macintosh, we had to install virtual PC and this slowed down the computers considerably. Further information on N6 can be found at http://www.qsrinternational.com/products/productoverview/N6.htm.

References

Apple, M. (1979) *Ideology and Curriculum.* London: Routledge.

Bélanger, J. (1996) Language awareness in the high school classroom. Paper given at the Shifting Strands Conference (NCTE) in Vancouver, British Columbia, April.

Bilash, O. and Tulasiewicz, W. (1995) Language awareness and its place in the Canadian curriculum. In K. McLeod and Z. De Koninck (eds) *Multicultural Education: The State of the Art. A National Study* (pp. 49–54). Ottawa, Ontario: Canadian Association of Second Language Teachers.

Billiez, J. (ed.) (1998) *De la didactique des langues à la didactique du plurilinguisme, hommage à Louise Dabène.* Grenoble: CDL Lidilem.

Billiez, J. (2000) Un bilinguisme minoré: Quel soutien institutionnel pour sa vitalité ? *Notions en Questions* 4, 21–40.

Bourdieu, P. (1977) The economics of linguistic exchanges. *Social Science Information* 16, 645–668.

Bourdieu, P. and Passeron, J.C. (1977) *Reproduction in Education, Society and Culture.* London: Sage.

Candelier, M. (ed.) (2003a) *L'Éveil aux langues à l'école primaire: Evlang. Bilan d'une innovation européenne.* Bruxelles: De Boeck-Duculot.

Candelier, M. (2003b) Le contexte politique: Un ensemble de principes et de finalités. In F. Heyworth (ed.) *Défis et ouvertures dans l'éducation aux langues: La contribution du Centre européen pour les langues vivantes 2000–2003* (pp. 19–32). Strasbourg: Centre Européen pour les Langues Vivantes/Conseil de l'Europe.

Castellotti, V. and Moore, D. (2002) *Représentations sociales des langues et enseignements. Étude de référence: Guide pour l'élaboration des politiques linguistiques éducatives en Europe. De la diversité linguistique à l'éducation plurilingue.* Strasbourg: Conseil de l'Europe.

Cenoz, J. (1998) Multilingual education in the Basque Country. In J. Cenoz and F. Genesee (eds) *Beyond Bilingualism: Multilingualism and Multilingual Education.* (pp. 175–191). Clevedon: Multilingual Matters.

Cenoz, J. and Genesee, F. (eds) (1998) *Beyond Bilingualism: Multilingualism and Multilingual Education.* Clevedon: Multilingual Matters.

Cenoz, J. and Gorter, D. (2006) Linguistic landscape and minority languages. *International Journal of Multilingualism* 3, 67–80.

Cenoz, J., de Bot, K., Gorter, D., Huebner, T., Shohamy, E. and Spolsky, B. (2004) Linguistic landscape and multilingualism: Theoretical and methodological issues. Colloquium presented at the American Association of Applied Linguistics Annual Conference, Portland, May 1–4.

Dabène, L. (1994) *Repères sociolinguistiques pour l'enseignement des langues.* Paris: Hachette.

Dagenais, D. (2003) Accessing imagined communities through multilingualism and immersion education. *Language, Identity and Education* 2 (4), 269–283.

Dagenais, D. (2005) Recognizing multilingual immersion students. *American Council on Immersion Education Newsletter* 8 (Spring) 4–5.

Dagenais, D. and Berron, C. (2001) Promoting multilingualism through French immersion and language maintenance in three immigrant families. *Language, Culture and Curriculum* 14 (2), 142–155.

Dagenais, D. and Day, E. (1998) Classroom language experiences of trilingual children in French immersion. *The Canadian Modern Language Review* 54, 376–393.

Dagenais, D. and Day, E. (1999) Home language practices of trilingual children in French immersion. *The Canadian Modern Language Review* 56, 99–123.

Dagenais, D. and Jacquet, M. (2001) Valorisation du multilinguisme et de l'éducation bilingue chez des familles immigrantes. *Journal of International Migration and Integration* 1, 389–404.

Dagenais, D., Day, E. and Toohey, K. (2006) A multilingual child's literacy practices and contrasting identities in the figured worlds of French Immersion classrooms. *International Journal of Bilingualism and Bilingual Education* 9, 1–14.

de Courcy, M.C. (2002) *Learners' Experiences of Immersion Education: Case Studies in French and Chinese*. Clevedon: Multilingual Matters.

de Pietro, J-F. (1998) Demain, enseigner l'éveil aux langues à l'école? In J. Billiez (ed.) *De la didactique des langues à la didactique du plurilinguisme, hommage à Louise Dabène* (pp. 323–334). Grenoble: CDL Lidilem.

Fairclough, N. (1992) *Critical Language Awareness*. New York: Longman.

Freire, P. (1970) *Pedagogy of the Oppressed*. New York: Continuum.

Giroux, H.A. (1983) Theories of reproduction and resistance in the new sociology of education: A critical analysis. *Harvard Educational Review* 53, 257–293.

Goldstein, T. (2003) *Teaching and Learning in a Multilingual School: Choices, Risks and Dilemmas*. Mahwah, NJ: Lawrence Erlbaum.

Green, J. and Wallat, C. (eds) (1981) *Ethnography and Language in Educational Settings*. Norwood, NJ: Ablex.

Harter, S. (1998) The development of self-representation. In W. Damon and N. Eisenberg (eds) *Handbook of Child Psychology, Vol. 3, Emotional and Personality Development* (pp. 553–618). New York: Wiley.

Hawkins, E. (1984) *Awareness of Language: An Introduction*. Cambridge: Cambridge University Press.

Hawkins, E. (1992) Awareness of language/knowledge about language in the curriculum in England and Wales: An historical note on twenty years of curricular debate. *Language Awareness* 1 (1), 5–17.

Heller, M. (2003) *Crosswords: Language, Education and Ethnicity in French Ontario*. Berlin: Mouton de Gruyter.

Hornberger, N. (ed.) (2003) *Continua of Biliteracy*. Clevedon: Multilingual Matters.

Hurd, M. (1993) Minority language children in French immersion: Additive multilingualism or subtractive semi-lingualism? *The Canadian Modern Language Review* 49, 514–525.

Ibrahim, A. (1999) Becoming Black: Rap and hip-hop, race, gender, identity and the politics of ESL learning. *TESOL Quarterly* 33, 349–371

Labercane, G., Griffith, B. and Feurerverger, G. (1997) Critical language awareness: Implications for classrooms in a Canadian context. Unpublished manuscript (1 17), University of Calgary.

Lamarre, P. (1997) Review of the literature on immigrant students and French immersion. Unpublished manuscript, Canadian Association of Immersion Teachers, Ottawa, Ontario.

Landry, R. and Bourhis, R.Y. (1997) Linguistic landscape and ethnolinguistic vitality: An empirical study. *Journal of Language and Social Psychology* 16, 23–49.

LeCompte, M. and Preissle, J. with Tesch, R. (1993) *Ethnography and Qualitative Design in Educational Research*. San Diego, CA: Academic Press.

Maraillet, E. (2005) Étude des représentations linguistiques d'élèves au 3ᵉ cycle du primaire, en milieu pluriethnique à Montréal, lors d'un projet d'éveil aux langues. Master's thesis, Université de Montréal.

Moore, D. (1995) Éduquer au langage pour mieux apprendre les langues. *Babylonia* 3 (2), 26–31.

Moore, D. (ed.) (2001) *Les représentations des langues et de leur apprentissage: Références, modèles, données et méthodes*. Essais. Paris: Didier.

Muller, N. and de Pietro, J-F. (2001) Que faire de la représentation? Que faire des représentations? Questions méthodologiques et didactiques à partir des travaux sur le rôle des représentations dans l'apprentissage d'une langue. In D. Moore (ed.) *Les représentations des langues et de leur apprentissage: Références, modèles données et méthodes* (pp. 51–64). Collection CRÉDIF Essais. Paris: Didier.

N6 (2002) Non-numerical unstructured data indexing searching & theorizing. Qualitative data analysis program (Version 6.0). Melbourne: QSR International.

Norton, B. and Toohey, K. (2004) *Critical Pedagogies and Language Learning*. Cambridge: Cambridge University Press.

Pennycook, A. (1999) Introduction: Critical approaches to TESOL. *TESOL Quarterly* 33, 329–348.

Pennycook, A. (2001) *Critical Applied Linguistics: A Critical Introduction*. Mahwah, NJ: Lawrence Erlbaum Associates.

Perregaux, C., de Goumoëns, C., Jeannot, D. and de Pietro, J-F. (eds) (2003) *Education et ouverture aux langues à l'école*. Neuchâtel: CIIP.

Rolstad, K. (1999) Effects of two-way immersion on the ethnic identification of third language students. *Bilingual Research Journal* 21 (1), 43–63.

Rowney, S. (1994) Language awareness through the use of literature in the classroom. *Language Awareness Newsletter* 1 (1), 2–3.

Sabatier, C. (2004) Rôle de l'Ecole dans la construction et le développement du plurilinguisme chez des enfants issus de la migration maghrébine en France. Nouveau Régime Doctoral Dissertation, Université Stendhal Grenoble 3.

Swain, M. and Johnson, R.K. (1997) Immersion education: A category within bilingual education. In R.K. Johnson and M. Swain (eds) *Immersion Education: International Perspectives* (pp. 1–16). Cambridge: Cambridge University Press.

Swain, M. and Lapkin, S. (1991) Heritage language children in an English/French bilingual program. *Canadian Modern Language Review* 47, 635–643.

Swain, M. and Lapkin, S. (2005) The evolving sociopolitical context of immersion education in Canada: Some implications for program development. *International Journal of Applied Linguistics* 15, 169–186.

Taylor, S. (1992) Victor: A case study of a Cantonese child in early French immersion. *Canadian Modern Language Review* 48, 736–759.

Walsh, N. (2005) Collaborer pour s'ouvrir aux autres: L'éveil aux langues dans une classe d'immersion française. Master's thesis, Simon Fraser University.

Chapter 11

Restoring Aboriginal Languages: Immersion and Intensive Language Program Models in Canada

MERLE RICHARDS and BARBARA BURNABY

Introduction

Canadian Aboriginal languages are all at risk of extinction; if they are lost here they are gone forever. That fact alone distinguishes the role of Aboriginal language education from the teaching of other languages. In the 2001 Canada Census, about one million people, or just over 3% of the Canadian population, identified themselves as of Aboriginal origin. Of their approximately 60 languages, only three have more than 10,000 mother tongue speakers – Cree (72,880), Ojibwe (21,000) and Inuktitut (29,005) (Statistics Canada, 2002). Most Canadian Aboriginal languages have fewer than 1000 speakers; some have already become extinct. In this chapter, we will sketch how Canadian Aboriginal peoples have used various models (school core subject, school immersion, adult immersion, language nests and summer camps) within formal and community education in their struggle to develop, maintain and revive their ancestral languages. Focus here is on indigenous immersion programs for adults.

History: Aboriginal Language Education Programs

By the 1970s, most Aboriginal children in southern Canada used English as their primary language, and communities were becoming alarmed at the decline of their languages and cultures (National Indian Brotherhood, 1972). In the 1970s, federal, provincial and band-controlled[1] schools slowly began to offer Aboriginal languages as a subject of instruction in so-called Native as a Second Language (NSL) programs (Ontario Ministry of Education, 1975). These were *core language programs*, i.e. where language is taught as a core curricular subject 20–40 minutes per day.

From the 1980s, some northern jurisdictions where children still learned the local Aboriginal language as their mother tongue (mainly the Northwest Territories, and the Cree and Inuit in northern Quebec) began to offer vernacular school programs in the primary grades, using the home language as the medium of instruction to ease the transition from the family environment to the English curriculum of the higher grades (e.g. Burnaby & MacKenzie, 2001). Elsewhere in Canada, Aboriginal language immersion programs for children who did not speak their ancestral language were being established, usually in kindergarten and the early primary grades.

Several studies provide an overall picture of the numbers and characteristics of Canadian Aboriginal language programs. In a survey by the Canadian Education Association of about 500 federal, band, and provincial schools (Kirkness & Bowman, 1992), questions about Aboriginal language programs yielded useful data:

(1) 35% of the 458 schools in the sample taught a First Nations (FN) language;
(2) more band and federal schools (87%) offer a FN language than public/ provincial schools (26.7%);
(3) a higher FN enrolment in the schools typically resulted in a greater number of FN language programs;
(4) over two-thirds of sampled schools began teaching a FN language prior to grade one, most (61%) no longer do so beyond grade 8;
(5) 29 of Canada's 54 FN languages are taught in the schools;
(6) only 4% of responding schools use the FN language as a medium of instruction in the primary grades, all but one of these being Inuktitut bilingual schools located in the Northwest Territories. These bilingual schools use the vernacular in the primary grades, gradually moving towards full English-language instruction by grade 5 or 6. Unlike the French one-way immersion schools in Canada, whose pupils are usually English speakers, these schools cater to pupils whose home language is Inuktitut or another Aboriginal language.

Discussing the findings of the survey, Kirkness and Bowman observe that few FN language offerings fully respond to the needs of the Aboriginal communities or are integrated into the school curriculum. The notable exception is the Inuktitut bilingual programs mentioned above. Although the sampling and return rate of this survey certainly resulted in some existing Aboriginal language programs not being represented, this material is the most complete of the general data we have on Aboriginal language programming.

The Assembly of First Nations (AFN) (1990) conducted a survey directed at a rationalized sample of bands rather than directly at schools.

However, valuable data on language programs in schools were obtained. In line with Kirkness and Bowman's findings that schools with a high percentage of First Nations students had much higher numbers of language programs, the AFN data show proportionately more Aboriginal language programming available to the respondents. Because the survey focused not on schooling but on Aboriginal language, broader questions were asked, for example, about community-based pre-school and adult programs and community attitudes to programs. Findings from this survey shed light on the nature of FN language programming as well as community member needs and concerns:

FN language programming

(1) Two-thirds of respondents offer FN language programs at the elementary level (often limited to grades 1–3), only 31% offer programs at the secondary and 19% in adult education programs.
(2) While programming at the pre-K and K–3 level is often either immersion (for native English speakers) or bilingual (for students with Aboriginal home languages), most FN language classes are taught for 20–30 minutes a day as core subject and offer more cultural awareness than language instruction.
(3) FN language programs are lacking in basic resources, and 30% of communities do not have a writing system or curriculum materials; assistance in these areas is specifically needed in adult education.
(4) Critical FN languages with fewer than 10 fluent speakers in the community have the fewest resources and only 1 in 5 operates a language program at all.

Community member needs and concerns

(1) Community members stressed the need to have FN language taught from nursery to grade 12.
(2) Community members believed FN language education should hold similar curricular standing as Core French and that Native children should be able to enrol in Native language classes in lieu of French.
(3) Common community concerns included school-based teaching of FN language as not in keeping with traditional ways of learning through participation, FN language learning as school-based language-as-subject learning only, the importance of elder participation in passing on the legacy of culture and language, and that the teaching of language not be separate from the teaching of cultural ways and Native spirituality.

Importantly, the AFN report states that the current aim of Aboriginal language education, even when used as a medium of instruction, is transition to the official language, not maintenance of the FN language. In this way these programs parallel the transitional bilingual programs briefly described by Genesee in Chapter 2. The school system is not viewed as a means to language conservation. The report continues by calling for more programs in provincial schools, for resources such as instructors and curriculum materials, and for additional teacher recruitment and professional development opportunities. Funding for Aboriginal language programming is very unfavourably compared with the much greater amounts available for French. One further finding of the survey concerns a question about where the Aboriginal language was used in the community. Of all the locations noted by respondents, the school was the place where the Aboriginal language was used *the least*, even in communities that had flourishing Aboriginal languages. The report rather pessimistically concludes that the relative non-use of FN languages in the communities effectively negates efforts of language personnel' (Assembly of First Nations, 1990: 37).

A recent study (Burnaby, 2002) of provincial governments' policies and programs on Aboriginal languages and cultures found that only the largest Canadian provinces had detailed policies regarding Aboriginal programming and that all provinces generally had very little data on how these were being implemented, especially in urban areas. Only those where the Department of Indian Affairs was paying the costs seem to have been identifiable in most cases. The availability of suitable teachers for Aboriginal language programs was mentioned as a major obstacle to the implementation of language programs; support for pre-service and in-service training of such teachers was noted as minimal or non-existent in many cases.

In sum, Aboriginal language programming in schools is substantial but is haphazard in its distribution, quality and available resources. It is highly concentrated in the early grades and, for those children who speak an Aboriginal language as a mother tongue, it is seen as a transitional program to the standard English-medium school curriculum. For those children who are not mother-tongue speakers of the traditional language, the programs have been criticized as ineffectual in language development. Acting on these concerns, many communities where the children do not speak the traditional languages have, since the time of the Kirkness and Bowman (1992) and the AFN studies, implemented Aboriginal language immersion programs aimed at developing real fluency.

Aboriginal Language Immersion Programs for Schoolchildren

Aboriginal languages in Canada have continued to decline rapidly, with few children learning their ancestral language at home. Aboriginal communities seeking to revitalize their languages have therefore looked to stronger solutions than core language programs. In the late 1960s, taking a cue from the growing popularity of French immersion programs in the general Anglophone population, an Ojibwe immersion program was attempted at West Bay, Ontario (Wasacase, n.d.), but it encountered concern about the overall impact on the children's education and closed after one year. In the early 1980s, an immersion program in Mohawk was initiated at Kahnawake, Quebec, and soon after, immersion programs in Mohawk and Cayuga began at Six Nations, Ontario. Following the success and persistence of these groundbreaking programs, immersion programs for English-speaking schoolchildren with indigenous roots have extended greatly across the continent. However, most of these are confined to the early grades, with the result that children seldom achieve functional levels of proficiency in the Native language. This is in contrast to reports on many Maori and Hawaiian immersion programs, which aim toward additive bilingualism and often exceed the percentage of time devoted to the minority language that is typically found in immersion programs, as explained in Chapter 1. To our knowledge, there has been no broad survey of Aboriginal language immersion programs in Canada or the US, although several reports have been written on particular immersion programs (e.g. Boyer, 2000; Kipp, 2004; Norris-Tull, 2000; Richards & Kanatawakhon Maracle, 2005; Williams *et al.*, 1996).

The *Common Curriculum Framework for Aboriginal Language and Culture Programs: Kindergarten to Grade 12*, a curriculum resource document by the Western Canadian Protocol for Collaboration in Basic Education (2000), includes Aboriginal second language teaching in both core language and immersion settings. This framework has been subscribed to by all the western Canadian provinces and the three territories.

The Task Force on Aboriginal Languages and Cultures (TFALC, 2005) puts a strong emphasis on immersion programs for Aboriginal peoples of all ages, especially youth, as a means of revitalizing Aboriginal languages and as one approach to healing. In part, it states:

> It is our view that immersion language education can play an important role in language revitalization. Immersion programs should be available outside of schools as well and include summer programs for youth and short-term programs for family groups, particularly young families of parenting age. We are particularly conscious of the importance of

involving youth in their languages and culture. In the consultations, we heard many express grave concern that too many of our youth have lost their way, becoming involved in substance abuse, violence and gangs or, sadly, committing suicide. We have also heard how First Nation, Inuit and Métis youth benefit from the guidance and moral grounding that their language and culture can provide. Certainly, the many studies we refer to earlier confirm the intellectual and academic benefits of learning a second language. We believe it important that our youth be given the opportunity to learn their languages in the same way as youth who speak official minority languages [i.e. French/English spoken in parts of the country where English/French is the majority language of communication]. (TFALC, 2005: 88)[2]

At present, although schools offer Aboriginal language programming, most instruction is core language only and mainly for elementary-aged children. Hence, these patterns reinforce Churchill's (1986) findings for Organization for Economic Co-operation and Development countries. He states that policies for indigenous groups are largely at the lower levels of policy development since most are for the youngest children, only for a few years, inadequately funded, and basically transitional to the official language education of their respective countries.

Issues in Aboriginal Immersion Programs for Schoolchildren

The resurgence of attention to indigenous cultural identity and the view that traditional languages are essential to cultural identity have led many Aboriginal parents to desire strong language programs for their children. In regions where the Native languages are spoken at home, this has led to successful implementation of vernacular medium curricula. In areas where families speak English at home, parents may choose immersion as a way of initiating their children into the ancestral language and culture when they themselves cannot do so. The following are some of the issues that arise.

Aboriginal parents' concerns about educational priorities

Even where Aboriginal immersion programs for children and adolescents have existed since the early 1980s, few have flourished. Enrolments have been low (Kaweienon:ni Cook-Peters, 2005) because, although parents may want their children to learn their ancestral language, they often fear that lack of instruction in English will deprive the children of life chances or a basis for further formal education. Even in exceptional circumstances, as in Kahnawake (discussed below), with fluent teachers and a well-prepared curriculum, most families continued to choose the regular English-language program with core Mohawk instruction.

The fluency/teacher development dilemma for immersion teachers

Aboriginal immersion programs must depend on the presence of fluent speakers who may not be trained teachers and who are not familiar with the grammatical structures of the language; they are therefore seldom prepared to develop lessons that will guide students into successful language learning. During year-end evaluations of an adult immersion program at Six Nations (Richards & Kanatawakhon Maracle, 2003), participants recounted their experiences as language learners. One learner expressed the frustration of years of school language programs thus:

> My grandparents spoke it and different people around the community. In school, it never really worked up until the course I'm taking now... Our teachers in the past – they were fluent speakers, right, and that was their first language, but they didn't know how to take it all apart and show how it all goes back together.... They were teaching it word by word, and that works a little bit but not like how it is here. I learned more here in a week than I did at public school to high school, because they show you how it all works: like pronouns, suffixes – all the little things that make a sentence. (Richards & Kanatawakhon Maracle, 2003: 11)

An exception was the Mohawk immersion program at Kahnawake, where five trained teachers who knew the language, led by Kariwenhawe Dorothy Lazore, spent a year preparing a program and preparing themselves to teach it. They carefully studied aspects of the formal usages still known among the elders, for example, using full pronunciations instead of the elisions and contractions of ordinary 'kitchen' Mohawk (Kariwenhawe, personal communication, 1995). When the school was opened, a curriculum and many resources were in place.

Unlike Kahnawake, few southern Canadian communities have been fortunate enough to have trained teachers sufficiently fluent to teach even in core language programs, let alone in immersion. When immersion programs in Mohawk and Cayuga began at Six Nations, for example, around 1987, fluent speakers were recruited to teach in the system. Most were in their 40s or 50s; a few were teachers of core language classes who had taken summer courses in indigenous grammar, but with no training in immersion teaching strategies. Some opted to take a teacher education program offered on the reserve by Brock University, but many felt that the deliberate use of teaching strategies was an alien, mainstream concept. They preferred a *natural* approach to classroom language, using the language so that the children would learn it through experience. This worked adequately in the early years, but parents became concerned that the children were not learning the skills and knowledge they would need for success in high school. Several transferred their children out of immersion while others promoted an immersion high school, Gaweniyo, which, though small, has since graduated several cohorts of speakers (Key, 2005).

In many communities, fluent speakers are often those who remained living on a reserve rather than go away to seek an education; they may therefore not be familiar with the concepts of the school curriculum beyond the primary years. This is one reason why immersion programs are frequently limited to the pre-primary and primary grades. Most reserves have adopted at least parts of the provincial curricula but, without suitable training and curriculum resources in the language, fluent teachers lack the framework for addressing the provincial curriculum through the Native language. Where there are now too few young fluent speakers to become teachers, it becomes necessary to select excellent teachers or potential teachers and enable them to learn their languages to a high degree of proficiency.

The dialect issue

Another problem with Aboriginal school immersion programs is the issue of dialect. When French immersion programs were first introduced, parents debated whether *French French* or *Canadian French* should be taught. However, another overriding concern was to engage good teachers familiar with the local curriculum and school traditions. Teachers were therefore hired from many parts of Canada and abroad; now many French immersion teachers are themselves graduates of such programs, unconcerned about dialect variations. In First Nations communities, however, dialect is an important aspect of identity, and parents are concerned that their children may not learn *our ways*. This has added to the difficulty of finding fluent speakers to become teachers, because language teachers cannot easily move to other communities. Residents of isolated reserves are no longer accustomed to hearing many varieties of their language and may criticize teachers who do not speak as their grandparents did. This criticism may be strongest among parents who are not themselves fluent, but who grew up hearing the language spoken. Shaw addresses the challenge of dialect diversity within FN language revitalization programs:

A major motivation for language retention and revitalization is the deep-seated recognition that language is an integral part of identity. However, one's unique identity is intimately defined by one's own local dialect. Therefore, to teach a different dialect, a recognized marker of *another* group's distinctive identity, is fundamentally at odds with the vital affirmation of one's own identity that language constitutes. (Shaw, 2001: 51)

Community values for the Aboriginal language

A somewhat different situation has prevailed at Ahkwesahsne, a Mohawk reserve that still has a large number of fluent speakers, including several qualified elementary teachers. This reserve, situated on the US–Canadian border with territory in New York, Quebec and Ontario, sends students to high schools off-reserve, and is sensitive to the fluctuating politics of language education. Here the community, expressing strong values of Native language and culture, has favoured elementary school immersion programs, but thus far, enrolment has remained small and the Council has only recently begun to provide adequate resources to encourage program expansion. Kaweienon:ni Cook-Peters views both low enrolments and scarce resources as signs of 'community resistance to the Native language' (Kaweienon:ni Cook-Peters & Richards, 2005: 2).

This apparent contradiction between expressed values and actual choices is consistent with the explanation offered by Edwards (1985). He points out that once a language becomes endangered, there may be strong emotional support for it as a symbol of cultural identity but little effort to retain it as an active mode of communication. As long as there are still people who can use the language, it retains its symbolic value. Ignace (1998: 2) comments that *'attitudes operate at a different level than actual use of a language, and positive attitude alone does not translate into speaking the language'* [italics added].

Burnaby and MacKenzie (2001) comment on the length of time required (a whole generation) before the Cree community at Chisasibi adopted a proposal to use Cree as the language of instruction in elementary school. Although first discussed in the 1970s, the program began only in 1993. By this time, children in many families were using English at home and at play, arriving at school with weak Cree language skills. For the first time, partly because of the arrival of television and other media, and partly because of an influx of families from outside the community, parents could no longer expect Cree language to continue to develop through constant use outside of school:

Therefore people in Chisasibi strongly lobbied the Cree School Board to institute a school programme using Cree as the language of instruction, at least for the first few grades. It is interesting to note that it was on account of opposition to such a program from that same community that the Tanner survey was commissioned in 1980 by the School Board, and that the policy to use Cree as the medium of instruction in kindergarten and pre-kindergarten was abandoned. (A. Tanner, cited in Burnaby & MacKenzie, 2001: 200)

At Ahkwesahsne, very few children now grow up with the ancestral language, although a few families are making an effort to use Mohawk as the language of the home. Both traditional and Christian adults use the language in connection with religious and cultural events, but the community depends on its elders to perform on their behalf. Kaweienon:ni Cook-Peters notes that language survival in the community now depends on education and prompt action to prevent further erosion. She states that the language will survive:

If, and only if, we as community members ... parents and grandparents, and any people who are in positions [of influence] make decisions that will affect the future Seven Generations of speakers. The people who are in positions to make these ... decisions are anyone who works in education, sits on school boards, chiefs of elected councils, the traditional council and even the cultural centers.

Language has to be put on the agenda items as a topic of priority. It has to be implemented into the Early Years Programs such as the development of family centers (language nests), daycare centers and head start programs, in school immersion programs from pre-K to high school, and even into the post secondary programs. Our goal has to be clear and that is to develop programs whose end goals are fluency. If our community does not replenish the speakers at a young age, it will surely cease to exist by the year 2045 and it will not be the result of residential schools, but at the hands of our own community members and the decisions they make.

I, as a fluent speaker, and others who do not have the language have made a commitment to have our language survive so we push for the implementation of immersion programs and we make conscious [efforts] to learn and to teach language as best as we can, usually without the full support of the education system or the councils on both sides of the [imaginary] border. What it comes down to is ... how important is our language? If we 'say' it is important, what actions are we willing to take to support our words? Anyone can say, 'Yes, I support language' but the low numbers within our immersion programs show that people are afraid to fully support it. Many are still afraid that if their children aren't exposed to English literacy they won't succeed academically. As one of many immersion parents, I disagree. *Yes, we need to support our kids in immersion programs, but that goes for all parents across the board. All students should have parental and educational support no matter what the language and that isn't always the case* [italics added]. Many of our children still suffer from the effects of the education system in various ways and not only the students who are enroled in the immersion programs. *I emphasize the loss of language in Ahkwesahsne* [italics added] because we seem to be complacent and comfortable with the fact that we have the highest number of speakers. *However, like I wrote previously, if we don't make serious efforts to replenish speakers at the early years level it won't matter.* [italics added]. We even have to look at language from the concept of 'Cradle to Grave' and not just from the educational concept, because we still need people to learn the various birthing and naming speeches and the speeches needed upon one's passing into the spiritual world.

This is not a scare tactic, or a theory, but a reality for the survival of the Mohawk Language in Ahkwesahsne. It's up to us as an Ahkwesahsne community...it takes a village to raise a child; it will also take a village to raise our language level.

Nia:wen tsi wesewawennahno:ten. [Thank you for listening to these words.] (Kaweienon:ni Cook-Peters, 2005: 1)

Aboriginal immersion programs meet all the same challenges as other immersion programs. See, for example, Chapters 2, 3 and 4 of this volume for further discussion of challenges in immersion programs. However, the endangered status of the Aboriginal languages adds other unique dimensions, particularly the scarcity of appropriate fluent speakers to become teachers and the level of passion in the community about the outcomes. Also, the fact that most of these languages had small populations of speakers even when they were flourishing isolates each group in a number of ways from collaborating with each other.

Aboriginal Language Immersion for Adults

Rationale for and interest in language restoration through adult immersion

When Native elementary immersion programs were begun, parents hoped that their children would become fluent enough to use the language in everyday life and re-establish it as a principal language of the community. But after 20 years of school immersion programs, Native languages are rarely used even by those who have participated in these school programs. This is because too few students remain in such programs after the primary grades to become agents of community change, and also because the students have seldom gained the depth of language required for adult conversation or serious discussion; they consequently revert to English after exchanging initial greetings. Adult immersion is therefore designed to enable adults to speak the language, because it would appear from experience that only adults can truly assume responsibility for transmitting the language and keeping it alive (Richards & Kanatawakhon Maracle, 2002a).

The situation described by Kaweienon:ni may persist until the language has too few speakers to survive without deliberate efforts to revitalize and restore it as a means of communication. This has now happened in a number of Native communities all over the country, where almost no children learn the language at home and the few speakers who are left are past retirement age. For example, Tyendinaga, a reserve in Ontario with about 2600 residents, has lost the last people who spoke Mohawk as their only language in childhood. A handful of fluent bilingual speakers remain (some say only four). At this stage, there are no young speakers able to pass the language on to their children and few middle-aged speakers to act as teachers. Young adults have suddenly realized that the prediction they have heard from childhood – that soon no one will remember the language – will occur within their lifetime. This has led them to view adult immersion as a necessity if there are to be parents and teachers who can pass the language on to the next generation. One adult immersion student said:

> Because we have to bring our language back so everybody's got to learn. There is nobody who shouldn't speak Mohawk as far as I'm concerned. Everybody on the reserve should speak Mohawk and if they can't, then somebody's got to teach them. (Richards & Kanatawakhon Maracle, 2003: 4)

The purpose of adult immersion programs, then, is to build a cadre of speakers who can teach others, lead ceremonies and rituals, and begin to restore the language as a mode of communication in the community (Owennatekha, personal communication, 1999). Since 1996, when the first Mohawk adult immersion program began at Wahta, Ontario, this need for language restoration has been the chief motivation for adult immersion programs. Learners have a sense of mission: they know they stand between the language and its extinction (Richards & Kanatawakhon Maracle, 2002b). During year-end evaluations of the Six Nations adult immersion program (Richards & Kanatawakhon Maracle, 2003), a learner stated simply:

> I am determined that our language is not going to be extinct... We have to do this or language will disappear, because these guys here in this little school are not going to re-build language for the whole Mohawk nation;

it's too small. We need a whole bunch of little schools. (Richards & Kanatawakhon Maracle, 2003: 4)

Unlike foreign language immersion programs (showcased in this volume in Chapters 6, 7, 8, 10 and 12), which seek to enrich students through introduction to another culture, adult Aboriginal immersion programs are not intended simply for personal development or enrichment. Native immersion is committed to the transformational experience of finding one's place in one's own culture (Reyhner, 2005). For the Six Nations learners, this is a life-changing event. A middle-aged participant waxed eloquent:

> The power behind this program is that through those teachers you are beginning to see the world in a different world view and a different context, different philosophy – a whole different knowledge base that describes the world in a very unique way, and when you can begin to understand how beautiful that is, the description of those things will be the same way that our ancestors described them. To me, that made it so powerful and so beautiful because I'm seeing the world for the first time like my ancestors saw the world, and they open that world to me through my language.

> It helps me to understand what's going on in the world because I see the world through a whole different set of eyes. That's really powerful for me; I never had that before, I'd never seen how beautiful that was before, and to really see it and to feel it and to say it and to participate in it and understand it – oh, it's beautiful! (Richards & Kanatawkhon Maracle, 2003: 4)

Often the adult learners are people with young children for whom they wish to exemplify language learning and use; some have children in immersion programs or Native as a Second Language programs whose learning they support by trying to use the language at home. Older learners also enter immersion programs, hoping to fill a long-felt gap or void in their lives as Onkwehonwe (Native People) but also to honour the ancient role of grandparent as teacher and mentor.

Adult immersion and intensive language program models

Two important language program models in North America have evolved that enable adult learners to develop the language skills necessary for effective teaching. What these intensive language programs share is regular, sustained exposure to the language, with concentration on oral language skills and literacy as a support for language learning. One is the Master–Apprentice Program, which pairs a fluent speaker and a young learner who spend a great deal of time together using the Aboriginal language (Hinton, 2002); this might be considered an individualized intensive language program. More common, however, is the group immersion program, where several learners receive planned daily lessons in the language.

Adult immersion models for groups of learners have been delivered in a number of communities. An excellent example is the Mohawk immersion program that has been offered at Six Nations since 1999 and recently at Tyendinaga. This program, which will be described in a subsequent section, demands an extensive time commitment, with all-day classes five days a week from September until June. Many or most of the learners become near-fluent by the end of a school year. The year-long course has been followed up by weekly meetings for language use and a refresher course a year later. With this kind of time commitment, and with regular, ongoing use of the language, expectations for language retention and further growth are high.

Other types of intensive language programs have been developed in various places. For example, summer camps or schools provide an intensive language experience, although on a short-term basis. University courses with intensive exposure several times a week to the language for three or four years have also succeeded in creating near-fluent speakers. All such programs are valuable, although the intensive 10-month immersion program is likely the most successful way of taking essentially non-speakers and making them into speakers (Rice & Richards, 2002).

First case: Mohawk adult immersion program in Wahta, Ontario

The first Mohawk immersion program for adults took place at Wahta, Ontario, in 1996. The Mohawk adult immersion program established at Wahta was intended to develop language proficiency in at least six adults who would continue on to teacher certification programs. Following the example of English as a second language (ESL) classes, the instructors adopted communicative language methods, whereby the functional use of language in conjunction with daily experiences would lead to gradual language acquisition.

Although communicative language programs can take many forms, they share certain basic characteristics. They are designed to develop oral fluency and comprehension. In the immersion class, this usually means using the second language to learn and talk about personal experiences or lesson content. Content-based instruction and methods such as small-group discussion and language experience are common.

The overriding goal is communicative competence, not just linguistic correctness; that is, learners are expected to acquire functional language by using it in meaningful and unrehearsed ways. Fluency and accuracy are also goals, but, at times, the focus on accuracy is deferred in order to encourage active participation by the learners. Both receptive and productive language skills are developed in a context of natural language use, where spontaneous, message-centred communications take precedence over learning of forms and rules.

The initiative was planned as a community-based full immersion program, with both informal social aspects (such as cooking and eating meals together), and more formal language lessons. Oral fluency was the prime goal, with literacy skills to support it. Because no ready-made program existed, the Mohawk language course had to be developed entirely within six months. This became the heart of the program; it was theme-based, using cultural topics as content.

As part of the year-end program evaluation, the students were interviewed individually about their immersion learning experience, comparing it to previous language courses they had taken. They were also asked about factors that had helped or hindered their language learning during the immersion program. Their comments showed that the program had succeeded in enabling the students to develop language skills surpassing the results of all previous kinds of language learning they had experienced, but most acknowledged that the biggest hindrances were the heavy information load and their continued use of English, even when the instructors were trying to get them to use Mohawk.

A major difficulty was that the class was large and extremely diverse in terms of prior learning. It was therefore difficult to apply the principles of the communicative approach. It had been expected that perhaps a dozen students would register in the program. Instead, 22 people enrolled, ranging widely in age, educational experience and previous language study. Their attitudes to learning were also very different. Ironically, the students with the greatest experience in language study found it most difficult to adapt to the communicative approach; several advanced students enrolled in the course believing that their prior knowledge would provide the basis for fluency, and that all they needed was oral input and practice. But although, or perhaps because, they had studied Mohawk before, it seemed they were still approaching it from the perspective of unilingual English speakers, with expectations of similar grammatical structures and vocabulary. However, Mohawk grammar differs greatly from English, and its vocabulary is constructed differently. Therefore, although translation is possible, one-to-one correspondences between English and Mohawk expressions are rare. The felt need to use English to analyse and explain every utterance kept the advanced learners from the real usage they sought. They failed to distinguish between linguistic correctness and communicative competence and hence remained at a pre-communicative stage of language development, learning about the language instead of learning to use it. In contrast, the less experienced learners appeared able to adapt to the experience, using the language as well as they could without worrying too much about mistakes or precise translations.

The Wahta program provided useful lessons for the immersion programs that followed. Some, like the Cayuga immersion program at Six Nations, have continued to use the communicative approach, but with small groups of students at similar levels of language study.

Students understand that language acquisition is very slow in the initial stages, but that subsequent learning can be rapid. Hence, they need not feel that time is being wasted during the initial period of apparently slow progress. We find Krashen's (1981) distinction between language learning and language acquisition to be helpful, especially for those who have already done extensive language learning in sequenced lessons. They need to suspend their usual expectations and study habits while beginning the acquisition process. This justifies the advice to use whatever language resources they can to communicate, even before full comprehension and correct speech are possible. It should also be explained that stages of acquisition are not dependent on sequenced presentation and that any rich language context provides material for acquisition; this reduces concerns that items are not being presented in a *proper* order. Moreover, although challenging and apparently slower to the learner, language learning that stresses comprehension and listening first may lead to better retention. Again, the investment of time in the early phases seems worthwhile, especially if the immersion learning can be sustained over several years.

Second case: Mohawk adult immersion at Six Nations and Tyendinaga in Ontario

The Mohawk programs currently operating at Tyendinaga and Six Nations have taken a different route. The first cohort resembled the Wahta learners in their continual insistence on English translations and explanations, and constant note-taking, with the result that less actual language use occurred than had been planned by the instructors. As a result, the program was modified to provide a sequenced introduction to the grammar, with explanations and notes in English, followed by intensive oral exercises to practice the structures in various contexts.

Another reason for this change is that, in the past, Native language instructors, even when they were excellent teachers, usually lacked the formal instruction in grammar that would enable them to predict learning difficulties or provide deep explanations of apparent anomalies that are common to language learning. The Mohawk instructors have therefore departed from the usual pattern of communicative language classes and moved to intensive instruction based on the morphological structures of the language. Once these are firmly understood, communicative methods and the use of Mohawk are increased. Each day begins with the Hotinohsonni (Iroquois) Opening Address and ends with the Closing; as the year progresses, the students take responsibility for the daily recitations. A segment of listening and conversation time takes place away from the classroom with its wall charts and visual props, so that the learners must listen carefully in order to participate. As in the Wahta program, year-end evaluations include student interviews; the students have given permission for their words to be used in this chapter. On the issue of listening, one student comments:

> [Listening is the hardest] because you can put things together in your head, but when you're listening, they're going along and so then you pick out a word to try and figure out what it is, and then they are way off again. It's hard to keep up with anything. (Richards & Kanatawkhon Maracle, 2003: 12)

By the end of the program, most exchanges are in Mohawk. The learners therefore acquire both proficiency and an understanding of the grammar together with the cultural content they will teach to others. They reach a level that enables them to continue their language development by working with fluent speakers, practising with their friends and families, participating in ceremonies and rituals, and also attending follow-up immersion programs.

The intensive, adult immersion program provides an environment where Mohawk learners first develop basic language skills and apply them in limited conversational situations, and later interact more naturally among themselves and with fluent speakers from the local community. The intent is to provide an understanding of the structures of the language that will prepare learners to continue their language development after completing the program in order to restore Mohawk as a vital language of the community. A student who had studied Mohawk from childhood without gaining fluency described the process thus:

> We start out in English and then they slowly build words and vocabulary and ideas and concepts and processes in the language learning so it locates you in English and it moves your thinking from English to

Kanienkehaka. And that's the hard part, that's the part that nobody had really done before, because for us as adult learners, we are thinking in English and we're trying to reconstruct our language into – reconstructing the way what we want to say into Mohawk but it's actually just Mohawk speaking English thoughts. And what we need to do then is to be able to use English as a locator to figure out where we're at and then move over to that Mohawk kind of world and way of looking at the world through the language. And they [the instructors] begin to throw that English out, so that we are actually thinking and speaking in Mohawk rather than thinking in English and speaking in Mohawk. That's a hard leap, that's a big leap, so you're not going to get that kind of thinking by tapes or books or CDs or whatever. You've got to actually be in the classroom with those guys: 'What's the meaning of that word?' and they can deconstruct that word right in front of you and say 'Oh, that's the root word,' and 'What does that word mean?' and from there you just continue to add on. And unless you have somebody that can do that, the difficulty is that most teachers will say, 'That's the word, it is how it is, that's the word for whatever it is' and you are stuck with that – well what's the word mean – 'Well, it means bicycle' and you are looking at these things with two wheels and what it does. You actually need someone that can go in there and break those words down and reconstruct the way our English mind is working to be able to do the mechanics of it. There's no other program I've ever seen that can do that. (Richards & Kanatawakhon Maracle, 2003: 15)

Instructional practices in Mohawk adult immersion

As mentioned earlier, in year-end evaluations, the Mohawk immersion participants are interviewed about their experiences. Most are extremely positive, although they reflect diverse learning styles and preferences for different instructional strategies. Certain strategies have been deemed essential by most students in every cohort. Again, a few student voices represent the larger group:

We practice putting sentences together. We've seen that a lot now ... because even if we practice the words and the grammar and stuff, that's the hardest part ... putting sentences together. (Student A, year-end interview, 2004)

What's also been really good – and I never really thought about how important this really was until we actually did it– was the field trip stuff that you can actually go out and use [Mohawk]. It's just a simple thing, like we would go to a restaurant and have lunch there, and ... when you actually go out and you can converse together and you can practice it in the setting, see different things outside and ask different questions and do different things. One of the most memorable times for me is when we went to the market – the very first field trip we had – we went to the market and we learned like a series of maybe a dozen things about how much is this, which one is bigger, which one's fresher, which one is more expensive, all these different ideas and things that we talked about, so we practised all of those things ...We got to do it in a real life setting sort of thing – exciting for me because I never had that before. All the language learning that I had before was just done in blackboard – *house, car, bicycle*: that was it. (Student B, year-end interview, 2004)

The learners also hold strong opinions on the necessity for prior knowledge of the Mohawk language, agreeing that the introduction emphasizing pronouns, roots and particles was useful because it allowed them to incorporate what Mohawk words or phrases they already knew into new utterances:

When I first got here I could say all the words and stuff, I just didn't know how to build sentences and sentence structure and grammar and things ... For someone to come in here and take this course they should have prior language experience with a little bit of vocabulary and some working knowledge..because if people have an idea about knowing about the language, when they get into an immersion program they are not going to be stunned – at least they'll have an understanding of how the thing works. (Student C, year-end interview, 2004)

Conclusion

Experiences and issues in Aboriginal language instruction and those in other languages have much in common, but the context of the Aboriginal languages gives them heavy pressures and challenges. Under these circumstances, Aboriginal communities have expanded their repertoire of language teaching approaches (including immersion) and the scope of learners to target. From isolated evaluation studies, it appears that adult immersion programs have clearly been among the most successful. The adult learners' words above indicate that, along with language proficiency, they have gained confidence and self-understanding about learning processes and about themselves as learners.

I would tell anybody to take this course because other than this course, nothing else works. The bottom line is that we're producing speakers here – I'm not an eloquent speaker, but I can understand and I can say damned near anything. (Student B, year-end interview, 2004)

Some adult immersion learners have achieved their goals and are able to participate more fully in the life of their communities. But, for other adult immersion graduates, only the first step has been reached. Next, these graduates who want to do more feel they must reach out and provide for others in their communities the language learning that has been offered to them. Already, adult learners from previous cohorts are serving as assistants to both child and adult immersion programs in their regions and as teachers in elementary and high schools. If Aboriginal language immersion programs thrive and grow, there may yet be a future for these endangered languages.

Note

1. A band school is run by the band council of an Aboriginal community. The council receives federal funding to run the school. It hires staff and usually supervises curriculum, instruction and general management of the school.
2. The authors of this quote at times clearly use the term 'immersion' in its vernacular sense, as described in Chapter 1 of this volume.

References

Assembly of First Nations (1990) *Towards Linguistic Justice for First Nations.* Ottawa, Ontario: Education Secretariat, Assembly of First Nations.

Boyer, P. (2000) Learning Lodge Institute: Montana colleges empower cultures to save languages. *Tribal College Journal* 11, 12–14.

Burnaby, B. (2002) *First Nations Language and Culture Programs in Provincial Schools.* Ottawa, Ontario: Indian and Northern Affairs Canada.

Burnaby, B. and MacKenzie, M. (2001) Cree decision making concerning language: A case study. *Journal of Multilingual and Multicultural Development* 22 (3), 191–209.

Churchill, S. (1986) *The Education of Linguistic and Cultural Minorities in the OECD Countries.* Clevedon: Multilingual Matters.

Edwards, J. (1985) *Language, Society and Identity.* Oxford: Basil Blackwell.

Hinton, L. (2002) *How to Keep Your Language Alive: A Commonsense Approach to One-on-One Language Learning.* Berkeley, CA: Heyday Books.

Ignace, M.B. (1998) *Handbook for Aboriginal Language Program Planning in British Columbia: A Report Prepared for the First Nations Education Steering Committee Aboriginal Language Sub-Committee.* Kamloops, British Columbia: First Nations Education Steering Committee.

Kaweienon:ni Cook-Peters, M. (2005) Language: The final hour. Presentation at the Tahatikonsontonkie (Crying of Coming Faces) Conference, Ahkwesahsne, Quebec.

Kaweienon:ni Cook-Peters, M. and Richards, M. (2005) Struggling against community resistance to immersion. Paper presented at the annual meeting of American Educational Research Association, Montreal, Quebec.

Key, Taehowehs Amos, Jr. (2005) The success of immersion/bilingual education at Six Nations of the Grand River. *Wadrihwa* 19 (4), 2–8.

Kipp, D.R. (2004) American Indian millennium: Renewing our ways for future generations. Available online at http://www.pieganinstitute.org/renewing ways.html. Accessed 14.8.07.

Kirkness, V. and Bowman, S. (1992) *First Nations and Schools: Triumphs and Struggles*. Toronto: Canadian Education Association.

Krashen, S.D. (1981) *Principles and Practice in Second Language Acquisition: English Language Teaching Series*. London: Prentice-Hall International.

National Indian Brotherhood (1972) *Indian Control of Indian Education*. Ottawa, ON: National Indian Brotherhood.

Norris-Tull, D. (2000) Our language, our souls: Yup'ik bilingual curriculum. Available online at http://www.ankn.uaf.edu. Accessed 14.8.07.

Ontario Ministry of Education. (1975) *People of Native Ancestry: A Resource Guide for the Primary and Junior Divisions*. Toronto, ON: Queen's Printer.

Reyhner, J. (2005) Native language immersion. Available online at http://jan.ucc.nau.edu/~jar/NNL/NNL_1.pdf. Accessed 14.8.07.

Rice, K. and Richards, M. (2002) *Report to the Minister of Education on Aboriginal Language Teacher Education Concerns*. Toronto, ON: Ministry of Education.

Richards, M. and Kanatawakhon Maracle, D. (2002a) An intensive native language program for adults: The instructors' perspective. *McGill Journal of Education* 37 (3), 371.

Richards, M. and Kanatawakhon Maracle, D. (2002b) Learning from experience: Evaluating a Native language immersion program for adults: Year 2. Paper presented at the Canadian Association for Curriculum Studies/Canadian Society for the Study of Education Annual Conference, Toronto, ON.

Richards, M. and Kanatawakhon Maracle, D. (2003) Enlarging identity: A Native language immersion program for adults: The students' perspective. Paper presented at the annual meeting of American Educational Research Association, Chicago.

Richards, M. and Kanatawakhon Maracle, D. (2005) Restoring our language: Implementing language immersion for adults (Phase Two). Presentation at the CACS/CSSE Annual Conference, London, ON.

Shaw, P. (2001) Language and identity, language and the land. Available online at http://fnlg.arts.ubc.ca/pdfs/ShawLangLand.pdf. Accessed 14.8.07.

Statistics Canada (2002) Detailed mother tongue (160), sex (3) and age groups (15) for population, for Canada, provinces, territories, Census Metropolitan Areas and Census Agglomerations, 1996 and 2001 Censuses, 20% sample data. Cat. No. 97F0007XCB2001001. Online at http://www12.statcan.ca/english/census 01/products/standard/themes/. Accessed 14.8.07.

TFALC (2005) Towards a new beginning: A foundational report for a strategy to revitalize First Nation, Inuit and Métis languages and cultures. Available online at http://www.aboriginallanguagestaskforce.ca/e/e_index.html. Accessed 14.8.07.

Wasacase, I. (n.d.) *Bilingual 'Immersion' Native Language Ojibwe Pilot Project, West Bay, Ontario*. Ottawa, ON: Department of Indian Affairs and Northern Development.

Western Canadian Protocol for Collaboration in Basic Education (2000) The common curriculum framework for Aboriginal language and culture programs: Kindergarten to grade 12. Online at http://www.wncp.ca/. Accessed 14.8.07.

Williams, B., Gross, K. and Magoon, D. (1996) Lower Kuskokwim bilingual programs. In G. Cantoni (ed.) *Stabilizing Indigenous Languages*. Available online at http://www.ncela.gwu.edu/pubs/stabilize/additional/kuskokwim.htm. Accessed 14.8.07.

Chapter 12

Late Immersion in Hong Kong: Still Stressed or Making Progress?

PHILIP HOARE and STELLA KONG

Introduction

In this chapter we review and evaluate the state of development of late immersion education in Hong Kong since 1997, when the handover of Hong Kong from England to the People's Republic of China occurred, and we discuss its potential future development. We begin with a description of the post-1997 sociolinguistic context of Hong Kong with special reference to the status of each of the three main languages: Cantonese, English and Putonghua.[1] This context determines the parts these languages play in education, from policy decision to curriculum planning to classroom implementation, and these are described in the following section. We then explain the distinctive features of late immersion in Hong Kong and how these are a consequence of the sociolinguistic and language-in-education context. Following this, we review a number of recent studies that examined student outcomes and learning processes of late immersion in Hong Kong, and students' attitudes towards the three main languages after 1997. We end with a discussion of the implications of recent research findings and conclude that, given the improbability of contextual change, developments in implementation are essential if immersion education is to achieve its full potential in the Hong Kong context.

The Post-1997 Sociolinguistic Context of Hong Kong

Hong Kong is largely a Cantonese-speaking community, with other Chinese dialects, except for Putonghua, playing a significant but diminishing role (Bacon-Shone & Bolton, 1998; Census and Statistics Department, 2005). Putonghua, the standardised version of what used to be referred to in the West as Mandarin and is now the official spoken dialect of the People's Republic of China (PRC), has become more important as a second dialect in Hong Kong life since the mid-1990s. This has resulted from the return of Hong Kong to the PRC, the accompanying increases in immigration from the Mainland, and the rapid development in economic ties between Hong Kong and the Mainland. This rise in the importance of Putonghua, however, has not had a significant effect on the popularity or perceived importance of English. Even within the society at large where the language of everyday life is Cantonese for more than 90% of the population, most people claim to speak some English and the self-claimed levels of English are rising (Bacon-Shone & Bolton, 1998).

Moreover, the 1997 change in sovereignty has not led to a change in the status of English within Hong Kong society. English remains a language that most parents would like their children to know because it is still considered necessary for economic success. English is a prerequisite for entry into higher education and into many careers. In many professions in Hong Kong, such as medicine, law and engineering, practitioners are expected to be able to function more or less equally well in English and Cantonese. Despite this and its position as the colonial language, English in Hong Kong has never become a language of society at large. Even within the domains of government, business and education, where it remains very strong, English has been and still is more commonly used in writing than in spoken communication. It is the norm for a great many people to speak little or no English either at work or in any other facet of life. Hong Kong thus exhibits a sociolinguistic phenomenon where Chinese, the native language of more than 90% of the people, is socially and culturally valued while English, the colonial and now the international language, is economically valued. The demand for high levels of English proficiency for professional use in high status careers within a society where English is not used for social communication has important implications for education.

Language in Education in Hong Kong

The economic status of English means that its status in education as perceived by parents, in a society that places immense value on education and economic advancement, remains very high. About half of the parents surveyed in 1999 considered that it was 'more important to perform better in English than in other academic subjects' (Education Commission, 2005: 128). The education system, chiefly schools, is the route through which children are expected to acquire English, and English-medium schooling (one-way English immersion for Cantonese speakers) has been considered a critically important means of achieving this. English-medium education retains a high status in society because it is believed to give access to higher education, also largely in English, and ultimately to the linguistic prerequisites of more prestigious careers. The expectations of English-medium education by parents explain in large part the overtly political and public nature of the language-in-education debate in Hong Kong over many years.

Because of the social and cultural value placed on Chinese and the economic value placed on English, there is little argument that both should be taught in the Hong Kong school curriculum. The main debate is on *how*, how much and to which students each language should be taught, with the language of instruction being a major focus of argument. By virtue of its status as a colonial language, English was for a long time a language of instruction, especially at the secondary level and above. More recent debates have been influenced by changes from Hong Kong's colonial status to that of a Special Administrative Region (SAR) of China and from a manufacturing to a service-based economy.

To understand the current complex situation with regard to the language of instruction, a brief review of recent developments is helpful. The introduction of nine years of compulsory universal education in the 1970s moved the Hong Kong education system from *elite early immersion*, primary education through English for a minority of children, to *almost universal late immersion*, in which over 90% of the secondary schools claimed to use English as the language of instruction (Johnson, 1997: 171). The prestige of English in education led to irresistible parental pressure for English immersion. For two to three decades before 1997, the education system became one in which most primary schools were Chinese-medium and most secondary schools were English-medium. This is part of the scenario described by Johnson (1997: 171) which led to his characterisation of immersion education in Hong Kong being 'an extreme example of late immersion operating under stress.'

The stress that Johnson noted in the system before 1997 resulted in a number of features of teaching and learning in these late immersion classrooms that were not conducive to English language learning nor, indeed, to any learning. The focus on expansion in the 1970s and 1980s, with little or no attention being paid to the prerequisites for immersion success, resulted in a large number of teachers claiming to teach content subjects through English without sufficient proficiency in English to enable them to vary their language use to support students' learning (for example, by paraphrasing). They also lacked an understanding of essential teaching and programme implementation practices. A high proportion of students entered late immersion without a sufficient level of English proficiency to enable them to begin learning secondary-level content and there was no attempt to adjust any other aspects of curriculum and instruction to accommodate the expansion. These pressures led to the use of varying amounts of English, Cantonese and a mix of English and Cantonese, referred to locally as *mixed code*, for teaching and learning purposes. '[E]ven in the schools with the most able and best-motivated students, teachers used on average no more than 50% English' (Johnson, 1997: 175–176). Student talk in English was minimal and limited to single words or readings from the text-book. When students were required to write, they relied on copying or repro-ducing rote-learnt phrases. These inadequacies were frequently not reflected in the learning outcomes as they should have been because of the dominance of examinations that rarely required students to produce any English longer than a phrase or short sentence in the assessment of their content learning.

A number of language-in-education reforms in the early 1990s had little effect, as they were largely voluntary and could not overcome the pressures inherent in the system. They were followed by more rigorously enforced changes in 1998, which entailed a reduction in the proportion of students entering English late immersion education from around 90% to only about 32–40% (Education Department, 1997). This occurred despite vehement public opposition, which centred on a concern that many students were being denied the chance to become proficient in English and hence to the opportunities this proficiency opened up. After 1998, schools that wished to use English as the language of instruction were required to apply to the Education Department. The criteria for approval were (1) student ability to learn through English, as assessed by in-school measures of academic achievement, administered in Chinese except for English language assess-ment, in Primary 5–6 (grade 5–6) scaled across all schools; and (2) teachers' English language proficiency, as judged by the school principal. These 1998 changes have resulted, whether intentionally or not, in late English immer-sion education being restricted to the academically more able students (Education Department, 1997; Education Commission, 2005).

However, immersion in English-medium content instruction affects the education of more than just the academically-more-able students. All secondary schools are free to choose the language of instruction in the fourth year (Secondary 4, grade 10). Many schools that are *required* to be Chinese-medium during Secondary 1–3 (grades 7–9) by the 1998 policy change choose to use English for senior secondary classes (grades 10–13) to attract more students. Parents who fail to enter their children in an English immersion school at Secondary 1 (grade 7) often try to enter their children at Secondary 4 (grade 10) where there are more English immersion schools. Yet, regardless of when English-medium instruction begins in the content areas, no requirement exists for specialised qualifications for English immersion teachers.

The reforms in language-in-education policy since 1998 have not altered the low status of Chinese-medium schools, the persistent preference of parents for English-medium education, and teachers' and students' attitudes towards the language of instruction. Also, Hong Kong students' strong academic performance on international education achievement studies relative to counterparts in other countries, especially in science and mathematics (Programme for International Assessment, 2004), has made it difficult to persuade some stakeholders of the need for further change. Standards of English in schools and the language of instruction policy, however, remain controversial and are frequent topics of newspaper articles and editorials, student and parental comments, radio phone-ins and government pronouncements.

Distinctive Features of Immersion Education in Hong Kong

English-medium education in Hong Kong generally exhibits the eight core features of immersion education described by Swain and Johnson (1997: 6). Swain and Lapkin (2005) have proposed modifications to these features to take account of the greater ethnic and linguistic diversity of immersion students in Canadian schools and sociocultural theory, which posits that speaking and writing are tools for all learning, including language learning. This, they argue, suggests a role for student use of the L1 in the immersion classroom as it may support both content learning and the learning of the immersion language. These modifications are not directly relevant to Hong Kong, as the student population in public sector immersion schools remains almost entirely Chinese. The proposals may, however, eventually signal programme acceptance of some use of the L1 in the classroom, which is widely practised though officially frowned upon. Additive rather than replacive bilingualism[2] through immersion is clearly the aim in Hong Kong. Despite the apparent low status of Chinese-medium education, Chinese language and culture occupy a significant part of the school curriculum and a 'pass' in a Secondary 7 (grade 13) Chinese language and culture examination is a requirement for entry into higher education. Teachers are almost all bilingual to varying degrees (native speakers of Chinese who have acquired a sufficiently high level of English proficiency through the education system and are able to maintain English in the classroom). Immersion classes follow the same curriculum as those taught through Chinese. Despite the availability of English in the media, most Cantonese-speaking students do not need to use English outside school any more than the majority of French immersion students in Canada need French, despite its availability and status as an official language of the country.

Within the parameters established by the eight core features (Swain & Johnson, 1997), Hong Kong late immersion now exhibits a number of features that make it distinctive. These arise largely as a result of the sociolinguistic and educational context described above. On their own, these features are by no means unique, but together they create a context that provides very particular challenges to teachers and to the educational system. These features are late entry, the proportion of the age group that enters immersion, and the expected learning outcomes of immersion by the society at large.

Late entry

One of the few aspects of the language-of-instruction issue in Hong Kong about which there has been relatively little controversy is that of the starting age. Though proposals have been made to introduce early immersion, which is offered in a few schools largely outside the public school system, the main debate has been about access to late English immersion and how it should be implemented. The cultural and practical importance of Chinese (Lai, 2005) means that there is no question of Chinese literacy not being established as early as possible in primary schools. The challenge of learning the Chinese writing system leads some to question whether combining it with early immersion might put some children's initial literacy at risk. The scale of the demand for immersion also makes the early model a practical impossibility because there are too few primary teachers with satisfactory levels of bilingual proficiency and appropriate training. The cost of providing these skills would also make it non-viable.

Immersion in Hong Kong for the 30-40% of students allowed to pursue it begins in Secondary 1 (grade 7). In this respect, Hong Kong immersion is similar to late French immersion in Canada and in some European contexts (Fruhauf *et al.*, 1996). Immersion continues until the students leave school, either at Secondary 5 (grade 11) or Secondary 7 (grade 13, for those who enter university). Before the immersion programme begins, all students have been learning English for at least six years, with typically around three hours of English language instruction per week. However, English in primary schools does not specifically prepare students for academic study through the language, as much of the focus is, understandably, on the interpersonal domain. So-called bridging courses to help students manage the transition into English-medium schools are common but these frequently address only the English of classroom management and some content vocabulary. The failure to bridge the proficiency gap between students' English ability and the English level required to study content subjects through English further diminishes the programme's chances of success with the dual goal of content and language learning (Johnson & Swain, 1994).

English use extends across the curriculum in most English immersion schools, with only Chinese language and history taught in Chinese and, in some schools, subjects such as art, music and physical education. Despite the considerable opportunities the curriculum offers for students to engage in English, certain constraints imposed by the late-immersion model influence implementation. These have been recognised in other late immersion contexts. Time itself is, of course, one such limitation. Another is variation in the level of teacher commitment and ability across subjects, given that the subject specialisation typical in secondary schools means that a substantial number of different teachers are needed with the appropriate skills, knowledge and commitment (Berthold, 1995; Day & Shapson, 1996; Wolff, 2002). There is little time or space for a compromise between the drive for academic success in content area examinations and the need for high levels of English proficiency (Hoare, 2003). As a consequence, some teachers do not use English consistently in class, and many do not insist on spoken English by students as much as they should if a high level of English/Chinese bilingualism is the aim of immersion. While Swain and Lapkin (2005) propose that *some* use of the L1 may lead to enhanced learning of both content and the immersion language, many teachers assume that a great deal of student talk must be in the L1 if subject learning is to proceed. The notion of Chinese language usage *leading to* English learning, which is implicit in Swain and Lapkin's 2005 argument and made more explicit in the study they describe in Chapter 6 of this volume, is missing in these Hong Kong immersion classrooms. Though teaching materials are almost all in English, teachers give little language scaffolding to students who, consequently, are able to learn very little through reading and writing in English (Kong, 2004). Finally, though Berthold (1995) suggests that late immersion students have the advantage of being able to exercise more choice than younger students as to whether or not they should join an immersion programme, the context in Hong Kong denies this choice. The choice of the immersion school is almost automatic for students in the selected group because immersion goes hand in hand with high status.

Proportion of the age group

A second distinctive feature of immersion in Hong Kong, at least in comparison with North American and most European models, is that it provides for more than a quarter of the total student age group. This is a result of the perceived advantages for students of a high level of English proficiency by parents who put immense pressure on the education authorities to allow as many English immersion schools as possible.

The high proportion of students entering immersion means that it cannot be seen as a distinguishing feature or a competitive advantage for schools in Hong Kong, as it may be in some other parts of the world. Students (or their parents) choose immersion not because of a commitment to bilingualism as an objective but as the norm for any higher-ability student, and so schools do not feel the need to demonstrate their effectiveness as *immersion* schools. With such a high proportion of students and teachers involved, it is also impossible to demand that teachers have a special commitment as immersion teachers. This is especially so if, as we explain below, the measures of success are mainly associated with academic rather than language achievement.

The relatively high proportion of the overall age group that enters immersion education exerts pressure on the implementation and the outcomes of immersion in Hong Kong. It also gives immersion a higher public profile than it may have in many other contexts, influencing educational debate not just within immersion education but also across the entire educational spectrum.

Expected learning outcomes

The very high levels of Chinese/English bilingualism expected of some of Hong Kong's professionals have been described earlier in this chapter. The instrumental motivation this gives rise to is a third distinctive feature of immersion in Hong Kong. A significant proportion of students going into English immersion are expected to emerge ready to study for particular professional areas through English, and student effort and motivation is correspondingly focused almost entirely on acquiring English for work and education. Few students or teachers have a commitment to English that goes beyond the instrumental. Neither bicultural understanding nor engagement with literature or popular culture in English are goals of the education system (Hoare & Kong, 2001) and they are not widely pursued within the curriculum. As an example of this, the Secondary 7 (grade 13) examination in English required for entry to university called, revealingly, 'Use of English', was taken in 2006 by over 27,000 students. In contrast, Literature in English, available to the same students, was taken by 127 students (interestingly, only one of these was male) (HKEAA, 2007). At the same time, the correspondence between English immersion education and local prestige means that many schools, teachers and students feel they cannot afford to balance a focus on examination success with more serious engagement with English, either within the academic curriculum or outside it. *Success* in English immersion education is, therefore, somewhat paradoxically measured by academic success rather than by bilingual proficiency. There seems to be an assumption that students will acquire

English by being in English immersion schools though there is little emphasis placed on helping them to do so. As teachers and students are rewarded for academic success, they inevitably downplay any strategies which do not target this. Thus, although there are high expectations for both English and academic learning outcomes in late immersion schools, effort by both teachers and students is always focused on the latter.

The effects of the sociolinguistic and language-in-education context, therefore, are to impose an immersion system in which a substantial proportion of students have limited time to achieve very high standards academically as well as in the immersion language. The highly instrumental nature of student motivation, both at the individual and system levels, makes the teacher's task more difficult, in that neither teachers nor students exhibit great interest in developing the immersion language _per se_. Their concern is to achieve high academic standards. Yet, when the learning of the immersion language is constrained, academic learning also suffers.

Recent Research on English Immersion in Hong Kong

Since 1998, when English immersion became restricted to only a quarter of secondary schools, a great many more research studies have been published than was the case in the preceding decade. This research has focused more on learning outcomes and learning processes in English immersion than before. Findings provide opportunities to identify causes for the paradoxes that seem to beset immersion in Hong Kong and to offer the basis for research-driven development. The complexity of the issues, however, means that there remains a great deal to be researched. A number of these studies are reviewed below to provide an indication of where English immersion education currently stands in Hong Kong.

Studies of learning outcomes

Marsh _et al._ (2000) used data provided by the Education Department from a research project of their own (Education Department, 1998) to study the effects of instruction in the first language (Chinese) and in the second language (English) on students' achievement in these languages and in four content subjects (mathematics, science, geography and history). The data were collected before the 1998 policy changes, when about 90% of secondary schools claimed to be English immersion. The achievement of over 12,700 Secondary 1 (grade 7) students from 56 secondary schools within seven categories according to language of instruction and student ability was tracked for three years. Achievement tests were administered to students in the language of instruction in which the students learnt the subjects. Achievement scores were analysed, including prior achievement scores (i.e. placement scores at Primary 6 (grade 6), for entering secondary education), and standardised achievement test scores at Secondary 1–3 (grade 7–9) in English, Chinese, mathematics, science, geography and history. Multilevel growth modelling was used to compare growth in student achievement over time within and across different school types. In addition, when in Secondary 3, all students completed a questionnaire on the extent to which English was used in each subject studied (except Chinese). Separate factor analyses were conducted to explore the different dimensions of the responses. The number of students, the number of school subjects studied and the three-year duration of the research contribute to the robustness of the analyses.

Marsh *et al.* (2000) determined that immersion had a small positive effect on English and Chinese achievement but a substantial negative effect on subject achievement. The negative effect was especially strong in science, geography and history, and much less strong in mathematics. They also found that students with better academic results prior to beginning Secondary 1 did not learn content subjects through English better, but those with better English proficiency did. Moreover, the negative effects of instruction in English did not lessen over time. At Secondary 3, students learning science, geography and history through English were not achieving better scores than they were at Secondary 1. These results are contrary to those reported on late immersion studies done in Canada, referred to in Chapter 2 of this volume.

The conclusion of the original study by the Education Department is that the research 'does not support the general belief that attending an English-medium-instruction school would help students achieve higher English proficiency' (Education Department, 1998: i). Marsh *et al.* (2000) concur with this conclusion and further suggest that the findings of their study call into question a great deal of previous research on immersion education world-wide which shows that second language proficiency gains take place without any penalty in subject achievement. They propose that students will not be able to benefit from late-immersion education unless they reach a critical threshold level of English proficiency that enables them to learn subject content through English, but they do not specifiy what this threshold level can be. Though admitting that their study did not examine teaching quality, they argue that the fact that there was much less negative effect on mathematics (a subject which, they claim, relies much less on language skills), suggests that language proficiency, not teaching quality, is the major factor determining a student's potential for success.

While the results of these studies are clear and raise important concerns for late-immersion programme models in Hong Kong, these authors' contention that the language of instruction is the main determining factor for learning outcomes regardless of how that language is used is open to challenge. The thrust of language-in-education policies in the 1990s was to ensure that teachers were in a position to use language to support students' learning in the classroom by ensuring that students who were neither motivated nor approached a threshold level of English were not taught through English. The original study (Education Department, 1998) makes it clear (though Marsh *et al*. (2000) do not) that only three of the schools in the sample were recommended to use English, and these were included as part of a control group. The majority of the schools that chose to use English had been advised not to because their students did not meet minimum admission standards for immersion education. Few, if any, of the teachers were trained to deal with immersion classes of this sort. There is at least a possibility, therefore, that most students in the study who were studying through English were neither motivated to do so nor were they effectively supported in their learning.

Yip *et al*. (2003) report the first stage of a longitudinal study on the effects of the language of instruction on science learning using data collected after the 1998 policy changes. Their research is commissioned and supported by the Hong Kong Government. Secondary 1 (Grade 7) students' learning of science in 25 English-medium schools and 75 Chinese-medium schools were studied over a period of three years. As English-medium schools received approximately the academically top quarter of the student population, the 25 English-medium schools were proportionately represented in the study population. Twenty-five Chinese-medium schools were selected from each of three ability ranges, high, medium and low, totalling 75 Chinese-medium schools. It is worth noting that the Chinese-medium students in the high-ability band had lower prior academic ability than the English-medium students. The students were given science achievement tests, including multiple-choice and free-response questions, over three years. The tests were administered in Chinese to the Chinese-medium students, and in English to one third and in a bilingual version to two thirds of the English-medium students. Multilevel modelling analysis was used to measure students' progress in science achievement. Prior academic ability was taken into account by using data provided by the Education Department from standardised government tests administered in primary schools. Yip *et al*. (2005) report only up to the end of the second year of students' science results as measured by the achievement tests.

To date their findings show that English immersion students, despite higher prior academic ability, performed significantly worse than the high-ability students educated through their first language by direct comparison of mean scores on science achievement tests after two years of late immersion. When taking prior academic ability into account, all three levels of students learning through their first language outperformed their immersion counterparts. This was so in the majority of multiple-choice questions and all of the free-response questions. English immersion students were found to be particularly weak in questions that assess their understanding of abstract concepts, their ability to discriminate between scientific terms and their ability to apply science knowledge learnt in new and everyday experiences. Yip *et al.* (2005) interpreted these findings as suggesting that immersion students were handicapped by their inadequate levels of English proficiency in science learning especially in terms of conceptual understanding, which requires higher cognitive skills.

This is the only quantitative study of learning outcomes based on data collected after the 1998 change in policy and is, therefore, of considerable importance. The study strongly suggests that English immersion education in Hong Kong is not achieving its stated goal of academic content learning in at least one critical content subject.

Yip *et al.* (2005) recognise that the extent to which English was actually used in the English immersion classrooms is not accounted for in their results. This point also applies to Marsh *et al.* (2000). Yip *et al.* (2005) also built into their study a student questionnaire that elicited students' self-evaluation of their competence in science, and their views about the nature of the instructional activities. Lesson observations were recorded and transcribed to study the processes of teaching and learning, but these findings have not yet been reported. If English was not used consistently, then one contributing factor to English-medium student performance may be the lack of sustained support for learning the language of science. If the language of the classroom was frequently Cantonese and the language of written science texts was English, then students' learning of science through the language of science could have been seriously restricted. In particular, their ability to communicate their science understanding in English would likely have been very limited if this kind of language was rarely modelled by their teachers.

Studies of learning processes

Other compelling evidence for the apparent lack of effective content learning in late immersion in Hong Kong comes from studies of classroom teaching and learning processes undertaken since 1998 (Hoare, 2003, 2004; Kong, 2004). Both Hoare (2003, 2004) and Kong (2004) present qualitative case studies of the teaching and learning processes in late-immersion classrooms. Both also suggest that many Hong Kong immersion teachers do not have the pedagogical skills, nor the understanding of and commitment to immersion education, to integrate the teaching of language and content in the classroom in ways that can bring about the learning of both. Kong (2004) conducted a limited survey of 72 immersion teachers which provides initial research support for this finding.

Hoare (2003) studied immersion teachers' use of language to support students' learning in science. Five to six lessons comprising a unit on the topic of neutralisation from six Secondary 2 (grade 8) science teachers were taped and transcribed for detailed analysis of how the teachers' language use helped students to learn science. The six teachers filled in a question-naire, which provided information to gauge their level of awareness of the role of language in science learning. Three teachers were rated as 'more language aware' and three as 'less language aware'. The teachers were also interviewed to discover the rationale behind their use of language during the lessons. Their students completed an achievement test on the topic after the unit was finished. The test required the students to write a few sentences to answer questions eliciting understanding of key topic-related concepts. Three pairs of students from each class (a total of 36), of high, middle and low levels of academic ability as judged by the teachers, were interviewed to find out more about how their teachers supported their science learning through English and what aspects of classroom practice they found useful.

Hoare (2003) found major differences among the six science immersion teachers in their awareness of the roles of language in learning and the effects these had on their teaching. The tests showed that teachers who were 'more language aware' were more effective in making science content accessible to their students through English. These teachers built up science meanings through careful use of the English of science and, at the same time, helped their students to use the science genre to make science meaning. For instance, students brought to their lessons the concept of salt as a food additive or flavouring. By introducing a scientific term for salt, sodium chloride, and, gradually over time, characterising it with chemical language as a white solid, the product of sodium hydroxide reacting with hydrochloric acid, and as one salt of a class of salts that are products of acid–alkali reactions, the 'more language aware' teachers enabled students to transform the word *salt* into other words that make up the language of science. They also helped students put their experiences of science, mainly experiments, into words, thus making those experiences meaningful and potentially generalisable. Hoare showed that, in these six cases at least, the language-related strategies teachers employed in the classroom had a major effect on students' content learning, and this indicated the need for teacher education in this area.

Kong (2004) studied the use of writing in biology and history in four late immersion classrooms to find out whether and how writing was used to support students' learning of subject content and English. Relevant curriculum materials such as the subject syllabi, examination papers and textbooks were analysed for the writing demands. A total of 285 scripts of Secondary 4 (grade 10) students' writing in biology and history, sampled from more than 800 scripts of all the writing students did in the second semester, were analysed. The scripts selected represented high, middle and low levels of performance as judged by the two biology teachers and two history teachers participating in the study. The four teachers were interviewed about their classes' general writing practices and their views of the uses of writing in their classroom. Three pairs of students, each of high, middle and low levels of performance as judged by teachers from each of the four classes (a total of 24), were interviewed about their views of the uses of writing in biology and history. The four teachers and 68 others teaching various subjects in different immersion schools also completed a questionnaire eliciting similar information to the interviews.

Kong (2004) found that the writing demands in biology and history at Secondary 4 were highly subject-specific in terms of the content and the genres required. Students, however, mostly failed to meet these writing demands. In fact, Kong found that there was more copying than writing. When students did not copy, their language use never brought out the meaning adequately. The interview data, from both teachers and students, clearly showed that these immersion participants lacked an understanding of how language is used to represent meaning. Both teachers and students considered the presence of key subject concept vocabulary in writing as most important, but thought that grammar and subject-specific genres would not affect the meaning very much. Both teachers and students saw writing more as a ritual to demonstrate understanding and to score marks than as a process to learn. Clearly, these immersion teachers were not using writing in the context of the subject area to help students learn the subject and the language.

These two studies that focus on the learning process within the immersion classroom context suggest that teaching strategies often do not support students' learning through a second language. This may explain, at least in part, the learning outcomes documented by Marsh *et al.* (2000) and Yip *et al.* (2003).

A study of students' language attitudes

The most thorough survey of Hong Kong students' attitudes towards Cantonese, English and Putonghua after 1998 was conducted by Lai (2005). Lai administered a questionnaire to 1048 randomly selected students in their fourth year of secondary education (grade 10) in 2001. The students surveyed belonged to the first cohort of students to have had all of its secondary education after the change of language policy in 1998. Lai compared students' instrumental and integrative orientation towards the three languages. She used Gardner and Lambert's (as cited in Lai, 2005) dichotomy of instrumental and integrative motivation towards language learning to measure orientations to the languages. Lai elicited student responses to statements intended to reveal their individual attitudes towards each language (e.g. 'I like Cantonese') and their attitudes towards users of each language or the status of each in Hong Kong (e.g. 'A person who speaks English is usually educated, intelligent and well-off' or 'Putonghua is not an important language in Hong Kong'). She then derived a composite mean from the responses to the statements, which provided a clear basis for comparison (see Table 12.1 for details).

Lai (2005) concluded that the first cohort of Hong Kong students to go through their secondary education since the handover and change of language policy had a strong integrative orientation towards Cantonese, though they did not believe that it was as important as English in economic terms. At the same time they had a strong instrumental orientation but a weaker integrative orientation towards English. There was little evidence of Putonghua replacing English as the chief language of power as, Lai suggests, many people had expected. Lai points out that there have been significant changes in students' attitudes towards English and Cantonese since the early 1980s. At that time Pierson, Fu and Lee (as cited in Lai, 2005) found that the status of English was seen as a threat to Cantonese and Hong Kong people's feelings of *Chineseness*. Lai claims that her study shows that decolonisation reinforced Hong Kong people's sense of identity mainly as

Table 12.1 Integrative and instrumental orientations of Hong Kong school students towards Cantonese, English and Putonghua

	Cantonese	*English*	*Putonghua*
Integrative orientation	3.43	3.05	2.47
Instrumental orientation	3.19	3.51	2.66

Note: Composite means on a Likert scale of 4 (4 = strongly agree).
(adapted from Lai, 2005: 375)

belonging to Hong Kong rather than China, and that students feel this identity is exemplified by Cantonese/English bilingualism, which distinguishes them from residents of the Mainland. At the same time, their beliefs in the importance of English as the most valuable language in economic terms are confirmed.

These findings are important, as they provide a possible key to one of the paradoxes of Hong Kong immersion education. The strong instrumental orientation towards English provides a rationale for the overwhelming belief among parents that their children need to acquire as much English as possible even at the expense of other learning (Education Commission, 2005). At the same time, teachers' and students' feelings that the combination of Cantonese and English signifies their identity as Hong Kong people, together with their integrative orientation towards Cantonese, reinforce their urge to use it in the classroom at the expense of English, the supposed language of instruction (Johnson, 1983; Hoare & Kong, 2001). This is, however, not conducive to the learning of the immersion language (English) or of subject concepts through English.

Implications and Future Development

The language-of-instruction policy changes introduced in 1998 were intended to improve learning across the curriculum and to ensure that all students are educated through a language in which they can learn effectively. The most obvious conclusion we can draw from the studies described in the last section is that this aim has largely not been achieved with respect to English immersion. Yip *et al.* (2003) show convincingly that students in English immersion are not achieving gains in content learning equivalent to those of students in mainstream mother tongue education. This finding mirrors the results found by Marsh *et al.* (2000) using data before the 1998 policy changes. These results are plainly not what is expected from immersion education. Yip *et al.* (2003) confirm that the 1998 policy changes have resulted in better learning generally across most subjects except English, as measured by examination results, by many students who are now educated through Chinese. These outcomes are backed up by analyses of public examination results (Education Commission, 2005: 155). There is little evidence, however, of a corresponding improvement in content learning outcomes in English immersion schools despite recent limitations on access to immersion education to those students who can supposedly most benefit from it.

The apparent weakness in subject content learning, despite the emphasis placed on it at the expense of English learning, is clearly a matter for concern. There is also evidence that the standard of English language in immersion schools is not as high as might be expected (see, for example, Kong, 2004). Some of the reasons for this apparent failure of immersion may be found in the evident degree of misunderstanding of immersion education currently in Hong Kong. Yip *et al.* make a telling comment in the conclusion to the report of their study. When discussing English immersion students' seeming failure to learn science as well as their Chinese-educated peers, they say that the students' 'English proficiency may not have been high enough to enable them to learn science effectively' (Yip *et al.*, 2003: 314). This statement reflects a prevalent view that content learning through the immersion language can occur *because* students already have high proficiency rather than understanding that the aim of the programme itself is to help them attain this proficiency. This view is shared by Marsh *et al.* (2000: 343) and is echoed in the most recent debates about language education policy. There is very little corresponding discussion about the specialised teaching strategies needed to help students develop both content and language learning within immersion classrooms (Hoare & Kong, 2001).

In this chapter we have shown how Hong Kong's immersion system is shaped by its sociolinguistic and language-in-education context. It is hard to escape from the societal demand for English immersion education because of the prevalent belief in the importance of English. Late immersion is probably the only viable model to achieve this. The expectations of immersion are high and, as they are rooted in societal beliefs and attitudes, they are unlikely to change. Failure, therefore, is not an option, as there is no likelihood that English immersion education will fall out of favour. Recent policy changes (Education Commission, 2005) have not been welcomed by parents because they limit access to English immersion, and it is politically inconceivable that access should be further limited. The 2005 report and several others (e.g. Education Commission, 1990; Education Commission, 1996) were produced because there is a societal demand for English immersion education that must be acknowledged.

If the system cannot be changed, the only avenues for change are in its implementation, and it is in this area that there are grounds for cautious optimism. The studies described in the last section represent just a few of the research studies undertaken since 1998 (see others by, for example, Chan, 2002; Chen, 2001; Choi, 2003; Evans, 2000; Lai & Byram, 2003; Lin, 2000; Poon, 2000; So, 2002; Tsui, 2004; Tsui *et al.*, 1999; Wong 2001). The growth in research provides the basis for consideration of models of instruction that might lead to better content and language learning (e.g. Hoare, 2003, 2004; Kong, 2004). Hoare and Kong (2006) point to a heightened level of understanding of the aims of immersion education among teachers which, they suggest, was not evident before. Interviews with 20 teachers and accompanying videotaped and analysed lesson observations reveal an acceptance of their responsibility to develop students' English with subject content knowledge, though reservations about how to appropriately balance the push for academic achievement with time spent on English development remain.

Government measures being introduced indicate some recognition of immersion as distinct from Chinese-language educational programmes, though some measures appear to be intended to monitor performance rather than improve it. Beginning in 2009, all English immersion content teachers will have to demonstrate a minimum level of English proficiency (Education Commission, 2005). Some generous staff development provisions are in place but no formal certification of immersion teachers is likely to be required in the foreseeable future. Guidance for teachers and samples of teaching materials integrating language and content are now available (e.g. Evans *et al.*, 2001; Polias, 2005). Each six years, immersion schools will be subject to a quality assurance review to determine whether they should be permitted to remain as immersion schools, though this inspection regime is mediated by grants to enhance cross-curricular language support. While a minimum English proficiency level will be required of immersion teachers from 2009, the recommended minimum level is disturbingly low and does not match the level achieved by the best 15% of Secondary 7 (grade 13) students each year (HKEAA, 2006).[3] Given the history of immersion in Hong Kong there has to be some question as to whether an appropriate combination of carrot and stick has been employed. It may be that pressure will result in more, not less, stress to the system. Looking back over the period since 1997, it is apparent that many of the stresses that Johnson (1997) identified remain, but there are signs of progress.

Conclusion

In this chapter we have summarised the background to late-English-immersion education in Hong Kong and how this unique sociohistorical context has shaped the current system. The choice of late rather than early immersion, the demand for a high proportion of the age group to be admitted, and the high expectations of learning outcomes for both language and content are all consequences of the social and educational context. These features, in combination, make Hong Kong immersion distinctive and especially challenging to students and teachers. That these challenges are not being fully met is revealed by the increasing range of research undertaken since 1997. We have reviewed some of the major studies and their relevance to the intense and continuing debate on languages in education. We have pointed out that, because the features of the system are rooted in the context, there is little potential for these to change. Thus, if immersion is to achieve its potential, it is the implementation of immersion programmes, especially teacher knowledge and skills, that must be developed. We have concluded that while there are few signs of positive outcomes at present, there are reasons to suppose that changes might yet occur as a result of the improved understanding of immersion resulting from research.

Notes

1. The use of the two terms 'languages' and 'dialects' in this chapter may require some explanation. Cantonese and Putonghua can be considered Chinese dialects because they both refer to a spoken variety of Chinese, though they share the same writing system. Cantonese is the dialect of native people of Hong Kong. Putonghua is the standard dialect now used across the whole of the People's Republic of China, in addition to local dialects such as Cantonese, and is an attempt to standardise what used to be referred to in English as Mandarin, which is still the term used in Taiwan. In Hong Kong, Putonghua, as a dialect of Chinese, was not commonly used before the 1990s but it has become increasingly more important since then. However, it is not uncommon for people in Hong Kong to refer to Putonghua as a language for sociolinguistic and sociopolitical reasons. The Hong Kong Government's language education aim is to produce 'trilingual and biliterate' students, able to speak Cantonese, Putonghua and English, and read and write standard written Chinese and English. The use of Cantonese in Hong Kong and Putonghua in Mainland China constitutes a key difference between Hong Kong Chinese and Mainland Chinese societies, a difference that Hong Kong people are eager to maintain. So for people in Hong Kong, there are currently three languages commonly used: Cantonese, English and Putonghua.

   We have used *Cantonese* when we are referring to only the spoken variety and *Chinese* when we are referring to either only the written variety or any spoken dialect (generally Cantonese or Putonghua in this chapter) with the written variety. We refer, therefore, to the use of Cantonese in the English immersion classroom, meaning spoken Cantonese. On the other hand, we refer to Chinese-medium education, meaning that the language of instruction is (in almost all cases) spoken Cantonese and standard written Chinese.

2. Replacive bilingualism means a situation in which a learner becomes proficient in L2 in place of the L1 rather than in addition to the L1 (additive bilingualism). For example, becoming academically proficient in L2 instead of L1. This is not the same as subtractive bilingualism, which we take to mean being not fully literate in either L1 or L2.

3. In international terms the recommended minimum proficiency level in English represents a score of 213 (computer-based), 550 (paper-based) or 79–80 (Internet-based) or above in the Test of English as a Foreign Language (TOEFL), or Band 6 or above in the International English Language Test System (IELTS).

References

Bacon-Shone, J. and Bolton, K. (1998) Charting multilingualism: Language censuses and language surveys in Hong Kong. In M.C. Pennington (ed.) *Language in Hong Kong at Century's End* (pp. 43–90). Hong Kong: Hong Kong University Press.

Berthold, M. (1995) Pioneer and lighthouse: The Benowa experience. In M. Berthold (ed.) *Rising to the Bilingual Challenge* (pp. 19–36). Canberra: National Language and Literacy Institute of Australia.

Census and Statistics Department (2005) Population aged 5 and over by usual language, 1991, 1996 and 2001. Online at http://www.censtatd. gov.hk/major_projects/2001_population_census/main_tables/population_aged_5_and_over_by_usual_language_1991/index.jsp . Accessed 20.8.07.

Chan, E. (2002) Beyond pedagogy: Language and identity in post-colonial Hong Kong. *British Journal of Sociology of Education* 23 (2), 271–286.

Chen, P. (2001) Language policy in Hong Kong during the colonial period before July 1, 1997. In N. Gottlieb and P. Chen (eds) *Language Planning and Language Policy: East Asian Perspectives* (pp. 111–128). Richmond, England: Curzon.

Choi, P.K. (2003) 'The best students will learn English': Ultra-utilitarianism and linguistic imperialism in education in post-1997 Hong Kong. *Journal of Education Policy* 18 (6), 673–694.

Day, E.M. and Shapson, S.M. (1996) *Studies in Immersion Education.* Clevedon: Multilingual Matters.

Education Commission (1990) *Education Commission Report No. 4.* Hong Kong: Government Printer.

Education Commission (1996) *Education Commission Report No. 6.* Hong Kong: Government Printer.

Education Commission (2005) *Report on Review of Medium of Instruction for Secondary Schools and Secondary School Places Allocation.* Hong Kong: Government Logistics Department.

Education Department (1997) Hong Kong: Government circulars.

Education Department (1998) *Evaluation Study on the Implementation of Medium Instruction Grouping in Secondary Schools.* Hong Kong: Government Printer.

Evans, M., Hoare, P., Kong, S., O'Halloran, S. and Walker, E. (2001) *Effective Strategies for English-medium Classrooms: A Handbook for Teachers.* Hong Kong: Hong Kong Institute of Education.

Evans, S. (2000) Hong Kong's new English language policy in education. *World Englishes* 19 (2), 185–204.

Fruhauf, G. Coyle, D. and Christ, I. (eds) (1996) *Teaching Content in a Foreign Language: Practice and Perspectives in European Bilingual Education.* Alkmaar: European Platform for Dutch Education.

HKEAA (2006) Hong Kong Examinations and Assessment Authority Examination statistics. Available online at http://eant01.hkeaa.cdu.hk/hkea/switch. asp?p_left=hkale_left.asp&p_clickurl=exam_reports.asp?p_exam=HKALE. Accessed 20.8.07.

HKEAA (2007) HKALE entries and results statistics over the years. Hong Kong Examinations and Assessment Authority. Available online at http://eant01. Hkeaa.edu.hk/hkea/switch.asp?p_left=hkale_left.asp&p_clickurl=exam_reports.asp?p_exam=HKALE. Accessed 20.8.07.

Hoare, P. (2003) Effective teaching of science through English in Hong Kong secondary schools. Unpublished doctoral dissertation, University of Hong Kong.

Hoare, P. (2004) The importance of language awareness in late immersion teachers. In M. Bigelow and C. Walker (eds) *Creating Teacher Community: Selected Papers from the Third International Conference on Language Teacher Education* (pp. 235–257). Minneapolis, MN: Center for Advanced Research on Language Acquisition.

Hoare, P. and Kong, S. (2001) A framework of attributes for English immersion teachers in Hong Kong and implications for immersion teacher education. *Asia Pacific Journal of Language in Education* 4 (2), 79–106.

Hoare, P. and Kong, S. (2006) *Enhancing Teacher Education for English-medium Teachers: Report of a Teaching Development Project.* Hong Kong: Hong Kong Institute of Education.

Johnson, R.K. (1983) Bilingual switching strategies: A study of the modes of teacher-talk in bilingual secondary classrooms in Hong Kong. *Language, Learning and Communication*, 2, 267–285.

Johnson, R.K. (1997) The Hong Kong education system: Late immersion under stress. In R.K. Johnson and M. Swain (eds) *Immersion Education: International Perspectives* (pp. 171–189). Cambridge: Cambridge University Press.

Johnson, R.K. and Swain, M. (1994) From core to content: Bridging the L2 proficiency gap in late immersion. *Language and Education* 8, 211–229.

Kong, S. (2004) Writing in the Hong Kong immersion classroom: Developing students' content knowledge and English language proficiency. Unpublished doctoral dissertation, City University of Hong Kong.

Lai, M.L. (2005) Language attitudes of the first postcolonial generation in Hong Kong secondary schools. *Language in Society* 34, 363–388.

Lai, P.S. and Byram, M. (2003) The politics of bilingualism: A reproduction analysis of the policy of mother tongue education in Hong Kong after 1997. *Compare* 33 (3), 315–320.

Lin, A. (2000) Deconstructing 'mixed code.' In D.C.S. Li, A. Lin, and W.K. Tsang (eds) *Language and Education in Postcolonial Hong Kong* (pp. 179–194). Hong Kong SAR: Linguistic Society of Hong Kong.

Marsh, H.W., Hau, K.T. and Kong, C.K. (2000) Late immersion and language of instruction in Hong Kong high schools: Achievement growth in language and non-language subjects. *Harvard Educational Reviews* 70 (3), 302–346.

Polias, J. (ed.) (2005) *Improving Language and Learning in Public-sector Schools.* Hong Kong: Quality Assurance Division, Hong Kong Education and Manpower Bureau.

Poon, A.Y.K. (2000) *Medium of Instruction in Hong Kong: Policy and Practice.* Lanham: University Press of America.

Programme for International Assessment (2004) *Learning for Tomorrow's World: First Results from Pisa 2003.* Paris: Organization for Economic Cooperation and Development.

So, D.W.C. (2002) Whither bilingual education in Hong Kong: Views of stakeholders on the way forward. In D.W.C. So and G.M. Jones (eds) *Education and Society in Plurilingual Contexts* (pp. 199–229). Brussels: Brussels University Press.

Swain, M. and Johnson, R.K. (1997) Immersion education: A category within bilingual education. In R.K. Johnson and M. Swain (eds) *Immersion Education: International Perspectives* (pp. 1–16). Cambridge: Cambridge University Press.

Swain, M. and Lapkin, S. (2005) The evolving sociopolitical context of immersion education in Canada: Some implications for program development. *International Journal of Applied Linguistics* 15 (2), 169–186.

Tsui, A.B.M. (2004) Medium of instruction in Hong Kong: One country, two systems, Whose language? In J.W. Tollefson and A.B.M. Tsui (eds) *Medium of Instruction Policies: Which Agenda? Whose Agenda?* (pp. 97–106). Mahwah, NJ: Lawrence Erlbaum Associates.

Tsui, A.B.M., Shum, M.S.K., Wong, C.K., Tse, S.K. and Ki, W.W. (1999) Which agenda? Medium of instruction policy in post-1997 Hong Kong. *Language, Culture and Curriculum* 12 (3), 196–219.

Wolff, D. (2002) Content and language integrated learning: An evaluation of the German approach. In D.W.C. So and G.M. Evans (eds) *Education and Society in Plurilingual Contexts*. Brussels: VUB Brussels University Press.

Wong, M.M. (2001) Assessing medium of instruction policy on secondary school internal management. Unpublished Ed.D. thesis. Hong Kong: The Chinese University of Hong Kong.

Yip, D.Y., Tsang, W.K. and Cheung, S.P. (2003) Evaluation of the effects of medium of instruction on the science learning of Hong Kong secondary students: Performance on the science achievement test. *Bilingual Research Journal* 27 (2), 295–331.

Synthesis for the Volume

Chapter 13

Concluding Thoughts: Does the Immersion Pathway Lead to Multilingualism?

G. RICHARD TUCKER and DEBORAH DUBINER

Introduction

Worldwide linguistic diversity

Despite pressures and influences toward commonality from a seemingly pervasive mass media, the residents of the world continue to speak an amazing array of mutually unintelligible languages (see, for example, Gordon, 2005). These languages vary in typological characteristics, geographical spread and number of speakers. If written, they also vary in terms of the type of system that is used to record them (e.g. alphabetic, logographic, syllabic-alphabetic). Although people frequently observe that a small number of languages such as Arabic, Bengali, English, French, Hindi, Malay, Mandarin, Portuguese, Russian and Spanish serve as important link languages or languages of wider communication around the world, these are very often spoken as second, third, fourth or later-acquired languages by their speakers, and they may or may not have official status in various countries (see, for example, Cheshire, 1991; Comrie, 1987; Edwards, 1994; Faingold, 2004; Graddol, 1997, 2006).

Pervasive North American monolingualism

Within this broader context, we find it to be an enduring paradox of life and education in many parts of Canada and the United States that bilingualism, becoming bilingual, and the encouragement of innovative language education programs within the core or basic curriculum of public education are so often viewed as *problematic, difficult* or *undesirable*. As we are all aware, the demography of both Canada and the United States has been changing dramatically over the past three decades, and concomitantly that of the school systems and of the workplaces. We are becoming collectively markedly more culturally and linguistically diverse. The number of foreign-born as a percentage of the total population and the percentage of individuals who typically speak a language other than English at home in the United States or a language other than English or French in Canada have increased rapidly since 1980. More and more of the entrants to our schools and to our workforce are so-called language-minority individuals, and this trend will continue for the foreseeable future. These changes have profound implications for our educational systems and for the types of individuals who provide services to our students.

Clearly, as the composition of the North American population continues to change, individuals who possess at least some degree of even latent bilingual proficiency will increasingly comprise the pool of prospective students and members of the workforce. However, if present educational practices continue, these individuals will *not* be encouraged, nor will they even be assisted, to nurture or to maintain their native language skills as they add English (or French) to their repertoire. They will comprise a rapidly expanding pool of individuals that Wallace Lambert (1980) has characterized as 'subtractive bilinguals.'

Is there some alternative pathway that might lead in a different direction? The present volume, *Pathways to Multilingualism: Evolving Perspectives on Immersion Education*, presents a collection of papers that examine various facets of *immersion* programs as implemented in differing settings in North America, Europe and Asia with students from a variety of ethnolinguistic and social backgrounds. In this chapter, we propose: (1) to identify and to comment briefly on six overarching themes that we have identified running through these contributions, and (2) to identify some research lacunae to which we believe additional attention would seem to be warranted.

Overarching Themes

The following themes emerged as particularly prominent ones for us in these contributions:

(1) the need for teachers to focus continually on language development within the teaching of content;
(2) the need for additional focus on form and function;
(3) a concern with more effective ways to promote literacy and academic development;
(4) an emphasis on the role of the teacher as an agent for social change;
(5) the desirability of broadening the traditional base of those to be included in immersion education;
(6) the need to prepare students for life in the global village.

We turn now to a few brief comments on each of these themes that cross program contexts.

A focus on language development within the teaching of content

Numerous contributors (e.g. Lindholm-Leary and Howard, Lyster and Mori, Met, and Swain and Lapkin) called attention to the fact that, without a continuing focus on language development (including, but not limited to, vocabulary development) participants in immersion programs (both one-way and two-way) will have difficulty mastering the content knowledge required for academic success. They argue that, when dealing with higher-level academic texts in immersion programs, it is necessary to formally and explicitly transmit to immersion students pertinent language codes and lexical items that do not emerge in social interaction and cannot be learned incidentally. Various contributors underscore the need for a combination of incidental/implicit and explicit vocabulary instruction and learning. Language development is perceived as a springboard to literacy development and ultimate school success. The contributors argue that this language growth must be facilitated concurrently with regular treatment of subject matter content in core classes and that, without such attention, the academic progress of many students will be severely hampered.

The need for additional focus on form and function

The question of *how* best to provide explicit language instruction is raised by many contributors to the volume. Genesee, for example, discusses the enhanced importance of the content-based, activity-oriented *curriculum* (in comparison to length of exposure to a language, or *time on task*) and its relationship to ultimate/eventual attainment, while Swain and Lapkin investigate the role of *repetition* in lexical learning and language development. Lyster and Mori discuss *instructional counterbalance* (balancing different kinds of teacher feedback with instructional approaches and student styles) as a way of 'reconstructing interlanguage' and facilitating students' achievement of target forms. They elaborate on the interplay between various types of feedback/error correction and program/student orientation. Met describes different ways of (1) providing opportunities for *use* of new words, as well as (2) *explicitly* teaching vocabulary, and (3) utilizing *output* for language enrichment while presenting examples of how language can be optimally integrated into the curriculum. She stresses the intimate link between *content* and *language* in immersion program lessons. Södergård's study examines teacher–student interaction against the backdrop of the *focus on content* vs. *focus on form* dichotomy. This ethnographic study highlights a teacher's behavior that intends to elicit non-random L2 use following specific strategies to achieve definite goals in language achievement alongside the teacher's treatment of subject matter content. These contributions each address ways of implementing research findings so that attention to language development does not become over-shadowed by the exclusive focus on meaning that is characteristic of some immersion programs.

Promoting literacy and academic development

Various studies such as that cited by many contributors (e.g. Thomas & Collier, 2002) demonstrate the powerful effects that programs such as two-way bilingual (immersion) programs can have on youngsters. Nonetheless, the question remains how best to encourage the continuing development of literacy and academic development for students. Fortune, Tedick and Walker, in their contribution, focus on the kind of teaching that needs to occur for there to be successful integration of language and content and thus academic development on the part of students. Their most salient finding was that their teachers were constantly *aware of language* in the classroom, regardless of the subject being taught. This sensitivity results from, and may result in, teachers' conscious efforts to make language a focus of attention while dealing with curricular subject matter. In a complementary vein, Met also focuses on techniques for identifying features of language that need to be taught to assist students to achieve higher-order academic language proficiency and thus move toward content mastery.

Lindholm-Leary and Howard, on the other hand, stress the need to attend to a broad array of factors such as school environment, staff quality, opportunity for professional development and family involvement when attempting to understand and to predict ultimate academic achievement. Met stresses the potential power of providing children from less advantageous socio-economic backgrounds with experiences that will aid them in acquiring the building blocks necessary for participation in the school's community of learners.

The teacher as agent for social change

Met, in particular, views the teacher not only as an agent for educational change but also as an agent for *social* change. She reminds the reader that teachers provide all students with skills necessary to participate in the academic community, thus helping blur differences that stem from divergent socio-economic backgrounds. This stance is in tandem with Hall's (2002: 45) sociocultural approach to teaching, which calls for the formation of communities of learners in the classrooms – where learning is viewed as 'socially situated, collaborative, and mutually beneficial.' According to

Hall, the teacher plays two roles: helping learners 'appropriate knowledge,' and helping them to become aware of this new knowledge so they can use it in achieving their goals.

Similarly, various other contributors (e.g. Richards and Burnaby, Dagenais, and Palmer) each focus on the role of the teacher in an immersion program as an agent of social change – the addition of a language for instrumental (but explicitly not for integrative) reasons, language restoration or maintenance through participation in an indigenous language immersion program; language awareness activities to enhance knowledge of language as resource rather than as object of marginalization, the role of the teacher as a shaper of alternative discourses. They remind us that it is important to understand the sociocultural context in which immersion programs operate and the power of such programs for social as well as linguistic and cognitive change upon students, parents, teachers and others in the community.

Broadening the base for participation in immersion education

Several contributors argue for the desirability of ensuring that diverse others have opportunities to participate in immersion programs. For example, Richards and Burnaby describe the challenges, and the limited success, of Aboriginal immersion programs for indigenous peoples. Although the target populations for their chapter are quite different from those of other contributors, the goals remain similar with respect to maintaining or reviving a cultural heritage through a focus on language development (see also the chapters by Palmer and Lindholm-Leary and Howard).

Several of the contributions (e.g. Dagenais, Palmer) also brought issues of diversity to the forefront (for example, in terms of broadening the traditional base of participation or in terms of the forms and content of classroom discourse). Dagenais described an important social facet of immersion education, that of fostering diversity, multilingualism and language awareness. Once again, social change in immersion settings is positioned in the foreground alongside the more traditional linguistic focus. The close relationship between 'critical language awareness' and diversity as described by Dagenais adds to the extant literature on change of attitudes and deconstruction of stereotypes brought about through language education.

Furthermore, diversity in the immersion classroom teaches not only respect for, and equity among, students (and in the broader sense, peoples) from different origins. In Palmer's contribution we are reminded that there is much to be learned from, and changed about, local classroom interactions lest they perpetuate situations that are reflected by inequity in classroom discourse. By curbing these inequities in the classroom, immersion programs transmit a message that can be extrapolated to the world outside the school – that one values diversity and the contributions of all participants in the discourse. This message serves to empower minority children both culturally and linguistically.

Preparing students for life in the global village

It can be argued that a primary goal of education today is to prepare students to participate effectively in the so-called global knowledge economy of the 21st century. The ever-growing need for *additive bilingualism* is well served by participation in available dual language programs. Likewise, the multilingualism present in local communities, and the diversity represented by it, demand a language awareness without precedent on the part of both minority- and majority-language speakers. A number of the contributors (e.g. Genesee, Hoare and Kong, Richards and Burnaby) focus explicitly on the ways in which participation in various types of immersion education programs can help to prepare students to function in an increasingly complex society where benefits accrue to those with dual language proficiency and cross-cultural competence.

Neglected Areas in which Research is Warranted

As we read these contributions, we felt that three areas stood out as ones deserving additional attention by researchers and teacher educators. We believe that there has been a relative paucity of attention to date to:

(1) the special needs of *newcomers* joining immersion programs at varying grade levels following the beginning of the program in a particular school or district;
(2) the potentially special needs of *students with severe disabilities* – that is, those with sensory-perceptual, cognitive or socio-affective disorders;
(3) the phenomenon of *transfer*.

Newcomer participation

Little attention seems to have been paid in the literature, or in this volume, to the case of *newcomers*. There seems almost to be an implicit understanding that if the program begins at kindergarten, or grade 7 or whenever, an intact class or cohort of children will begin the program and will remain with it throughout the life of the intervention. Of course, this is not the case – particularly in certain areas where there is high mobility, transfer and other coming and going. In particular, the issue of teachers' assistance to new students in bridging the language gap created by a delayed entrance to the program needs to be addressed. For example, a child who in, say, fourth grade moves to a neighborhood whose school has a language program, has missed three to four years of second language instruction. How can this child be successfully integrated into the language program? What kind of program needs to be designed in order to best serve the needs of this *newcomer* in order to help her become a full-fledged participant in her class's level? What special challenges does a youngster face who joins an immersion program in grade 3 that began in kindergarten? What are the linguistic, affective and other challenges? Will all children do well in such a transition? What types of special summer programs or academic-year support programs will best ease the transition for such youngsters to ensure their likely success? When analyses are done of the effects of program participation, does length of participation become a covariate? What practical advice should be given to educators and to parents concerning the likely successful integration of their child into a program he/she has entered after inception? Since mobility is normative rather than exceptional, we believe that this is a topic deserving serious and prompt attention.

Participation for children with severe disabilities

Likewise, as Genesee and Lindholm-Leary and Howard note, relatively scant attention has been paid to the effects of participation in innovative immersion programs by children with severe disabilities, such as dyslexics, deaf children and children with Asperger's syndrome. As the numbers of students with Individualized Education Programs (IEP)[1] seems to grow – at least in the United States – this is a topic to which new research attention is warranted. Should such students be encouraged to participate? Should they be discouraged? If they do participate, what type of accommodation is most appropriate for what set of circumstances? Not all IEPs are similar. What can we learn from studies that examine the current participation patterns of children with differing IEPs? How can and should the special education teacher or resource person within a school be best prepared to work with the language specialist to formulate an appropriate plan for the student? These and myriad other questions remain, to the best of our knowledge, unanswered (see, for example, LeLoup & Ponterio, 1997).

The phenomenon of transfer

Thirdly, we believe that we still have much to discover if we are to understand the nature of transfer, the relationship between social language development and cognitive language development, and the relationship between cognitive language development in the mother tongue and in the second language – constructs or conceptual linkages that are critical when our goal is to help the student ultimately develop the highest possible degree of content mastery and dual-language proficiency. Much has been written about the supposed effects of positive transfer, but in actuality, our knowledge base remains quite limited.

For example, O'Malley and Chamot (1990) describe the use of first-language transfer as a strategy used by both teachers and students. Transfer, however, does not happen automatically, and students do not necessarily transfer concepts and skills from their first language to an additional language (McLaughlin 1987). Additionally, Durgunoglu (2002) emphasizes the benefits of positive transfer as realized in metalinguistic strategies such as application of first-language writing conventions and construction of meaning by active reading and reader–text interaction. Does the integration of transfer as a learning strategy take place in the class-room, and if yes, how? Is it explicitly used by teachers? What is the students' level of awareness about the benefits of language transfer? O'Malley and Chamot (1990: 192) also discuss the transfer of cultural experiences and cultural schemata in the understanding of second-language stories. Are second-language programs making use of the connections between 'new information and previous cultural knowledge and experience' as a teaching tool?

Furthermore, educators have faced the challenge of students with difficulties in second language acquisition. What role does language transfer play in this field? Durgunoglu (2002) offers an innovative view of language transfer as a diagnostic tool:

> If LLs [language learners] have certain strengths in their L1, and those strengths are known to transfer across languages, then we can expect that the LLs will develop those proficiencies in their L2 as their L2 proficiency develops. ... However, if children have had reasonable exposure and instruction in their L1 and still had not developed certain metacognitive/metalinguistic skills, then we can suspect cognitive/developmental deficits that are likely to affect both L1 and L2 literacy development. (Durgunoglu, 2002: 9)

Again our point is that this is an area requiring additional attention.

Concluding Observation

We would like to conclude by referring to three of the questions posed in the foreword and indicate some of the ways in which these questions are addressed in the contributions to this collection:

What is the impact of sociocultural context on immersion programs?

Hoare and Kong discuss the high prestige of both English and Cantonese, which leads to the implementation of late-immersion programs, which in turn may cause achievement, language and content mastery problems. Dagenais stresses the impact that the value attributed to the home language has on the success of the immersion program: in her chapter we see, for example, how immersion leads to 'critical bilingualism.' Richards and Burnaby's chapter also shows how an immersion program shapes, and is shaped by, the sociocultural context in which it takes place.

How can language learning opportunities in the classroom be optimized?

Södergård analyzes a number of classroom strategies applied by a teacher to promote and sustain L2 use in a kindergarten classroom. Fortune, Tedick and Walker focus on actions with long-term implications for the L2 development of L2 students, such as improving teachers' conditions and abilities and continued development of language awareness of all participants in the classroom L2 interactions. Palmer studies the way teachers handle a multilingual classroom's interactions in a way that provides all students with a fertile ground to develop their linguistic, cultural and academic identities.

How can immersion instruction better support high levels of academic achievement?

Lindholm-Leary and Howard underscore the fact that positive educational outcomes are influenced by a number of factors in immersion programs, ranging from school to curriculum to family involvement. Timing becomes an important consideration in the implementation of immersion programs that strive for academic excellence. Indeed, Hoare and Kong describe the *negative* effect of *late* immersion on academic achievement in Hong Kong. Met points to the clear connection between literacy, language and academic achievement. She stresses that teachers face the challenge, and have the obligation, of providing students in multilingual settings with appropriate opportunities to develop language (particularly a robust vocabulary), an essential factor leading to academic achievement in immersion programs.

Finally, we would like to call attention once again (see Tucker, 1999) to the need for longitudinal research and its importance. Here we refer to *longitudinal studies* as ones that follow the students over the entire educational span and later collect information following graduation. A model of a study of this kind is described in Lambert and Tucker (1982). We believe that studies such as this could serve as the basis for the further dissemination of successful educational practices to others; and that it could also – and perhaps equally importantly – help to portray bilingual students and immersion programs developed to promote bilingualism in a more favorable light.

We propose that thought be given to carrying out a series of truly longitudinal studies to track cohorts of immersion students throughout the varied educational programs in which they have participated. Students would be followed over a number of years following their initial enrollment, progression through the system, and 'graduation' – using the model of the Terman 'gifted-student' studies (Terman & Olden, 1959) – to document the cumulative effects of various types of program participation as well as to describe clearly the social and affective correlates and consequences of developing bilingual proficiency.

We believe based on the available evidence that immersion education can provide a clear, and pedagogically attractive, pathway to multilingualism for many, many students. Indeed we are reminded of the lines in the poem *The Road Not Taken*, by Robert Frost (1924):

Two roads diverged in a wood, and I –
I took the one less traveled by,
And that made all the difference.

Note

1. In the US, a student who has been diagnosed with specific learning disabilities is assigned an Individualized Education Program (IEP), which documents in detail specially-designed instruction based on the student's unique academic, social and behavioral needs. By law, the IEP must include certain information about the child and the educational program designed to meet his or her unique needs.

References

Cheshire, J. (ed.) (1991) *English around the World: Sociolinguistic Perspectives.* Cambridge: Cambridge University Press.

Comrie, B. (ed.) (1987) *The World's Major Languages.* New York: Oxford University Press.

Durgunoglu, A.Y. (2002) Cross-linguistic transfer in literacy development and implications for language learners. *Annals of Dyslexia.* Baltimore, MD: Orton Dyslexia Society.

Edwards, J. (1994) *Multilingualism.* London: Routledge.

Faingold, E.D. (2004) Language rights and language justice in the constitutions of the world. *Language Problems and Language Planning* 28 (1), 11–24.

Frost, R. (1924) *Mountain Interval.* New York: Holt.

Gordon, R.G. Jr (ed.) (2005) *Ethnologue: Languages of the World* (15th edn). Dallas, TX: SIL International.

Graddol, D. (1997) *The Future of English*. London: The British Council.

Graddol, D. (2006) *English Next*. London: The British Council.

Hall, J.K. (2002) *Methods for Teaching Foreign Languages: Creating Communities of Learners in the Classroom*. Upper Saddle River, NJ: Prentice-Hall

Lambert, W.E. (1980) The two faces of bilingual education. *NCBE Forum* 3.

Lambert, W.E. and Tucker, G.R. (1982) Graduates of early French immersion. In G. Caldwell and E. Waddell (eds) *The English of Quebec: From Majority to Minority Status* (pp. 259–277). Lennoxville, QC: Institut Quebecois de recherché sur la culture.

LeLoup, J. and Ponterio, R. (1997) Language education and disabilities. *Language Learning and Technology* 1 (1), 2–4

McLaughlin, B. (1987) *Theories of Second Language Learning*. London: Edward Arnold.

O'Malley, M. and Chamot, A.U. (1990) *Learning Strategies in Second Language Acquisition*. New York: Cambridge University Press.

Terman, L.M. and Olden, M.H. (1959) *Genetic Studies of Genius. The Gifted Group at Mid-life: Thirty-five Years' Follow-up of the Superior Child* (Vol. 5). Stanford, CA: Stanford University Press.

Thomas, W.P. and Collier, V. (2002) A national study of school effectiveness for language minority students' long-term academic achievement. Available online at http://www.crede.ucsc.edu/research/llaa/1.1_final.html. Accessed 14.8.07.

Tucker, G.R. (1999) The applied linguist, school reform, and technology: Challenges and opportunities for the coming decade. *CALICO Journal* 17 (2), 1–25.

Index

Authors

278

Subjects